HEMINGWAY AND AGAMBEN

HEMINGWAY AND AGAMBEN

Finding Religion Without God

◆ ◆ ◆

MARCOS ANTONIO NORRIS

EDINBURGH
University Press

Edinburgh University Press is one of the leading university presses in the UK. We publish academic books and journals in our selected subject areas across the humanities and social sciences, combining cutting-edge scholarship with high editorial and production values to produce academic works of lasting importance. For more information visit our website: edinburghuniversitypress.com

© Marcos Antonio Norris, 2023, 2025

Edinburgh University Press Ltd
13 Infirmary Street
Edinburgh EH1 1LT

First published in hardback by Edinburgh University Press 2023

Typeset in 12/15 Adobe Sabon
by Manila Typesetting Company

A CIP record for this book is available from the British Library

ISBN 978 1 3995 1678 5 (hardback)
ISBN 978 1 3995 1679 2 (paperback)
ISBN 978 1 3995 1680 8 (webready PDF)
ISBN 978 1 3995 1681 5 (epub)

The right of Marcos Antonio Norris to be identified as the author of this work has been asserted in accordance with the Copyright, Designs and Patents Act 1988, and the Copyright and Related Rights Regulations 2003 (SI No. 2498).

CONTENTS

1. **Hemingway, Sartre, and the Secular** — 1
   - An Introduction — 1
   - A Word on Secularization — 14
   - Hemingway as Religious Believer — 22
   - Sartre as Religious Believer — 26
   - Returning to Hemingway — 32
   - Book Summary — 41

2. **Sovereign Decisionism and the *Imago Dei*** — 57
   - The Failed Atheism of Jean-Paul Sartre — 57
   - The Biographical Origins of Sartre's Failed Atheism — 61
   - Agamben and the Creation of Mankind — 67
   - Looking at Sartre through Agamben's Eyes — 79
   - Hemingway's Youth as an Oak Park Congregationalist — 88
   - A Change in Hemingway's Religious Temperament — 94
   - Hemingway the Existentialist — 104
   - Hemingway the Catholic — 108
   - Hemingway the Un/Believer — 114

3. **The Problem with Human Exceptionalism** — 123
   - Approaching the Masculine in Hemingway's Fiction — 123
   - "On the Quai at Smyrna" — 128
   - *Death in the Afternoon* — 136
   - Hemingway's Stance on Animal Equality — 146

4. **Hemingway's Masculine Hero**   167
   There Are No Happy Endings   167
   On the Use of Ritual   178
   Suicide as Cowardice   188
   The *Faena*, or Becoming Like God   207
   The Masculine, Existential Hero   215
   Finding Religion Without God   229
   Cause for Question in Hemingway's Posthumous Works   237
   Conclusion: The Death of God, the Death of Man   245

Bibliography   260
Index   270

CHAPTER 1

HEMINGWAY, SARTRE, AND THE SECULAR

An Introduction

Ernest Hemingway has long been considered either a nihilist or a secular existentialist. "A vast number of critics," writes Joseph Prud'homme, "have deemed Ernest Hemingway a nihilist. As an individual, they contend, Hemingway spurned religious truth and espoused absurdist nihilism.... The art and artist express the same worldview."[1] Robert Penn Warren writes that Hemingway's protagonist in the 1933 short story "A Clean, Well-Lighted Place" is "obsessed by ... the meaninglessness of the world, by nothingness, by nada."[2] William Bache likewise asserts that the story's protagonist represents a "nihilistic way of life."[3] And Judith P. Saunders argues that the story's protagonist experiences "existential panic" in the face of his mortality when confronted with the old man's suicide. She says that his "cynical parody" of two Roman Catholic prayers—the Hail Mary and the paternoster—is "insistently blasphemous."[4] But existentialist interpretations of Hemingway's fiction extend far beyond "A Clean, Well-Lighted Place." One can look to a handful of his better-known short stories—like "The Killers," "The Snows of Kilimanjaro," and "The Short Happy Life of Francis Macomber"—to see that Hemingway at the very least sympathized with an existentialist worldview. As Warren states elsewhere, "The typical Hemingway hero is the man aware, or in the process of becoming aware, of nada."[5] Hemingway's own confrontation with mortality, meaninglessness, and the freedom to make of this life whatever one chooses profoundly shaped his worldview, and you can see this influence throughout his body of work. As José Antonio Gurpegui notes in *Hemingway and Existentialism*, a search of the combined "words 'Hemingway' and 'existentialism' in Google showed 354.000 results on August 2013."[6] As of December 2022, that number has grown to 481,000.

Writing decades apart, Ben Stoltzfus and John Killinger take an existentialist interpretation of Hemingway's fiction a step further. As an unbeliever, Hemingway was not a Kierkegaardian existentialist,[7] but neither would he align himself with Nietzsche, despite the considerable overlap in their views.[8] Rather, Hemingway's own brand of existentialism resembled that of his contemporary, the twentieth-century French philosopher Jean-Paul Sartre. Like Sartre, Hemingway did not believe in God or a spiritual afterlife. This meant that one's death resulted in everlasting nonexistence and, consequently, that one's life was devoid of lasting significance. Both Sartre and Hemingway believed, in light of these sobering realities, that each person is free to create the meaning and value of their own life. What makes Hemingway particularly Sartrean, for both Killinger and Stoltzfus, is his belief that individual choice is the locus of metaphysical value. Stoltzfus elaborates on this point in a 2005 article entitled "Sartre, *Nada*, and Hemingway's African Stories":

> Sartre views death—his own, as well as God's—as the essential clue to facing life and living it authentically. It is this one "capital" possibility, always in view from the outset, from which all other possibilities derive their status of

radical contingency. What dread, or despair, or alienation reveal to every man is that he is cast into the world in order to die there. To live with death as the supreme and normative possibility of existence is not to reject the world or to refuse participation in daily events. On the contrary, it is a refusal to be deceived. To accept death is to heighten the capacity for living, and that in turn leads to a heightened sense of authentic personal existence.[9]

Killinger made the same point forty-five years earlier in *Hemingway and the Dead Gods: A Study in Existentialism* (1960), writing that "God is dead in our time and the traditional ethic is invalid. Hence every man is directed to himself for the formation of a new ethic which will stand in an intimate relation to him alone."[10] Without a "God in heaven," life loses its metaphysical purpose, and each person is left, Killinger observes, to be "his own creator, giving form to his own life."[11] Reading Killinger, Gurpegui adds that "there are no values or rules that show a path to follow or a goal to reach. . . . existence is an experience of complete freedom."[12] So it is not that Hemingway was an atheist whose nihilism ruled out the possibility of transcendent moral values; it is that, for Hemingway, every individual possessed the radical freedom to fashion their own identity, create their own moral values, and ascribe a temporary meaning to their ephemeral existence. It is that Hemingway wrote specifically from a Sartrean point of view and believed, in unison with Sartre, that *existence precedes essence*, that one's human nature, to paraphrase the famous dictum, is determined by the inherently free choices of the individual themselves.

Killinger wrote in 1960 that "there has been no liaison between [Hemingway] and the existentialists, either personally or intellectually, and neither has ever formally recognized a kinship to the other."[13] For Killinger, the Sartrean point of view reflected in Hemingway's fiction is not the result of Sartre's influence on Hemingway or even the outcome of their professional collaboration because the two of them, Killinger explains, never met and never claimed to be influenced by the other's work. But Killinger is simply wrong on this count, and how he brings himself to make such a sweeping claim is not entirely clear. It may be that in 1960 Killinger did not have access to the biographical material that is available today; it may also be that he was simply unaware of Sartre's 1946 publication in the *Atlantic Monthly*, "American Novelists in French Eyes," which speaks directly about Hemingway's influence on French existentialist writers. As Sartre explains in the article, Albert Camus made use of Hemingway's innovative writing techniques to "express his philosophical experience of the absurdity of the world," techniques that draw our attention to a character's freedom of choice over against a deterministic view of the character's internal psychology.[14] In his reflections on Hemingway's fictional characters, Sartre "recorded in his diary a fantasy of becoming a man of unreflective action,"[15] Louis Menand notes, as such a man would be "handsome, hesitant, obscure, slow and upright in his thoughts; . . . [a man] who thought little, spoke little and always did the right thing."[16] Sartre claims that he, Simone de Beauvoir, and Albert Camus were all influenced by Hemingway, so it is certainly possible that Sartre, who was publishing as early as 1936 (when Hemingway was less than midway through his writing career), had likewise influenced the American Francophile, who lived in Paris throughout the 1920s and would later celebrate the experience in his memoir, *A Moveable Feast*.

Indeed, we learn in James D. Brasch's and Joseph Sigman's *Hemingway's Library: A Composite Record* that Hemingway read the *Atlantic Monthly* often,[17] so he likely encountered Sartre's 1946 essay. Moreover, Hemingway was an avid reader of the French literary magazine *Nouvelle Revue Française*, which published a translation of "Fifty Grand" in 1927, so it is likewise possible that Hemingway encountered many of Sartre's publications in the magazine, including essays on John Dos Passos and William Faulkner, which no doubt would have interested the writer. More to the point, however, is that Hemingway owned many of Sartre's books, including *Sartre par lui-même* (1955), *Situations I* (1947), *The Age of Reason* (Eric Sutton's 1947 translation), *Les Chemins de la liberté*, volumes 1 and 2 (1945), *Le mur* (1939), and *La nausée* (1938).[18] There is no question, then, that Hemingway was a reader of Sartre. We learn in Matthew Bruccoli's and Judith Baughman's *Hemingway and the Mechanism of Fame*, moreover, that Hemingway, in his own words, subscribed to "three French magazines" and read "any French books Sartre sends me."[19] Thus, not only was Hemingway a reader of Sartre; he also read the books that Sartre personally recommended.

Which brings us to my next point: Hemingway's relationship with Sartre was not merely one of literary influence. As Hemingway's fourth wife, Mary Welsh, records in her 1976 autobiography, Sartre and de Beauvoir made a personal visit to Hemingway in December 1944 when Mary and Ernest were working in Paris as war correspondents. Sartre would visit Hemingway again in Cuba in 1949, by Mary's account, and though these are the only two meetings I am personally aware of, the accounts show that Sartre and Hemingway knew each other on a more intimate level. The night of Sartre's 1949 visit, he brought a female companion to dine with him and the Hemingways at their home, Finca Vigía, but, as Mary confesses, "the evening was a disappointment for me. I had hoped for surveys and reviews of the 'inside gen' of the French existentialist movement. But our two conversationalists, the men, passed it by lightly."[20] Instead, Sartre and Hemingway "talked like businessmen," discussing "percentages" and how the American and French publishing markets differed from each other.[21] The dinner came to an end and Mary recalls that, "for once, Ernest made no offer to introduce Sartre to the sea."²² The fact that she emphasizes "for once" indicates that Ernest had made the same offer to Sartre multiple times before. This means that by 1944, at the very latest, the two were friends as well as professional acquaintances; they dined with each other, they talked shop, and both men, in their own ways, fervently pursued in their writings the pressing existential questions of the age.

But there remains the question of who influenced whom. Hemingway had already published three novels, two books of nonfiction, and multiple short story collections before Sartre published *The Transcendence of the Ego* in 1936. It would be another two years before Sartre's famous novel *Nausea* would appear, and another seven years before the publication of *Being and Nothingness*, his philosophical magnum opus. One might reasonably assume, on these grounds, that it was Hemingway who first influenced French existentialist writers like Sartre, and not the other way around.²³ "Sartre was right to salute the influence of the American author," Stoltzfus writes, because Hemingway's "preoccupation with death and with the consequences of inauthentic behavior adumbrate many of Sartre's preoccupations."²⁴ The popular stereotype of Hemingway as anti-intellectual is challenged by critics Philip Young and Robert Evans,²⁵ but the fact remains that Hemingway was not a trained philosopher, so the extent to which his fiction may have influenced Sartre's philosophical development is questionable. We can at least speculate that Sartre's key philosophical ideas were inspired by Hemingway's fiction, which appears to model these concepts, but it seems more likely that both Sartre and Hemingway were socialized in a burgeoning existentialist culture, Hemingway during his expatriate years in Paris, Sartre while he was studying at the École Normale Supérieure, and that this is partly the reason we see significant overlap in their works. "It is entirely possible," Killinger writes, "that the young American who lived in an attic where Verlaine had once lived, and who always loved

Paris more than any other city in the world, imbibed the spirit of existentialism in the bars and bistros of that city in the nineteen-twenties."[26] During this time, Sartre was "frequenting the same cabarets as Hemingway," so "the similarities in their worldviews are due not to collaboration," Killinger proposes, "but to living in the same milieu," a milieu composed of disillusioned young artists and intellectuals who, in the aftermath of an unprecedented war, were attempting to break loose from the heavy chains of tradition.[27]

Literary modernism shared an important overlap with twentieth-century French existentialism, in this regard. Both cohorts imagined the individual subject born anew, thrown into the world as a kind of orphan who, bereft of a Father in Heaven, was left to recreate existence in his own image, according to his own liking. This so-called *lost generation*—an appellation coined by Hemingway's mentor and patron Gertrude Stein and thereafter popularized by Hemingway's novel *The Sun Also Rises*—was a group of disillusioned artists whose faith in the religious, cultural, and political institutions of Western society was, along with their faith in God, torn away from them after they witnessed the brutalities of World War I, or so the narrative goes. This all-too-familiar rendering of the lost generation appears afresh when viewed through the lens of French existentialism; indeed, we do not often associate Sartre's radical freedom with the Poundian maxim to *make it new*. But the similarities between the two are nevertheless striking, and as George Cotkin writes in his 2003 study *Existential America*, we should perhaps think of the modernist avant-garde as existentialist in its philosophical orientation. Cotkin writes:

> the Lost Generation of the 1920s had declared, in the words of F. Scott Fitzgerald, that they had "grown up to find all Gods dead, all wars fought, all faiths in man shaken." Ernest Hemingway, armed with these assumptions, depicted a

generation often stunted by boredom and impotency, captured most fully in the characters of Jake Barnes and his drifting friends in *The Sun Also Rises* (1926). At its best, the work of the Lost Generation enunciated a metaphysical condition of despair and alienation. But all too often there is more than a hint of ennui in such renderings, a feeling that the important questions have been decided once and for all. As Jake announces, "I only wished I felt religious." But he doesn't and that is that. Thus Lost Generation writers and intellectuals embraced an essentially existential perspective. And the problems they confronted were the stuff that defined much of the existential style of thinking.[28]

Reflecting on the American drama critic Joseph Krutch, who, in the 1920s, was among only a handful of Americans to espouse an existentialist worldview, Cotkin says that Krutch's esthetic was "as barren and impotent as the world inhabited by many of Hemingway's characters," for, much like Hemingway, Krutch recognized that "man was alone" in a world that had been "shorn of meaning and certitude."[29] Alongside of both American and French existentialists, the modernist avant-garde was cultivating a view of radical freedom that had likewise, according to Cotkin, grown out of their confrontation with nothingness. "To be existential is, ultimately, to join with Camus's Sisyphus in a tragic acceptance of the limitations of existence while exulting in each affirmative breath of life, in each push of the stone up the mountain."[30]

In their brazen rejection of history, tradition, and cultural convention—at its heart a disavowal of God, the afterlife, and metaphysical transcendence—both existentialism and literary modernism lionized individuality, originality, and thinking for oneself. In the modernist spirit, James Joyce, at University College Dublin, famously renounced the Roman Catholic faith of his youth, while Virginia Woolf, herself a committed atheist, was outraged to learn in 1927 of T. S. Eliot's shocking conversion to Anglicanism. The lost generation, from which Hemingway would emerge as one of the most important literary voices of the twentieth century, was existentialist in its philosophical orientation before the term became associated with Sartre and his coterie of followers. It should therefore come as little surprise that Hemingway too, as a modernist convert, had renounced his childhood religion. Most critics agree that, as an adult, Hemingway would come to believe in nothingness, *nada*, or a world evacuated of predetermined meanings.

Significantly, twentieth-century French existentialism was atheistic on principle, and as Catholic scholar Una M. Cadegan shows in her 2002 article "Modernisms Theological and Literary," so was the philosophical perspective of the modernist avant-garde. Cadegan advances this argument, first, by describing the basic tenets of literary modernism. She then contrasts these tenets against the theological commitments of Roman Catholicism to pinpoint where exactly their incompatibility lies. She writes that

> literary modernists saw in world events a radical break from history, tradition, and convention, which on the one hand could lead to despair but on the other offered significant opportunities for the liberation of humanity from political and social constraints. Formally, this resulted in the need for a new language and style to express a new way of perceiving the world, to express the alienation, dissociation, and fragmentation believed unique to post-Great War Western society. . . . In many if not most of its defining elements, literary modernism seemed tailor-made to alienate Catholics. Philosophically it at least toyed with and at worst entirely rejected all the propositions neoscholasticism depended on to exist. Socially it mocked and flouted, in the name of self-expression and human freedom, conventions that for many Catholic observers were grounded in timeless moral law.[31]

The modernist rejection of history was also a rejection of God, his worldly institutions, and the Christian metanarrative largely responsible for suffusing the Western tradition with metaphysical authority. Foisting a blank slate over the linear progression of Christian history, literary modernists imagined for themselves a new beginning, fraught with creative potential. There was no longer a transcendent purpose to life, essential human nature, or God-given morality to guide our creative choices, so "Catholic writers and critics opposed literary modernism to the extent that it seemed to embrace meaninglessness, fragmentation, and nihilism."[32] Cadegan argues over a decade later in *All Good Books Are Catholic Books: Print Culture, Censorship, and Modernity in Twentieth-Century America* that the Roman Catholic Church privileged community over the individual, orthodoxy over iconoclasm, repetition over innovation, and closure over openness; literary modernism was, in principle, irreconcilable with Catholic belief.[33]

This is why Hemingway's conversion to Roman Catholicism in 1927 has been cast by numerous critics and Hemingway scholars as nominal at best and, at worst, a total sham. Hemingway's first biographer, Carlos Baker, dismissed the author's religious conversion as a matter of mere ceremony, writing that Hemingway's marriage to Pauline Pfeiffer was indeed "nominal" and even required that Hemingway act with "duplicity" to convince the Church that his religious confession was sincere.[34] According to Baker, Ada MacLeish, a close acquaintance of the writer and a friend to Pauline, "tried her best to swallow the disgust she felt over Ernest's efforts to persuade the Catholic Church" that he was a true believer.[35] Evidence would show that, after being injured during the war, Hemingway was in fact baptized at a field hospital in Fornaci, Italy, but, in Baker's account, there is even more evidence to suggest that, following the war, Hemingway's attitude toward life and death took an atheistic and, one might even say, a nihilistic shift, as Ada seems to have understood at the time. By most accounts, Hemingway converted to Catholicism in 1927 not because he was moved to religious belief but because his marriage to the devoutly Catholic Pauline Pfeiffer in large part depended on his religious conversion. God's death was a central part of Hemingway's philosophical worldview; as both an existentialist and a literary modernist, he recognized the cultural bankruptcy of our religious institutions. Therefore, it would only make sense that scholars would question the legitimacy of Hemingway's Catholic conversion, which seems to have been the result of his ulterior motive to marry Pauline Pfeiffer.

But critical changes have taken place in both Sartre and Hemingway scholarship over the past few decades that bring into question atheistic depictions of their work. Challenging the status quo, some scholars have argued that Hemingway's Catholic conversion was not only authentic but profoundly impacted the author's fiction. Hemingway was raised Protestant as an active member of the First Congregational Church of Oak Park. He would distance himself from Protestantism, however, after he graduated from high school and moved to Kansas City for his first professional job as a newspaper reporter. It was only years later as a young adult living overseas that he would convert to Roman Catholicism. But a number of Hemingway scholars contend that his faith in the gospel message remained consistent throughout this transitional period. Existentialist readings of Hemingway are inaccurate, they maintain, because Hemingway never lost his faith in the gospel message; he simply switched denominations, giving up Protestantism for Catholicism.

In similar fashion, recent scholarship in Sartre studies has demonstrated that the philosopher was not himself atheological, despite the important role that atheism played in his philosophy. According to some scholars,[36] in fact, Sartre does not entirely eradicate God from the picture, but instead replaces the deity with a secular form that fulfills what I call the "God-function"—the role played by a world-ordering metaphysical authority who determines the nature of absolute truth, which is to say, a univocal master-narrative that, at once, organizes human affairs and delegitimizes competing narratives. Egyptologist Jan Assman famously refers to this God-function in his 2009 study, *The Price of Monotheism*, as the "Mosaic distinction," a command given by Moses to the Israelites that they worship the one true God alone.[37] According to Assman, the historical development of monotheism introduced a metaphysical preoccupation with exclusionary truth, marking a theretofore unseen distinction between true and false religions, legitimate and illegitimate belief systems. By committing themselves to absolute truth, the secular philosopher becomes what Paul Tillich calls a "non-intentional theologian."[38] Tillich writes that "[n]o philosophy is without an ultimate concern in its background, whether this is acknowledged or denied. This makes the philosopher a theologian, always implicitly and sometimes explicitly."[39] For Adam Kotsko as well, theology is concerned with "systems of legitimacy, [or] the ways that political, social, economic, and religious orders maintain their explanatory power and justify the loyalty of their adherents."[40] In this sense, theology is not concerned with God as a living being but with the metaphysical "realities" that organize a believer's life. Building on this tradition of political theological thinkers, I argue that Sartrean existentialism is not properly atheistic, but is rather a *secularization* of theism, an atheistic worldview, in other words, that remains committed to the world-ordering operations of univocal, exclusionary truth.

Theism and atheism are not, by logical necessity, mutually exclusive in this sense because, as the current study will demonstrate, the latter often refashions the former into a secular version of itself. It is therefore possible, in light of this reasoning, that both schools of Hemingway scholarship, which at first appear fundamentally at odds, are correct—Hemingway was a practicing Roman Catholic but he was also, at the very same time, a secular existentialist. Attempting to reconcile the irreconcilable, mediating between seemingly exclusive claims, I argue that Hemingway's and Sartre's shared existentialist worldview secularizes theological transcendence and, in this way, builds a bridge between otherwise unbridgeable positions. Like Sartre, Hemingway replaced divinity with a secular form that enacts the God-function. An exhaustive account of what this means, what makes it possible, and why it matters to Hemingway studies will be charted in the following section.

Before moving on with this task, however, I should address one possible objection to my approach. Scholars of American literature may question my decision to read Hemingway as part of the French existentialist tradition rather than as part of an American tradition rooted in nineteenth-century transcendentalism given Ralph Waldo Emerson's promotion of self-reliance, individuality, and masculine autonomy over against the institutional pressures of cultural conformity—a question that stems, I think, from literary critical perspectives that, by default, read authors in terms of their national identities. Such a perspective wrongly assumes, however, that Hemingway should be read as an American author, steeped in national tradition, when in fact we know, by contrast, that Hemingway moved to Paris and immersed himself in the literary avant-garde precisely in order to break free from the traditions of his youth. Like Ezra Pound, Hemingway wanted to create a novel art form, so he looked outside of the U.S. for personal, intellectual, and artistic fulfillment. If we perceive in Hemingway's secularized theism something akin to Emersonian self-reliance, we should not take this as proof that Hemingway was influenced by Emerson, or, at the very least, we should not take this as proof that Hemingway was influenced by Emerson alone, or, alternatively, that Hemingway was consciously influenced by Emerson.[41] Indeed, Hemingway's influences are wide and varied, and, as I will attempt to show at various times in this study, what contributed the most to Hemingway's secularized theological views were the muscular theology of Oak Park Congregationalism, Roman Catholicism, the innovative spirit of the modernist avant-garde, and twentieth-century French existentialism. There is certainly value in considering an author's national identity, and, to this end, it is clearly worth deliberating over Hemingway's place in "the American literary canon," but the author was himself an international citizen with global concerns. For these reasons, I have chosen to read Hemingway in terms of his international belonging and the traditions with which he was most directly engaged.

A Word on Secularization

I employ the word *secularization* throughout this study to describe the process whereby avowed atheists unwittingly replace God with moral absolutes, a secular version of transcendence that retains the world-ordering operations of theology—i.e., the God-function. In my view, it is difficult to eliminate God from any belief system without also eliminating moral absolutes, which can only be guaranteed by a deity. Atheists may object that moral absolutes are part of the metaphysical nature of reality, with or without God, but this is a profoundly consequential claim in need of verification; were it possible to verify the existence of moral absolutes, after all, there would no longer be ground for moral disagreement. But proving that one person's moral values are objectively right and that another person's moral values are objectively wrong is impossible;[42] it follows a circular logic that verifies moral absolutes on the basis of human values and that justifies human values on the basis of moral absolutes.

If we distance ourselves from the anthropocentric presuppositions of monotheism—in particular, the presupposition that mankind was created with moral purpose by a loving God who determines the metaphysical nature of being—then holding up as our moral standard an infant species on an obscure planet buried among trillions of galaxies in a vast and possibly timeless universe may be seen as not only absurd but desperately egocentric—what Nietzsche calls "the most arrogant and mendacious minute of 'world history.'"[43]

Modern-day secular society continues to live under God's shadow, failing to eradicate the divine, which lives on in secular dogma like absolute morality and its corollary, the legal protection of human rights. Stated differently, secular society still organizes around a belief in divine transcendence, which has changed its form but not its function—the difference is that we no longer recognize it as divine. In my view, the ostensible disagreement here between form and function is what characterizes secularization today. That being said, because my definition of secularization is not one that every person is already familiar with, and because many people will disagree with my claim that secular society disguises religious authority in the form of non-religious sources, a discussion of the very term *secularization* is necessary to clarify my position.

Make no mistake: my definition of secularization does not represent how the term is generally understood. The secular has been offset by the sacred in the modern imagination as this-worldly, immanent, and as limited to all matters nonreligious. Indeed, secularization is commonly understood as a general decline in religious practice, as the institutional separation of church and state, and as a demystification of religious superstition by advancements in science and technology. "[T]he general sentiment that science has caused, is causing, and will cause, a decline in the power of religious faith is relatively common in works of popular science, in the polemical writings of the 'new atheists' and, indeed, in the apologetic writings of some conservative Christians," Peter Harrison writes in a 2017 issue of *Intellectual History Review*. "The idea that the forces of science and modernity have inexorably pushed the gods into an involuntary redundancy . . . and the notion of a fundamental opposition between science and religion is often thought to be characteristic of Western modernity."[44] Indeed, the prevailing view since the Enlightenment is that science has rendered God unnecessary and that, eventually, secularization will eliminate the deity from an intelligible universe. But not everyone agrees with this view.

Among the scholarship challenging the standard secularization narrative is Charles Taylor's watershed tome *A Secular Age* (2007), around which critical debates of secularization now pivot. According to Taylor, declining religious belief in the modern age is not the result of scientific advancements, but of ideological shifts that took place within Christianity itself. Taylor argues that the economic theories of John Locke and Adam Smith, among a host of other influences, transformed Christianity into a Deistic worldview that reimagined a personal, loving God as a distant, impersonal *first cause* who no longer intervened in human lives. Therefore, it was on theological grounds rather than scientific grounds that Western culture transitioned from an enchanted world haunted everywhere by transcendence to an immanent world entirely devoid of transcendence, from a culture that regarded atheism as virtually unthinkable to one where theism is now the more difficult concept to swallow. This transformation was accomplished, Taylor says, through an anthropocentric shift that rendered human significance this-worldly, when in the past, human significance was regarded as other-worldly by people who lived in anticipation of the afterlife. "A race of humans has arisen," Taylor observes, "which has managed to experience its world entirely as immanent."[45] Taylor does not argue that secularization has failed to take place; he simply argues that its causes were religious rather than scientific. Today, even Christian believers are secularists at heart, according to Taylor, because religion has been reduced to a fashionable interest in *spirituality* that lacks any real investment in theological transcendence.

Taylor is revered within the academic community for his work on *A Secular Age* but, like any scholar of note, he has detractors.[46] Furthermore, there are alternate theories of secularization that have gained just as much notoriety in recent decades, including the theory advanced by contemporary political philosopher Giorgio Agamben, who describes secularization not as a widespread cultural shift toward the immanent, as Taylor describes it, but as the reformulation of theological transcendence. Taylor argues that modern Western society has emptied religion of its transcendent theological elements, but Agamben argues, in concert with the position advanced in this book, that these elements have merely been disguised as secular. The philosophers therefore adopt opposing positions: according to Taylor, no one takes the transcendent seriously anymore; according to Agamben, however, we regard the transcendent as seriously as ever, but we no longer recognize it as God. Building on the assertion of the Nazi legal theorist Carl Schmitt in *Political Theology* (1922) that "[a]ll significant concepts of the modern theory of the state are secularized theological concepts,"[47] Agamben writes in his 2007 *Profanations* that

> Secularization is a form of repression. It leaves intact the forces it deals with by simply moving them from one place to another. Thus the political secularization of theological concepts (the transcendence of God as a paradigm of sovereign power) does nothing but displace the heavenly monarchy into an earthly monarchy, leaving its power intact. Profanation, however, neutralizes what it profanes. Once profaned, that which was unavailable and separate loses its

aura and is returned to use. Both are political operations: the first guarantees the exercise of power by carrying it back to a sacred model; the second deactivates the apparatuses of power and returns to common use the spaces that power had seized.[48]

Agamben's model of secularization is diametrically opposed to the model advanced by Taylor. In his philosophical effort to decrease political violence and encourage social reform, Agamben urges readers to embrace a world devoid of the transcendent political structures he sees at work in the dictatorial emergency powers of modern democratic nations.[49] Functionally, secularization does not extinguish theocratic rule through the institutional separation of church and state. Rather, it "leaves intact the forces it deals with by simply moving them from one place to another." In this manner, secularization removes God from the picture but retains the metaphysical division between transcendence and immanence. It is only after "profaning" the sacred—or that which has been set apart as transcendent—that a truly immanent realm emerges with no relationship to transcendence whatsoever. Agamben's "profanation" evacuates the world of metaphysical authority, instating what *true* secularization should look like. So it is not that a "race of humans has arisen which has managed to experience its world entirely as immanent,"[50] as Taylor argues, but that the human race, seemingly against all reason, no longer identifies the transcendent with God.

Agamben develops his theory of secularization to expose the theological character of dictatorial power. But his critique applies beyond forms of state governance to the freely made choices of every individual in a world without God, choices that, for the sovereign decision maker, are thought to take on the metaphysical authority of divine law. As Schmitt writes, "[a]ll law is 'situational law.' The sovereign produces and guarantees the situation in its totality. He has the monopoly over this last decision. Therein resides the essence of the state's sovereignty, . . . not as the monopoly to coerce or to rule, but as the monopoly to decide."[51] Zeroing in on this secularized theological notion of sovereign decisionism—where human choices are afforded the creative power of divine will—Agamben will argue, in a seeming reversal of the argument advanced by Taylor, that, in the secular age, even atheists retain an unconscious belief in theological transcendence. Secularization only appears to eliminate divinity from the world by effectively transferring its metaphysical authority to non-religious sources, but this, for Agamben, simply disguises the theological, which maintains its operative presence in the world.

For this reason, secularism should instead be described as secularized theism, a point of view that hollows out the transcendent metaphysical structure of Christianity, for example, to eliminate or significantly transform its ideational content. In effect, theological notions like the *imago Dei*,[52] virtue, and sin may be transformed, respectively, into secular notions like human worth, good, and evil, which are then subsequently ascribed an a priori, metaphysical value. For Taylor, Christianity is reformulated within the immanent frame, but, for Agamben, the secular is reformulated as transcendent. Taylor is concerned with the ideational content of Christianity while Agamben is concerned with its theological structures. Even though religious believers may no longer take God seriously, in Taylor's account, in Agamben's view, they will nevertheless worship secular forms charged with the theological force of metaphysical transcendence. In certain respects, Taylor's watershed study is a force to be reckoned with, but, as Agamben's work reveals, Taylor's representation of immanence ignores the deification of secular forms. For Taylor, human significance was first rendered this-worldly within the confines of Christianity itself, but it is precisely this kind of anthropocentric gesture that reaches beyond immanence to the transcendent realm by displacing metaphysical authority from God to mankind. Taylor understands the secularization of Christianity as a reconfiguration of theological concepts within the immanent frame, but Agamben shows that even the immanent frame, in the modern age, retains a commitment to transcendent metaphysical notions like *truth*, *morality*, and *human worth*—all of which play an operative role in Sartrean existentialism, as I will show in the sections to follow.

I will seek to demonstrate, in particular, that Sartre's portrayal of human freedom parallels Schmitt's portrayal of sovereign decision making. Schmitt's assertion, for example, that "[a]ll law is situational law" mirrors Sartre's assertion that morality is "an absolute in the midst of the relative."[53] It is absolute because moral decisions presuppose their metaphysical authority; it is relative because all such decisions are made in accordance with the individual's free will, which can change at any time. This is why Sartre identifies the sovereign subject as a "legislator" in his famous 1946 lecture *Existentialism Is a Humanism*.[54] The sovereign subject enacts the metaphysical authority of their every decision by presupposing its absolute moral value. It is the sovereign leader of the state, however, who, backed by brute military force, is most able to materialize the effects of their decisions, asserting their legal authority over state citizens. The lawmaking decisions of a sovereign political leader are relative insofar as they are freely chosen; they are absolute because the sovereign presupposes their metaphysical authority. Sartre and Schmitt have a shared understanding of sovereign freedom, but the latter applies its legislative power to political leadership while the former applies it to every individual in a world without God.

Nevertheless, both models of secularized theism are, at their core, manifestations of the same basic phenomenon.

They broadly fall under what Terry Eagleton calls *culture*, a human collective that, since the Enlightenment, has produced countless God-surrogates, all of which prop up humanity in God's place as a transcendental, organizing value. Eagleton argues in his 2014 monograph *Culture and the Death of God* that religion since the Enlightenment has assumed a number of cunning, secularized disguises that have prevented people from developing an "authentic [form of] atheism."[55] According to Eagleton, Friedrich Nietzsche is an outstanding exception to this rule whose *Übermensch* marks the death not only of God but also of humanity as a transcendent source of absolute moral value. Eagleton writes:

> Perhaps it is with Nietzsche that the decisive break comes. He has a strong claim to being the first real atheist. Of course there had been unbelievers in abundance before him, but it is Nietzsche above all who confronts the terrifying, exhilarating consequences of the death of God. As long as God's shoes have been filled by Reason, art, culture, *Geist*, imagination, the nation, humanity, the state, the people, society, morality or some other such specious surrogate, the Supreme Being is not quite dead. . . . Man is a fetish filling the frightful abyss which is himself. He is a true image of the God he denies, so that only with his own disappearance from the earth can the Almighty truly be laid to rest. Only then can timorous, idolatrous Man pass beyond himself into that avatar of the future which is the *Übermensch*. Only somewhere on the other side of Man can authentic humanity be born.[56]

For Eagleton as for Agamben, true secularization carries out the death of God by moving forever beyond humanism, a secularized theological worldview that disguises the *imago Dei* as inherent human value, around which modern culture and, in particular, human rights discourse is organized. In Chapter 2 of this book, I will discuss how the existential beliefs of

Hemingway and Sartre lead, in their metaphysical presuppositions, to a deification of human nature. For the time being, I turn to the scholarship surrounding Hemingway's and Sartre's own secularized theism, which has garnered scholarly attention in recent years and deserves our attention as well.

Hemingway as Religious Believer

The research surrounding Hemingway's religious orientation is rather limited. To my knowledge, Larry Grimes, H. R. Stoneback, and Matthew Nickel are the only scholars to have conducted serious research on this neglected topic.[57] In the foreword to Nickel's 2013 *Hemingway's Dark Night: Catholic Influences and Intertextualities in the Work of Ernest Hemingway*, Nickel's mentor and scholarly predecessor H. R. Stoneback observes that his career as a Hemingway scholar has been "a lonesome business" because the writer has traditionally been viewed as irreligious.[58] "This was especially true in the 1970s," Stoneback observes, when "the Papa Myth generally held . . . that he was some kind of atheist or agnostic or secular existentialist, a man and writer who wanted nothing to do with religion, organized or disorganized."[59] So the scholarship of Grimes, Stoneback, and Nickel is like a voice crying in the wilderness, a body of dissenting literature that reimagines Hemingway—the secular existentialist—as a devout Christian believer.

In contrast with Stoneback and Nickel, who concern themselves primarily with the Catholic influences on Hemingway's life and work, Grimes focuses on the author's Protestant upbringing. He agrees with Stoneback and Nickel that Hemingway's conversion to the Catholic faith was sincere, acknowledging that a Catholic presence can be seen in *The Sun Also Rises* and *A Farewell to Arms*, but he insists that a Protestant ethos, instilled in Ernest as a child, permeates the entire Hemingway canon. This influence can be seen most strikingly in his early works but also in the works that follow his divorce from Pauline, a period that resulted for Hemingway in a loss of faith. He argues in *The Religious Design of Hemingway's Early Fiction* that the author grew up under a liberal form of Congregationalism. While the denomination was historically Calvinistic, Congregationalism lacked a central authority, leaving every church body to govern itself independently. Many Congregationalist churches fell under a Unitarian influence as a result and succumbed to liberal views of "the social gospel, the perfectibility of human life, the higher criticism of the Bible, and the convergence of the American Dream and the Kingdom of God."[60] For Grimes, this particular brand of Protestantism had an indelible impact on Hemingway that would show up in various ways for the rest of the author's life.

Stoneback, however, believes that Hemingway's fiction reflects far more of his Catholic conversion than it does his Protestant upbringing. "[F]rom the earliest short stories" to *The Old Man and the Sea* "and on through all the posthumously published work to *True at First Light*," Hemingway's fiction "is rooted in his religious sensibility, and the work is most deeply accessible," Stoneback asserts, "through an understanding of his Catholic vision."[61] Stoneback questions the biographical accounts advanced by Carlos Baker, Kenneth Lynn, and Jeffrey Meyers that present Hemingway's Catholic conversion as merely nominal. For Stoneback, the biographical evidence shows that Hemingway converted to Catholicism "long before"[62] his marriage to Pauline Pfeiffer; and his fiction from the period bears out deeply Catholic structures through the use of symbols, subtexts, rituals, and landscapes. "The ever-recurring center of Hemingway's work," Stoneback writes, "is the notion of pilgrimage," a spiritual quest to sacred places "rendered numinous by the millennial motions of millions of pilgrims who have traveled that way before."[63] According to

Stoneback, Jake Barnes of *The Sun Also Rises* walks the paths of these symbolic landscapes for the purposes of "renewal and redemption" in a novel written before Hemingway's purportedly nominal conversion to Roman Catholicism.[64] Stoneback proposes that from 1925 to 1937 Hemingway was devoutly Catholic, that from 1937 to 1947 he endured a period of "spiritual dryness" and "confusion," which led him to question his faith in Catholicism, and that from 1947 to 1960 the author underwent a period of "resurgent belief," only to lose his faith completely, Stoneback asserts, in the years leading up to his suicide.[65]

Using as his scaffold the biographical research conducted by Stoneback, Nickel performs a literary analysis of Hemingway's major works of fiction to prove that the author was more than just a nominal Catholic. According to Nickel, a close reading of his novels confirms, first, that Hemingway converted to Catholicism after being injured in the war (nearly a decade before his marriage to Pauline), and second, that his devotion to the Catholic faith was continuous and conscientious from this time on throughout his marriage to Pauline, their divorce, and the remainder of his life. Una M. Cadegan, however, is critical of Nickel's literary analysis, writing that

> Nickel reiterates key concepts, themes, and images to the point that there seem to be no references to fish in the novels that are not invoking the *ichthys* symbol of the early Christians, no references to darkness or night or *nada* that are not explicitly to Juan de la Cruz and the dark night of the soul. The analysis strikes the same limited notes again and again, rather than exploring how Hemingway's sharply honed sense of irony interacted with the culturally multifaceted and historically tumultuous nature of Catholicism.[66]

However limited his study may be, Nickel's emphasis on Hemingway's mystical affinities provides an entry point for further analysis that will prove important to the current study. Honing in on one element of an otherwise complex issue has its merits, and while Nickel's approach may be reductive, as Cadegan argues, his single-minded focus nevertheless draws our attention to elements of Hemingway's fiction that should not be lightly discarded.

According to Nickel, Hemingway's Catholic faith was profoundly informed by the mystic tradition represented by Saint Teresa of Ávila and Saint John of the Cross, with whose teachings Hemingway was well acquainted. The mystic's apophatic approach to God *via negativa* is a passage toward divine mysteriousness, Nickel says, that appears as *nada* in Hemingway's fiction. Making this claim, Nickel elaborates upon the arguments already advanced by Stoneback, who writes that *nada* is Hemingway's "path to the Allness of God and owes nothing to fashionable secular existentialist notions about nothingness."[67] Nickel himself writes that "nada is more dark night of the soul—that passage toward mystery—than death."[68] Hemingway's relationship to Catholic mysticism is a point of interest for the current study because recent scholarship maintains that Sartre's existential atheism was itself a secularized version of Catholic mysticism. It may be that Hemingway's existentialism, which is characteristically Sartrean, shares the same elements of Catholic mysticism that Sartre is believed to have secularized. If this proves to be the case, then binary debates over Hemingway's religious orientation miss the point, as Hemingway might be best understood as neither an atheist nor a theist, strictly speaking, but as a secularized theist, which is a nuanced combination of the two.

Scholars on both sides of the debate have provided substantial evidence to prove, on the one hand, that Hemingway was a secular existentialist, and, conversely, to prove on the other hand that Hemingway was a religious believer. Rather than become immobilized by this binary division, which offers up compelling evidence on both sides of the aisle, I offer an alternate route, an interpretation of the existing literature that aims to make sense of this critical deadlock rather than exacerbate it, resolving the conflict between these seemingly irreconcilable positions. I argue that Hemingway secularizes the Oak Park Congregationalism of his youth into a metaphysical view of free will that prepares the writer—as a secular existentialist—to embrace the mystical elements of Roman Catholicism. Hemingway scholars have regarded theism and atheism as mutually exclusive for obvious reasons, but the secularized version of theism adopted by Hemingway complements Sartrean existentialism, with which it shares important theological structures: specifically, both resort to a transcendent view of free will, both rely on *nothingness* as an ontological category, and both operate under the anthropocentric assumption that humanity is inherently superior to the rest of nature (a belief that I will frame later as the *imago Dei*, or sacred image of God). Following the model of secularization outlined in the previous section, Sartrean existentialism claims to rid itself of God but the philosophy is nevertheless founded upon tacit theological elements. Because Hemingway's existentialism was characteristically Sartrean, we can harness a reading of the philosopher to understand Hemingway's relationship to both Catholic and Protestant Christianity.

Sartre as Religious Believer

Jerome Gellman begins his 2009 article "Jean-Paul Sartre: The Mystical Atheist" with an account of the philosopher's materialistic approach to religious disbelief. According to Gellman, God's nonexistence is first intuited by Sartre as a boy, long before the philosopher sought to vindicate atheism in *Being and Nothingness*, his philosophical magnum opus. There, Sartre argues that no creaturely being—not even God—can simultaneously exist as being-in-itself and being-for-itself,[69] which, to translate these Sartrean terms, means that no creaturely being can exist at once as both ontologically fixed and yet totally free. Building on the childhood account depicted in his autobiography *The Words*, Sartre recounts this early experience in a late interview with his lifelong romantic partner and philosophical colleague Simone de Beauvoir:

> When I was about twelve . . . in the morning I used to take the tram with the girls next door . . . One day I was walking up and down outside their house for a few minutes waiting for them to get ready. I don't know where the thought came from or how it struck me, yet all at once I said to myself, "But God doesn't exist!" It's quite certain that before this I must have had new ideas about God and that I had begun solving the problem for myself. But still, as I remember very well, it was on that day and in the form of a momentary intuition, that I said to myself, "God doesn't exist."[70]

At the time, Sartre "looked upon" the revelation of God's nonexistence "as a manifest truth that had come to [him] without any foregoing thought"; it was "an intuition," he says, "that rose up and . . . determined [his] life."[71] But, as Gellman points out, the Christian mystic intuits God's existence in the same way that Sartre intuited the deity's nonexistence. Moreover, both Sartre and the Christian mystic realize that, in God's absence, human beings lack a fixed ontological nature. The mystic goes on to conclude that their true essence as being-in-itself is attained by uniting with the deity who created them, while Sartre is forced to conclude in light of God's nonexistence that human beings altogether lack a fixed ontological identity. Gellman writes that "Sartre is seeing through a glass darkly what the Christian mystic has discovered—that a person has no distinct self-being, because he exists only in the encompassing being of God."[72] Like the mystic, Sartre will argue that there is no predetermined meaning to human life without God, and that, in the absence of the deity, we are totally free to create its meaning for ourselves.

According to Gellman, "Sartre interprets the emptiness of self-being as the exclusionary category of the for-itself, and misses the true import of his insight"—namely, that he unwittingly derives from Christian theology his ontological view of human nature.[73] Gellman charges Sartre with advancing a theological system that has been emptied of its deity and central organizing figure. If God is the source of humanity's ontological nature, as the Christian mystic believes, then humanity lacks an ontological nature without him. Following this line of reasoning, this complete lack of being, which Sartre refers to as *nothingness*, would in turn be the source of humanity's radical freedom. But Sartre's conclusion that human beings are radically free begins with the theological presupposition that human ontology is derived from God. As Gellman argues, materialistic atheism is Sartre's "own brand of mystical experience."[74]

In her 2017 monograph *Sartre on Sin: Between Being and Nothingness*, Kate Kirkpatrick argues in agreement with Gellman that Sartre is a secularized theist. According to Kirkpatrick, Sartre's atheism took shape under a literary tradition largely influenced by the Catholic mystic of nothingness, Pierre de Bérulle, whose Augustinian view of sin profoundly shaped the intellectual landscape of seventeenth-century France. Sartre's philosophical predecessors from the era—René Descartes, Blaise Pascal, and François Fénelon—followed in Bérulle's footsteps to argue, in line with Saint Augustine, that sin is the privation of being. Kirkpatrick affirms that, under the rubric of Christian mysticism, all being-in-itself is contingent upon God, who "perpetually wills being into being."[75] Kirkpatrick therefore agrees with

Gellman that, in the mystic tradition as well as the orthodox Augustinian tradition, God is the source from which all other essences derive their being. Sartre professes God's death at the same time that he advances a Christian hamartiology,[76] reformatting an Augustinian view of sin to fit his atheistic worldview. For Augustine, any violation of God's will reduces the sinner quite literally to nothingness, or the negative ontology of being-for-itself. This is why Sartre writes in *Being and Nothingness* that "[f]reedom is precisely the being which makes itself a lack of being."[77] Sartre evacuates the Augustinian system of its divine center to reveal the absolute freedom of every individual in a world without God. Therefore, Sartre is not simply a mystical atheist who intuits the deity's nonexistence but is rather, as Kirkpatrick proposes, a secularized theist, or theologically informed unbeliever, who adapts theological structures to frame his metaphysical view of humanity's nothingness.

One year earlier, in a 2016 article, John Gillespie argues that secularization merely transfers metaphysical transcendence from God to mankind. For Sartre, the death of God as a working concept in society pre-dates Friedrich Nietzsche's sociological study of secularization, but, according to Gillespie, Sartre was nevertheless "stimulated by Nietzsche's idea," so he "extends it" with the goal of accelerating "its long-drawn-out effects."[78] Sartre sought to accelerate the process because, as Nietzsche argues in *The Gay Science*, humanity has murdered God but continues to live under his shadow. Nietzsche says that the full realization of God's death is "on its way . . . [but] has not yet reached men's ears. Lightning and thunder need time, the light of the stars needs time, deeds need time, even after they are done, to be seen and heard. This deed is as yet further from them than the furthest star—*and yet they have done it*," Nietzsche writes, mankind has murdered their God.[79] God's death should result in the deauthorization of morality as such in what Nietzsche calls the transvaluation of values, but people continue believing in moral absolutes despite the fact that they no longer possess the conceptual grounding to do so. Ironically, Sartre counts himself among the secularized theists whose belief in moral absolutes contradicts their atheism, confessing to de Beauvoir that, throughout his long philosophical career, he continued to believe in moral absolutes even though it contradicted his philosophy.[80] As Gillespie notes, "[t]he Death of God leads [Sartre] to the secularisation of God in the person of the absolute free individual" who "is now God to himself, taking on a God-like mission of creative moral choice, asserting freedom and autonomy, not trying to become God but functioning as God for himself."[81]

As far as metaphysical absolutes are concerned, a godless universe is a morally neutral universe, so the death of God should bring with it the end of moral authority per se, but even modern-day secularists continue to believe in moral absolutes, around which they organize their personal ethics and to which they hold other people accountable. And yet, without a divine creator of moral values to sustain a univocal master-narrative—legitimizing the exclusionary truth that Jan Assman described in his discussion of the Mosaic distinction—there is no way, metaphysically speaking, to authorize your personal morals over against competing moral systems, which are not, as Christianity teaches, divinely instituted within nature but are, rather, culturally constructed and individually acquired in accordance with the ruling values of the day. So when Sartre confesses to de Beauvoir that his belief in moral absolutes logically implies that he must also believe in God, he is candidly recognizing a logical inconsistency in his thought. As Gillespie explains, Sartre takes on the God-function by asserting his personal values as moral absolutes.

It will be argued in Chapter 2 of this book that the law-making authority of God is tacitly transferred by Sartre to mankind, who, in the aftermath of God's death, takes over the deity's role as the ontological origin of moral value. Gillespie is right that the secularization of morality as a metaphysical absolute contradicts Sartre's assertion that nothing can be both in-itself and for-itself, ontologically fixed and yet totally free. As Sartre confesses to de Beauvoir, it is precisely in regard to morality that his atheism has failed. At the end of his long philosophical career, Sartre finally takes ownership of a persistent, underlying contradiction in his thought: his belief in moral absolutes is incompatible with his assertion that being-in-itself-for-itself is impossible. And yet, all throughout Sartre's philosophical project, we see moral absolutes that derive their authority solely from the individual who ascribes to them. It would appear that sovereign decisionism, for Sartre, is the metaphysical origin of moral law.

I introduce this material in preparation for Chapter 2 of this book, where it will be elaborated upon, clarified, and supported through an exegesis of Sartre's work. Chapter 2 will also explore this material in relationship to Hemingway, who develops a number of existential themes in his writing, the combination of which exposes Hemingway's own tacit commitment to theological transcendence. Readers should note the distinction I draw here between implicit and explicit beliefs. On the one hand, I make arguments about what Sartre and Hemingway explicitly state—take, for example, Sartre's repudiation of being-in-itself-for-itself in *Being and Nothingness*—but, on the other hand, I make arguments about the logical consequences of their statements, consequences of which the authors themselves were not always aware. We know in terms of the historical archive that Sartre denies the existence of theological transcendence, but we also know that Sartre's belief in moral absolutism logically requires that he *believe* in theological transcendence. Thus, I prioritize a logical analysis of the historical archive over Sartre's and Hemingway's "official" positions in order to expose a contradiction in their thinking: Sartre denies the existence of theological transcendence at the same time that he subconsciously bows to its authority, replacing God with a divine surrogate that remained hidden to the philosopher in a secular disguise until the final years of his life. It is my belief that Hemingway enacts some version of this as well.

Returning to Hemingway

Critics are right, in my view, to read Hemingway as a secular existentialist, but if this is the case—and we can say with confidence that Hemingway's fictional characters discover their metaphysical authority through an atheistic confrontation with nothingness—then we should consider Hemingway's existentialism in light of the philosophical discussion laid out in the previous section. In Sartre's tacit theological view, mankind is reduced to nothingness in God's absence, but God's removal from the Catholic theological system lays open a vacancy which is thereafter taken up by the sovereign individual. As a secular existentialist, Hemingway would similarly equate the loss of God with humanity's newfound freedom and, like Sartre, he would unwittingly supplant the missing deity with a deified individual who, in this exalted state, would come to regard himself as the ontological origin of moral law. Of course, Nickel will argue that Hemingway's "passion for the Christian mystics" leads to a confrontation with nothingness that his fictional characters encounter in the form of death, "either their own death or the death of someone close to them," but facing mortality eventually leads them to God, who reduces their moments of religious doubt, Nickel says, to a temporary *dark night of the soul*.[82] In my view, Hemingway never achieves this kind of religious resolve, despite his genuine interest in Catholicism. Perplexed by the unknowability of God, he is condemned to work out these moral decisions for himself.

But Hemingway's secularized theological view of moral decision making does not begin with Catholic mysticism or even with secular existentialism; it begins with the Protestant Congregationalism of his youth. In this section, I turn from the philosophical focus of the previous sections to conduct a biographical examination of Hemingway. Doing so will help demonstrate how the complex philosophical problems surrounding Hemingway's worldview grew out of the concrete conditions of his religious upbringing. I pursue this line of thinking in preparation for Chapter 2 of this book, which will provide an in-depth analysis of key events in Hemingway's life, including his near-death experience during the war and his Catholic marriage to Pauline Pfeiffer.

Raised in the staunchly religious town of Oak Park, Illinois, by a family of devout Congregationalists, Hemingway was socialized under a strict moral code that conflated masculinity with spiritual devotion. Under the combined efforts of Hemingway's father, Clarence, who would train the boy in traditional forms of masculine expression (hunting, fishing, camping and the like), and Oak Park's spiritual leader, the Reverend William E. Barton, whose *muscular* theology presented autonomy, self-determination, and thinking for oneself as the greatest of all spiritual virtues, Hemingway would come to regard free will—and the sovereign determination of one's own identity—as a theological truism that would help to legitimize his manhood. Of course, Hemingway's masculine training eventually culminated in a macho reputation of godlike proportions, and, as critics will note, the author's mid-century celebrity amplified "Papa" Hemingway's hypermasculine portrayal in popular society to the point of caricature. David M. Earle, for one, comments on just how pervasive an impact Hemingway's macho reputation had on print media, its depiction of gender stereotypes, and the collective imagination of mid-century America. He writes in his

2009 study *All Man! Hemingway, 1950s Men's Magazines, and the Masculine Persona*:

> Not only did *Modern Man* tout [Hemingway] as "America's No. 1 He-Man," but *Focus* labeled him one of the ten sexiest men alive (as did Zsa Zsa Gabor in *Show*), and *Rogue* gave him the honor of being a "Rogue of Distinction." Again and again Hemingway was held up as an example of manliness, a role model and tonic for the American male who was having trouble adjusting to a postwar suburbanization with its stress on domestic consumption. A *Man's Illustrated* article entitled "Ernest Hemingway's 5-War Saga" went so far as to state that "there aren't many men like Hemingway left in this soft-bellied world of ours. You may be one of them. If you are, then you belong to the select few who, along with Hemingway, are members of a vanishing breed of giants in a society dominated by women and women's ways."[83]

Known the world over for his manly endeavors—as bullfighter, boxer, big-game hunter, deep-sea fisher, womanizer, and war hero—Hemingway far exceeded the masculine goals instilled in him as a child by his father and Reverend Barton, two representatives of a highly gendered religious order that conflated sovereign decision making with traditional masculinity. Under the bravado of Hemingway's masculine exploits was always the deeper religious conviction that autonomy, self-determination, and thinking for oneself lay at the heart of masculine identity. The secularization of theological transcendence as sovereign moral decision making was also therefore a secularization of Hemingway's ever-inflating masculine authority.

Of course, Hemingway's reputation as the manliest of men is largely based on overblown stereotypes. The hypermasculine Papa myth with which so many of us are familiar has been dismantled through the years by feminist and queer scholars who uncovered in Hemingway's fiction complicated and, one might even say, progressive views of gender and sexuality. As early as 1977, Aaron Latham would question Hemingway's "exaggerated masculinity," writing that "a 'new' Hemingway may reclaim a lost generation of readers" who have become disenchanted with the Papa myth.[84] Likewise, in 1983, Bernice Kert challenged a misogynistic understanding of Hemingway in her biography on *The Hemingway Women*.[85] It has been argued, she writes, that Hemingway's "lifelong assertion of masculine power grew out of his emotional need to exorcise the painful memory of his mother asserting her superiority over his father, that his personal difficulties with women . . . originated with his determination never to knuckle under, as his father had done."[86] Kert decenters hypermasculine portrayals of Hemingway by focusing on the various women in Hemingway's life who tended to view him through a very different lens. Understanding Hemingway through their eyes has a subversive effect because, as we know, Hemingway's masculine reputation was in large part manufactured by the author himself. According to J. Gerald Kennedy, Hemingway depicts himself in *A Moveable Feast* as an "orthodox heterosexual" who "ridicules an effeminate homosexual named Hal, satirizes Fitzgerald's sexual uncertainties, and professes disgust at the lesbian practices of Stein and Toklas."[87] Kenneth Lynn similarly asserts that Hemingway "presented himself to the world as a man's man, and in both his published work and his very public behavior . . . his self-dramatizations hardened into myth."[88]

But, as Kennedy rightly observes, there is a countermasculine undercurrent in Hemingway's fiction that boils over in his posthumously published, unfinished novel *The Garden of Eden*. The novel deconstructs gender binaries by exploring Hemingway's "preoccupation with androgyny and the persistence of his fantasies about crossing the gender line."[89] As Cary Wolfe likewise observes, "we are beginning to understand that Hemingway—despite the hairy-chested persona of which he remains the nearly parodic literary exemplar—was, all along, intensely interested in the transgressive possibilities of gender performativity."[90] Thus, at work in Hemingway's life and fiction are conflicting currents—one that seeks to prove the author's masculinity through a preservation of rigid gender binaries, and another that seeks, in the words of Mauricio D. Aguilera Linde, to "unmask the arbitrariness, contradictions, and contingency of cultural conventions" that helped bolster Hemingway's macho reputation in the first place.[91] These revisionist approaches to Hemingway's oeuvre helped to demonstrate beyond the obvious deconstructive play of gender categories in *The Garden of Eden* that Hemingway's fiction is plagued by gender trouble, despite the heterosexual, gender normative matrix that others perceive in his work.

> What comes to the fore throughout his short stories and novels is a gallery of characters whose behavior blurs, transforms, questions, or puts a new perspective on gender: overtly gay (the bartender in "The Light of the World") and lesbian characters, closeted homosexuals ("Out of Season," "The Battler"), transvestites (*The Garden of Eden*), dephallused males (Jake Barnes in *The Sun Also Rises*), women dressed as men and guys adopting feminine features, men without sexual appetite and, in contrast, man-eaters (Brett in *The Sun*), perpetually unsatisfied in the quest for a non-existent macho male. The multitude of possibilities opened up by "gender-bending" analysis of Hemingway's life and works turns this traditionally most "misogynist" of men into a decidedly post-modern modernist writer.[92]

The purpose of revisionist scholarship of this kind is "not to destroy [Hemingway's] mythical status" as Papa, Linde writes, but to use the masculinist figure as "a case study in order to revise dogmatic principles and unexamined values, and to denaturalize" the gender categories to which Hemingway himself may at times have felt like a prisoner.[93] In a similar vein, Carl P. Eby argues in *Hemingway's Fetishism: Psychoanalysis and the Mirror of Manhood* that Hemingway experienced gender dysphoria, castration anxiety, and latent homosexuality in spite of—and indeed *because of*—the macho cultural scripts that imprisoned him. "Insofar as Hemingway was, and in some quarters still is, an icon of American masculinity, any revelation about the process by which he constructed his personal masculinity—and femininity—suggests something about how a multitude of men in our culture may have done the same," Eby writes; "if the ideal of the 'Hemingway man' struck a chord with many American men, it did so . . . in part because many of his *personal* concerns reflected, in an exaggerated form, wider *cultural* concerns of his day."[94]

My purpose in presenting Hemingway's masculinist upbringing is therefore not to challenge this body of revisionist scholarship; on the contrary, I join a long line of feminist and queer scholars who recognize the toxic effects of essentialist masculinity, what Jacques Derrida—and Judith Butler after him—called *phallogocentrism*, the conflation of male authority, metaphysical value, and a correspondence theory of language in the Western tradition. A biographical study of Hemingway's life and fiction clearly lends itself to a deconstructive analysis of gender categories. My purpose is to draw attention to the formative role that gender scripts— especially as they took shape under Reverend Barton's muscular Christianity—must have played in Hemingway's life. Not only was the boy raised to make morally righteous decisions; he was expected to do so in a way that proved his masculinity. The failure to self-determine reflected a constitutional weakness. Under Oak Park's gendered theological strictures, becoming a man was a moral pursuit.

The lasting impact of Reverend Barton's gendered theological teachings can be seen throughout Hemingway's life, even in his final years. Hemingway's close friend and biographer, A. E. Hotchner, recounts the first time he met Hemingway for an interview with *Cosmopolitan* magazine in 1948. Hotchner is dazzled by a man whose macho reputation precedes him, and at times he even appears intimidated, not by Hemingway's celebrity but by his masculine superiority. Upon their first encounter, Hotchner notes that

> His hair was dark with gray highlights, flecked white at the temples, and he had a heavy mustache that ran past the corners of his mouth, but no beard. He was massive. Not in height, for he was only an inch over six feet, nor in weight, but in impact. Most of his two hundred pounds was concentrated above his waist: he had square heavy shoulders, long hugely muscled arms (the left one jaggedly scarred and a bit misshapen at the elbow), a deep chest, a belly-rise but no hips or thighs. Something played off him—he was intense, electrokinetic, but in control, a race horse reined in. ... He had so much more in his face than I had expected to find from seeing his photographs.[95]

However scripted or artificial, Hemingway's embodied performance of the masculine ideal impresses Hotchner, who appears taken with the author's dominant energy and brute physical appearance. The old man oozes masculine bravado and Hotchner, who describes himself by contrast as a coward and "Horse's ass,"[96] seems to envy Hemingway as the superior male specimen. Undoubtedly, the popular and much-publicized image of Hemingway had a part in Hotchner's perception of the man, but the cultural narrative surrounding Hemingway appears to inform the author's self-perception as well. In the very first words he utters to Hotchner, Hemingway brags that he holds the local record for most daiquiris drunk in a single evening. The feat proves the author's male superiority under a traditional gender script that prizes heavy drinking as prototypical manly behavior; the fact that he brings up the accomplishment so quickly, however, demonstrates just how concerned he is with proving his manhood, even to a stranger.

Beneath this surface play of masculine signifiers is a deeper principle guiding Hemingway's choices that reflects the author's masculine training as an Oak Park Congregationalist. When the Hollywood starlet Marlene Dietrich confided to Hemingway in a phone conversation that she was debating whether to take a nightclub job in Miami, Hemingway replied to her in the following way: "Don't do what you sincerely don't want to do. Never confuse movement with action."[97] "In those five words," Dietrich says to Hotchner, Ernest "gave me a whole philosophy."[98] Making choices that are contrary to one's truest desires out of a sense of obligation or duty is to confuse movement with action, compelled choice with sovereign choice. The details of one's life ought to be deliberately chosen because the individual alone, Hemingway was taught to believe from a very young age, is morally responsible for the outcome of their life. Over time, this theological teaching of manly self-assertion would come into conflict with the expectations and moral standards of Hemingway's Oak Park community. But rather than abandon his quest for masculine self-realization, Hemingway would replace the moral standards of Oak Park Congregationalism with the principle of masculine autonomy, a secularized theological view of sovereign moral will that transfers metaphysical authority from God to mankind.

This "assertive manliness" is best exemplified by Hemingway's masculine characters, who insist upon themselves, Harvey Mansfield argues, in an attempt to establish their moral value.[99] As Mansfield explains, there is something at the heart of masculine superiority that extends beyond questions of gender binarism and patriarchal domination to larger queries about mankind's place in the universe. "Manliness is an assertion of man's worth because his worth does not go without saying. So too, because worth needs to be asserted it needs to be proved; in asserting, one must make good the assertion."[100] This is why masculinity inveterately attempts to prove itself through demonstrations of its superiority; the tendency to insist upon oneself—a well-known masculine stereotype—grows out of the need to establish value where it does not naturally exist. This need among humans to establish their lasting, metaphysical importance is a deeply religious impulse, as Mansfield explains:

> survival is not enough; it no longer holds in the leisurely ease of our civilization, and in any case, it never was enough. Human beings want quality time in their sojourn on the planet; they want more than self-sacrifice for the sake of keeping the species going. They are interested in *why* the species should be preserved—the point overlooked by Darwin. Why did primitive peoples, desperately poor by our standards, living on the margin of existence, and subject to daily risks we can hardly imagine, waste their time and substance on religion? They wanted to know that they matter, that's why; and they were willing to spend heavily for the answer to that question from time and resources they might have saved for their material well-being. Other animal species seek to survive; humans want to survive with honor. It is through manliness that humans insist that they are worthy of the attention of the gods and have an honored place in the scheme of things.[101]

Masculine virtues like autonomy, self-determination, and self-mastery are all manifestations of this religious self-assertion, the theological insistence that human life matters. That Hemingway exhibits an investment in self-determination is perhaps evidence that masculinity was itself a kind of religion for the writer. After all, self-determination was first taught to

Hemingway by Reverend Barton, whose theological view of free will was entangled with the concepts of masculinity, moral goodness, and human worth. Given his religious training as an Oak Park Congregationalist, it makes sense that Hemingway would later find homes with Roman Catholicism, which upholds the *imago Dei* as theological dogma, and with existentialism, which secularizes the *imago Dei* as a belief in superior human value, what I refer to as human exceptionalism. Our lives *must* matter, the masculine will asserts. The *imago Dei* and manliness are theological bedfellows.

Book Summary

In Chapter 1, I have proposed a novel understanding of literary modernism, of which Hemingway was an important mouthpiece and exemplar. I suggested that the lost generation was existentialist in its philosophical orientation before the term became associated with Sartre and his coterie of followers. The lost generation's defiant rejection of history, religious tradition, and cultural convention—in which this bohemian group of American expatriates had lost their faith—left these individuals without a transcendent authority figure to rely on, fatherless as newly born orphans in a world without God. Lacking a predetermined human nature and deprived of the moral commandments formerly written on their hearts, twentieth-century postwar writers embraced the radical freedom to create their own meaning, to construct their own moral values, and essentially to become gods unto themselves. For Hemingway, whose masculine reputation often preceded the actual man, this sense of willful determination, of thinking for oneself, and of crafting individual identity through the exercise of sovereign moral choices grew out of his confrontation with nothingness, or *nada*, which would become the founding concept of Sartrean existentialism. The surprising thesis advanced here, however, is that

Hemingway's existential freedom in the face of nothingness is precisely what made the author a secularized theist who, like Sartre, was amenable to the anthropological claims of Roman Catholicism. This study treats Hemingway's journey through secularization as a possible litmus test for twentieth-century secularization in general. If the modernist avant-garde was truly existentialist in its philosophical orientation, it would behoove us to reconsider its theological commitments in light of Hemingway, who appears to have straddled opposing worldviews as both an atheist and a secularized theist.

In Chapter 1, I have also summarized how competing scholarship in Sartre and Hemingway studies aligns both authors with secular existentialism and Roman Catholicism. What ties these seemingly opposing camps together, we discovered, is the belief that humanity lacks a fixed ontological identity in God's absence. Reconciling moral absolutes with his belief in God's nonexistence would prove difficult for Hemingway's existential compatriot, Jean-Paul Sartre, who brings these concepts together through a feat of philosophical gymnastics. Sartre preserves a place for moral absolutes in his philosophical outlook by secularizing—in the sense of the word elaborated by Carl Schmitt and Giorgio Agamben—theological transcendence in the form of sovereign decision making. It should come as little surprise, then, that Agamben and Schmitt are, for Sartre and even for Hemingway, important interlocutors whose philosophical conflict mirrors the inner turmoil of Sartre's and Hemingway's self-divided worldviews. Schmitt's political notion of sovereign decisionism models the decisionist metaphysics of Sartrean existentialism, while Agamben's critique of Schmitt—geared toward the deactivation and dismantling of theological transcendence—models the philosophical aims of materialistic atheism, which Sartre never fully achieved. My study of Agamben will provide crucial insight into my study of Sartre, and my study of Sartre will provide an interpretive framework for understanding Hemingway, whose atheism was of a religious nature, and whose religious commitments were atheistic at heart. Agamben is the essential piece, readers will observe, that holds the various parts of this study together.

Chapter 2 begins with a discussion of the incompatibility of secularism and moral absolutes. I argue that man-made morals cannot be authorized as objectively valuable without introducing the theological category of transcendence. Secular society operates under the presupposition that human rights are themselves objectively valuable, but in actuality, human rights secularize the theological category, replacing transcendence with a disguised version of the *imago Dei* that implicitly operates—for the morally authoritarian secularist—as the metaphysical origin of objective moral value. From here, I discuss the biographical origins of Sartre's failed atheism, which offers a clear example of how secular morality implies but also conceals a belief in the *imago Dei*. In order to establish my claim that Sartrean decisionism models the secularization of theism, I move from an analysis of Sartre's failed atheism to a discussion of Agamben's ontotheological critique of sovereign decisionism.[102]

In this more developed analysis, I show how secular morality gives birth to human rights discourse by dividing humanity from the nonhuman other, who is animalized or otherwise degraded and objectified by sovereign, lawmaking decisions. Having formed logical connections among secular morality, sovereign decisionism, and masculine domination, I turn to a biographical study of Hemingway's youth as an Oak Park Congregationalist. Hemingway was trained in macho self-determination, which he learned to associate with godly behavior, but after losing his faith after a near-death experience in the First World War, Hemingway was forced to separate his masculinity from his faith. The result was a secularization of the *imago Dei* that refashioned godly behavior as sovereign decision making. It was this secularized theological view of freedom that prepared Hemingway for his conversion to Roman Catholicism, which similarly adheres to masculine self-determination, human exceptionalism, and *nothingness* as an ontological category.

Chapter 3 applies this theoretical framework to an exegesis of Hemingway's short stories, novels, and works of nonfiction. Multiple themes are developed across the Hemingway canon that, when examined together, support my argument that Hemingway secularizes aspects of religion. First, I show that Hemingway's works problematize the human/animal divide, discovering in God's death the logical end of human exceptionalism. The dehumanizing effects of war convince Hemingway of God's nonexistence by reducing mankind to an animal species shorn of the *imago Dei*. But, as I argue in Chapter 4, Hemingway reaches this conclusion only to rebel against it. He recognizes, in other words, that human life lacks inherent value, but, in a move from nihilism to existentialism, he seeks to reassert human value through sovereign choice, or masculine self-determination. The highest expression of sovereign choice, for Hemingway as for Agamben, is killing, a gesture that separates human life from animal life, superior being from inferior being through the ultimate act of domination. Concluding this book, I then apply these findings to Hemingway's portrayal of religious pilgrimage, which is always a pilgrimage toward death, for Hemingway—first, as something that one must accept as their inevitable end, and second, as something that one must rebel against through positive affirmations of life. This, I conclude, is the two-part nature of Hemingway's secularized theism.

Notes

1 Joseph Prud'homme, "Hemingway, Religion, and Masculine Virtue," in *Hemingway on Politics and Rebellion*, ed.

Lauretta Conklin Frederking (New York: Routledge, 2010), 104.
2 Robert Penn Warren, "Hemingway's World," in *Readings on Ernest Hemingway*, ed. Katie De Koster (San Diego, CA: Greenhaven Press, 1997), 38.
3 William B. Bache, "Craftsmanship in 'A Clean, Well-Lighted Place,'" *Personalist* 37 (Winter 1956): 60–4.
4 Judith P. Saunders, *American Classics: Evolutionary Perspectives* (Boston, MA: American Studies Press, 2018), 209, 208, 208.
5 Robert Penn Warren, "Hemingway," *The Kenyon Review* 9.1 (Winter 1947): 7.
6 José Antonio Gurpegui, *Hemingway and Existentialism* (Valencia: Publicacions de la Universitat de València, 2013), 22.
7 That being said, José Antonio Gurpegui does notice similarities in their thought, despite the significant difference in their philosophical orientations. In his 2013 study *Hemingway and Existentialism*, Gurpegui writes that the "existentialist principles of interest to understand Hemingway's existentialism are referred to different authors: from Kierkegaard, the denial of universal values benefitting an individual and singular philosophy of the individual; from Heidegger, the conception of mankind as a 'being for death' (Sein-zum-Tode), deriving from the identification of 'being' with 'existing'; from Jaspers, the study of 'limit situations' and his transcendent worries; from Sartre, his nihilistic vision—not necessarily negative, as it has already been mentioned—of the human being" (29).
8 And there is considerable overlap. Nietzsche's ideas concerning master morality and the will to power appear to inform Sartre's notion of sovereign freedom, which is central to my study of Hemingway. Nevertheless, I have chosen to focus on Sartre over Nietzsche as one of Hemingway's philosophical influences for reasons that will be outlined in the coming pages.
9 Ben Stoltzfus, "Sartre, *Nada*, and Hemingway's African Stories," *Comparative Literature Studies* 42.3 (2005): 211.

10 John Killinger, *Hemingway and the Dead Gods: A Study in Existentialism* (New York: Citadel Press, 1965), 98.
11 Ibid., 99.
12 Gurpegui, *Hemingway and Existentialism*, 29.
13 Killinger, *Hemingway and the Dead Gods*, vii.
14 Jean-Paul Sartre, "American Novelists in French Eyes," accessed August 26, 2019, docs.sartre.ch/American%20Novelists.pdf, 5.
15 Louis Menand, *The Free World: Art and Thought in the Cold War* (New York: Farrar, Straus and Giroux, 2021), 82.
16 Qtd. ibid.
17 See James D. Brasch and Joseph Sigman, *Hemingway's Library: A Composite Record* (New York/London: Garland Publishing, Inc., 1981), 12.
18 Ibid., 328.
19 Matthew J. Bruccoli and Judith Baughman, eds., *Hemingway and the Mechanism of Fame: Statements, Public Letters, Introductions, Forewords, Prefaces, Blurbs, Reviews, and Endorsements* (Columbia: University of South Carolina Press, 2006), 109.
20 Mary Welsh Hemingway, *How It Was* (New York: Alfred A. Knopf, 1976), 244.
21 Ibid.
22 Ibid.
23 This is to say nothing, of course, of the many other existentialist influences on the two writers. We know, for example, that Hemingway read Fyodor Dostoevsky, Herman Melville, and Stephen Crane, all of whom are regarded as existentialists. Hemingway writes in *Green Hills of Africa* (New York: Charles Scribner's Sons, 1935) that "Crane wrote two fine stories. *The Open Boat* and *The Blue Hotel*" (22). Sartre, likewise, was influenced by predecessors, including Kierkegaard, Nietzsche, and Heidegger. There is no saying how much the two writers' influences overlapped, but Sartre and Hemingway were both avid readers; overlap would not be surprising.

24 Stoltzfus, "Sartre, *Nada*, and Hemingway's African Stories," 224.
25 See Philip Young's *Ernest Hemingway* (New York: Rinehart, 1952) and Robert Evans's "Hemingway and the Pale Cast of Thought," *American Literature* 38.2 (1966): 161–76. While Young zeroes in on the personal psychology of Hemingway, Evans focuses on Hemingway's literary works; both seek to undermine the stereotype that Hemingway was anti-intellectual.
26 Killinger, *Hemingway and the Dead Gods*, vii.
27 Ibid.
28 George Cotkin, *Existential America* (Baltimore, MD: Johns Hopkins University Press, 2003), 24.
29 Ibid., 26.
30 Ibid., 3.
31 Una M. Cadegan, "Modernisms Theological and Literary," *U.S. Catholic Historian* 20.3 (2002): 106.
32 Ibid., 108.
33 Una M. Cadegan, *All Good Books Are Catholic Books: Print Culture, Censorship, and Modernity in Twentieth-Century America* (London: Cornell University Press, 2013), 62.
34 Carlos Baker, *Ernest Hemingway: A Life Story* (New York: Avon Books, 1968), 238.
35 Ibid.
36 These scholars and their contributions to the study of Sartre's theological tendencies will be discussed later in the section "Sartre as Religious Believer."
37 Jan Assman, *The Price of Monotheism*, trans. Robert Savage (Stanford, CA: Stanford University Press, 2009), 2.
38 Paul Tillich, "Relation of Metaphysics and Theology," *The Review of Metaphysics* 10.1 (1956): 60.
39 Ibid., 59.
40 Adam Kotsko, *Neoliberalism's Demons: On the Political Theology of Late Capital* (Stanford, CA: Stanford University Press, 2018), 8.

41 Hemingway himself dismisses Emerson's work as derivative, pretentious, and too abstract, writing in *Green Hills of Africa* that great works of fiction do not "bear any resemblance to the classics" that preceded them (21). He nevertheless includes Emerson on a short list of "good" American writers, but he assures his listeners that the American canon of literature is entirely devoid of "great writers" (19). On this basis, it appears highly unlikely that Hemingway looked to Emerson for inspiration. But the case can still be made that Hemingway and Emerson bore certain similarities, among which included similarities in their aesthetic. See, for example, C. Hugh Holman, "Hemingway and Emerson: Notes on the Continuity of an Aesthetic Tradition," *Modern Fiction Studies* 1.3 (1955): 12–16. Moreover, Hemingway's mentor Gertrude Stein was herself a student of Emerson and it is certainly plausible (even likely) that Stein's Emersonian proclivities rubbed off on Hemingway, if indirectly. Indeed, Hemingway's commitment to sovereign individualism would seem to align the writer with a tradition of "strong poets" that, according to Harold Bloom, included Emerson. Ironically, Bloom would argue in *The Anxiety of Influence* that most writers end up merely regurgitating the insights of their predecessors, overwhelmed, as they regularly tend to be, by the challenge to *say something new*, but the emboldened "strong poet," of which Emerson is a prime example, deliberately misunderstands their predecessors in an unconscious way; this, in turn, allows them to present their insights as original, the writers "misreading one another, so as to clear imaginative space for themselves." See Harold Bloom, *The Anxiety of Influence: A Theory of Poetry*, 2nd edn (New York/Oxford: Oxford University Press, 1997), 5. Read from Bloom's perspective, it may be that Hemingway disavowed Emerson in order to establish his own reputation as the great American author, but this query is well outside the scope of the current project.

42 Sam Harris argues in *The Moral Landscape: How Science Can Determine Human Values* (New York: Free Press, 2010)

that objective morality can be proven by empirical research. Harris's argument, however, rests on the anthropocentric presupposition that human flourishing is inherently good when there is simply no reason to believe this, apart from the closely related anthropocentric presupposition that human life is inherently valuable. Harris must first prove that human life is inherently valuable in order to then prove that human flourishing is inherently good, but he makes no such attempt and appears blind to this logical necessity. Rather, Harris presupposes that human life is inherently valuable, concludes on this basis that human flourishing is inherently good, and then cites empirical data to prove that certain behaviors better support human flourishing. Harris completely misses the point. One cannot prove that certain morals are objectively valuable without first proving that human life, upon which those morals are based, is objectively valuable. The latter is an anthropocentric presupposition that Harris is unable to prove.

43 Friedrich Nietzsche, "On Truth and Lying in a Non-Moral Sense," in *The Norton Anthology of Theory and Criticism*, ed. Vincent B. Leitch (New York/London: W. W. Norton & Company, 2001), 874.

44 Peter Harrison, "Science and Secularization," *Intellectual History Review* 27.1 (2017): 48, 47.

45 Charles Taylor, *A Secular Age* (Cambridge, MA: Belknap Press of Harvard University Press, 2007), 376.

46 See, for example, Peter E. Gordon's "The Place of the Sacred in the Absence of God: Charles Taylor's *A Secular Age*," *Journal of the History of Ideas* 69.4 (2008): 647–73; Martin Jay's "Faith-Based History," *History and Theory* 48.1 (2009): 76–84; Daniel P. Horan's "A Rahnerian Theological Response to Charles Taylor's *A Secular Age*," *New Blackfriars* 95.1055 (2014): 21–42; William David Hart's "Naturalizing Christian Ethics: A Critique of Charles Taylor's *A Secular Age*," *Journal of Religious Ethics* 40.1 (2012): 149–70; and Marek Sullivan's "Cartesian Secularity: 'Disengaged Reason,' the Passions, and the Public Sphere

beyond Charles Taylor's *A Secular Age* (2007)," *Journal of the American Academy of Religion* 87.4 (2019): 1,050–84.
47 Carl Schmitt, *Political Theology*, trans. George Schwab (Chicago, IL: University of Chicago Press, 1985), 36.
48 Giorgio Agamben, *Profanations*, trans. Jeff Fort (New York: Zone Books, 2007), 77.
49 Like Gilles Deleuze and, before him, Baruch Spinoza, Agamben envisions the world as completely devoid of transcendental realities and the metaphysical divisions that follow—the most important of which include, for Agamben, the divisions between potentiality and actuality, existence and essence. This is why Agamben calls for a general *profanation* of the sacred, or that which divides the transcendent from the immanent. It is also why drawing the comparison between absolute immanence and Sartre's notion of materialistic atheism later in Chapter 1 of this study is helpful, for Sartre betrays his vision of materialistic atheism when he argues in *Being and Nothingness* and *Existentialism Is a Humanism* that existence converts into essence through sovereign acts of free will. Ostensibly, Sartre's account of human decision making reinstates the metaphysical division between existence and essence that materialistic atheism is believed to profane. This point, and the significance it bears in relationship to the *imago Dei*, will be developed in the context of Hemingway's fiction, insofar as Hemingway's characters and plot themes model the secularized theological views described by Agamben.
50 Taylor, *A Secular Age*, 376.
51 Schmitt, *Political Theology*, 13.
52 The *imago Dei*, or "image of God," is introduced in Genesis 1:26–7, where God is said to create humanity in his own image. Though it is tempting to take this passage literally, in context there is no indication that the first humans, Adam and Eve, were made to resemble God's physical image. In fact, what stands out in this passage is the occupational role afforded to humanity as image bearers. God says, "Let us make mankind in our image, in our likeness, so that they may

rule over the fish in the sea and the birds of the sky, over the livestock and all the wild animals, and over all the creatures that move along the ground. . . . Be fruitful and increase in number; fill the earth and subdue it" (Genesis 1:26–8). What characterizes the *imago Dei* in this passage and, moreover, what follows as a direct consequence of being created in the likeness of God is mankind's superiority over the rest of creation, which they are expected to subdue. According to the Catholic Church, the *imago Dei* refers to mankind's immortal soul, his intellectual capacity, his free will, and his unique place among creation. See Catholic Church, "The Dignity of the Human Person," in the *Catechism of the Catholic Church*, 2nd edn (Vatican: Libreria Editrice Vaticana, 2012). Wayne Grudem's *Systematic Theology* similarly identifies the spiritual, relational, and rational ways that human beings are thought to resemble God. See Wayne Grudem, *Systematic Theology: An Introduction to Biblical Doctrine* (Grand Rapids, MI: Zondervan, 2000). But, as Daniel P. Horan demonstrates in a 2019 article, the ways in which mankind is said to resemble God in ancient, medieval, and modern-day Christian theology are based on characteristics that, historically, were thought to distinguish humanity from the rest of creation as exceptional. To put this differently, theologians identified the ways in which human beings were superior to the rest of nature, and then attributed these characteristics to the image of God in humanity. Horan describes the *imago Dei* as a "placeholder for human uniqueness" that reflects Christianity's anthropocentric belief in human superiority. See Daniel P. Horan, "Deconstructing Anthropocentric Privilege: *Imago Dei* and Nonhuman Agency," *The Heythrop Journal* 60 (2019): 560. The argument could be made, however, that certain lifeforms exhibit the same spiritual, relational, and rational capacities as human beings and that these lifeforms should therefore be viewed as humanity's equals; the argument can also be made that all of creation bears the divine image because it was created by God with dignity and inherent worth; but arguments of this nature miss the point. The *imago Dei* does not explicitly refer to a set of godlike characteristics; the scriptures say nothing on this point. Rather, the *imago Dei* is a mark of superiority, indicating mankind's unique privilege as God's special interest in the throes of a cosmic drama. God values humanity over the rest of creation, which human beings as superior creatures are expected to exert their dominion over.

53 Simone de Beauvoir, *Adieux*, trans. Patrick O'Brian (New York: Pantheon Books, 1984), 439.

54 Jean-Paul Sartre, *Existentialism Is a Humanism*, ed. John Kulka, trans. Carol Macomber (New Haven, CT: Yale University Press, 2007), 25.

55 Terry Eagleton, *Culture and the Death of God* (New Haven, CT: Yale University Press, 2014), ix.

56 Ibid., 151–2.

57 That being said, there are two essays on the topic in editor Lauretta Conklin Frederking's *Hemingway on Politics and Rebellion* (New York: Routledge, 2010). In one essay, "Hemingway, Religion, and Masculine Virtue," which is cited on the first page of this book, Joseph Prud'homme compares the toxic masculinity embodied by the Promise Keepers movement and Mel Gibson's *The Passion of the Christ* with what he considers to be the admirable masculinity of Hemingway's Catholic Hero. Looking at *For Whom the Bell Tolls*, "Today Is Friday," and *The Old Man and the Sea*, Prud'homme vaguely represents Hemingway's Catholic Hero as someone who is not resentful of women or lost privilege, and who is strong but not arrogant. Personally, I do not see the utility in Prud'homme's definition of masculinity, and I do not believe his observations are relevant to the study at hand. The other essay, Harvey Mansfield's "Manly Assertion," is only circuitously related to the topic of Hemingway's religious orientation. According to Mansfield, the masculine performances of Hemingway's characters insist upon the value of human worth. This, he says, is an inherently religious gesture. I agree with Mansfield and will make use of his essay later, but Mansfield does not make

an argument about Hemingway's religious affiliation; he instead argues that masculinity itself is religious in nature.
58 Matthew Nickel, *Hemingway's Dark Night: Catholic Influences and Intertextualities in the Work of Ernest Hemingway* (Wickford, RI: New Street Communications, 2013), preface.
59 Ibid.
60 Larry Grimes, *The Religious Design of Hemingway's Early Fiction* (Ann Arbor, MI: UMI Research Press, 1985), 2.
61 H. R. Stoneback, "Pilgrimage Variations: Hemingway's Sacred Landscapes," *Religion and Literature* 35.2/3 (2003): 50.
62 H. R. Stoneback, "In the Nominal Country of the Bogus: Hemingway's Catholicism and the Biographies," in *Hemingway: Essays of Reassessment*, ed. Frank Scafella (New York: Oxford University Press, 1991), 109.
63 Stoneback, "Pilgrimage Variations," 50.
64 Ibid., 51.
65 Stoneback, "In the Nominal Country of the Bogus," 117.
66 Una M. Cadegan, "Hemingway's Dark Night: Catholic Influences and Intertextualities in the Work of Ernest Hemingway by Matthew Nickel," *American Catholic Studies* 125.4 (2014): 88.
67 H. R. Stoneback, "For Whom the Flood Rolls: Ernest Hemingway and Robert Penn Warren—Connections and Echoes, Allusion, and Intertextuality," *North Dakota Quarterly* 76.1/2 (2009): 12.
68 Nickel, *Hemingway's Dark Night*, 126.
69 The terms *in-itself*, *for-itself*, and *for-others* are used by Sartre throughout *Being and Nothingness*. Sartre defines *being-in-itself* as objects in the material world, among which he includes an inkwell and a drinking glass. These objects have autonomous self-presence and lack consciousness. *Being-for-itself*, by contrast, refers to human consciousness, which lacks a fixed ontological nature and is the source of our freedom. To be *in-itself-for-itself* is impossible because a being cannot be at once ontologically fixed and yet totally

free. God cannot exist, Sartre says, because a deity must possess both of these qualities. *Being-for-others*, moreover, refers to the state of being perceived by other people. We are recognized by people as another consciousness, but we are also perceived as an object in their world. This tension between subject and object is endlessly played out in our interactions with other subjects; we attempt to objectify them while they, in turn, attempt to objectify us. In bad faith, people often become enslaved to how other people perceive them. Sartre urges us to recognize our freedom as *being-for-itself* instead.

70 De Beauvoir, *Adieux*, 434.
71 Jerome Gellman, "Jean-Paul Sartre: The Mystical Atheist," *European Journal for Philosophy of Religion* 2 (2009): 127.
72 Ibid., 131.
73 Ibid.
74 Ibid., 133.
75 Kate Kirkpatrick, *Sartre on Sin: Between Being and Nothingness* (Oxford: Oxford University Press, 2017), 33.
76 *Hamartiology* refers to the theological study of sin. From the Greek ἁμαρτία, hamartia literally translates as "missing the mark, error." In Greek tragedy, hamartia refers to the fatal flaw of a heroic figure that eventually leads to their downfall. In Christian theology, however, hamartia refers to the original violation of God's moral law by Adam, the first man, the subsequent downfall of humanity, often referred to as "the fall of man," humanity's depraved sinful nature, which is inherited as a result of their fall, and the individual acts of rebellion committed by humanity against God's moral commandments. Taking these elements into account, hamartiology attempts to understand the precise nature of sin.
77 Jean-Paul Sartre, *Being and Nothingness*, trans. Hazel E. Barnes (New York: Washington Square Press, 1953), 725.
78 John Gillespie, "Sartre and the Death of God," *Sartre Studies International* 22.1 (2016): 53.
79 Friedrich Nietzsche, *The Gay Science*, trans. Thomas Common (New York: Dover Publications, 2006), 91.

80 De Beauvoir, *Adieux*, 439.
81 Gillespie, "Sartre and the Death of God," 48.
82 Nickel, *Hemingway's Dark Night*, 76.
83 David M. Earle, *All Man! Hemingway, 1950s Men's Magazines, and the Masculine Persona* (Kent, OH: Kent State University Press, 2009), 18.
84 Aaron Latham, "A Farewell to Machismo," *New York Times*, October 16, 1977, https://www.nytimes.com/1977/10/16/archives/a-farewell-to-machismo-a-story-by-any-other-name-hemingway.html.
85 Bernice Kert, *The Hemingway Women* (New York: W. W. Norton & Company, 1983), 9.
86 Ibid., 21.
87 J. Gerald Kennedy, "Hemingway's Gender Trouble," *American Literature* 63.2 (1991): 187.
88 Kenneth Shuyler Lynn, *Hemingway* (Cambridge, MA: Harvard University Press, 1987), 9.
89 Kennedy, "Hemingway's Gender Trouble," 207.
90 Cary Wolfe, "Fathers, Lovers, and Friend Killers: Rearticulating Gender and Race via Species in Hemingway," *boundary 2* 29.1 (2002): 223.
91 Mauricio D. Aguilera Linde, "Hemingway and Gender: Biography Revisited," *Atlantis* 27.2 (2005): 17.
92 Ibid., 25.
93 Ibid., 17.
94 Carl P. Eby, *Hemingway's Fetishism: Psychoanalysis and the Mirror of Manhood* (Albany, NY: State University of New York Press, 1998), 4.
95 A. E. Hotchner, *Papa Hemingway: A Memoir* (New York: Bantam Books, 1967), 6–7.
96 Ibid., 3.
97 Ibid., 28.
98 Ibid.
99 Harvey Mansfield, "Manly Assertion," in *Hemingway on Politics and Rebellion*, ed. Lauretta Conklin Frederking (New York: Routledge, 2010), 91.
100 Ibid., 94.

101 Ibid., 98–9.
102 According to Matthew C. Halteman, *ontotheology* accounts for the origin of ultimate being. He writes that, "[f]or Heidegger, 'ontotheology' is a critical term used to describe a putatively problematic approach to metaphysical theorizing that he claims is characteristic of Western philosophy in general. A metaphysics is an 'ontotheology' insofar as its account of ultimate reality combines—typically in a confused or conflated manner—two general forms of metaphysical explanation that, taken together, aim to make the entirety of reality intelligible to human understanding. These are an *ontology* that accounts for that which all beings have in common (universal or fundamental being) and a *theology* that accounts for that which causes and renders intelligible the system of beings as a whole (a highest or ultimate being or a first principle). Traditionally interpreted, Platonic metaphysics is a paradigm case of ontotheology in the Heideggerian sense insofar as it explains the existence of particular beings by recourse to universal forms (ontology) and explains the origin and intelligibility of the whole of beings by recourse to the Good as that from which everything else emanates (theology)." Agamben's critique of ontotheology follows the Heideggerian critique. Agamben demonstrates how sovereign decisionism positions itself as the originary source of universal being. See Matthew C. Halteman, "Ontotheology," *Routledge Encyclopedia of Philosophy*, ed. Edward Craig, https://www.rep.routledge.com/articles/thematic/ontotheology/v-1.

CHAPTER 2

SOVEREIGN DECISIONISM AND THE *IMAGO DEI*

The Failed Atheism of Jean-Paul Sartre

In the year following Sartre's death, Simone de Beauvoir published in *Adieux* a series of interviews she conducted with the philosopher in August and September of 1974. Toward the end of the final interview, Sartre says that his career as a professional educator helped him produce the publications through which he had hoped to achieve immortality—a kind of "quasi-survival" he imagined in the form of his literary reputation.[1] De Beauvoir uses this opportunity to shift the conversation from the figurative immortality Sartre hoped to achieve in his writings to the topics of religious belief, the immortality of the soul, and Sartre's own impending death. "[T]here is still one question that I should like to ask you," she says. "Has the idea of the survival of the soul, of a spiritual principle in us, a survival such as the Christians think of, for example—has that ever crossed your mind?"[2] Sartre replies to de Beauvoir that he expects there will be "nothing after death,"[3] but—intriguingly, and in spite of his atheism—he also admits that he has retained something akin to religious belief, a commitment to moral absolutes that, in Sartre's opinion, can only exist in a universe created and governed by a divine being. "In the moral field," he states, "I've retained one single thing to do with the existence of God, and that is Good and Evil as absolutes. The usual consequence of atheism is the suppression of Good and Evil. It's a certain relativism."[4] In a divinely governed universe, it would appear that moral absolutes are built into the metaphysical nature of being, not simply as axiological beliefs imposed on creation from above, but as an essential part of material reality itself. Arguably, this is why there are no moral absolutes in a world without God. The material nature of reality depends on a divine creator whose absence results—according to Sartre—in a morally neutral universe.

Sartre calls this perspective *materialistic atheism* because it moves beyond an *idealist atheism* (that rejects the mere idea of God) to reconsider the nature of material being in God's absence. Under this view, human beings, like all material reality, exist only by chance and natural processes, rather than by God's design, so unbelievers must divorce themselves from the theological belief that humanity was created with inherent value for a moral purpose. "[M]aterialistic atheism is the world seen without God," Sartre comments; it progresses from the mere "absence of an idea" to a new conception of being and of the human being in particular, who "is left among things and is not set apart from them by a divine consciousness that contemplates them and causes them to exist."[5] Like the rest of material reality, humanity lacks a moral purpose in the universe, so the materialistic atheist, in light of this knowledge, will create moral value if they so choose, but they will do so without falling into the authoritarian tendency to regard good and evil as transcendental principles. In response to Sartre's description of materialistic atheism, de Beauvoir quotes the Christian existentialist Fyodor Dostoevsky: "'If God does not exist, everything is allowed.'"[6] Sartre responds to de Beauvoir in the affirmative, but, as he immediately confesses, this is an aspect of materialistic atheism that he has failed to embrace. "In one way I clearly see what [Dostoevsky] means, and abstractly it's true," Sartre observes, "but in another [way] I clearly see that killing a man is wrong. Is directly, absolutely wrong; is wrong for another man; is doubtless not wrong for an eagle or a lion, but is wrong for a man."[7]

Sartre's embodied moral experiences are at odds with the philosopher's description of materialistic atheism, which should divest the phenomenal experience of its moral character. By Sartre's own admission, his moralist tendencies stem from a kind of *failed atheism*, an inability to realize fully God's absence in the embodied experience of everyday life. Sartre describes his morality as "an absolute in the midst of the relative,"[8] as if our moral actions could somehow demonstrate their unconditional authority within the relative conditions of particular circumstances. But Sartre's deeply felt experience of moral absolutes is the result of secularized theological views that contradict the philosopher's better judgment as an atheist. "Even if one does not believe in God," Sartre explains to de Beauvoir, "there are elements of the idea of God that remain in us and that cause us to see the world with some divine aspects."[9] This secularized theism results in the experience of good and evil as moral absolutes, but these absolutes are not abstract principles for Sartre. Rather, moral actions are measured as good or evil in light of their impact on human life, which is created by God as inherently valuable. As Sartre explains to de Beauvoir at a deeply revealing moment during the interview: "I don't see myself as so much dust that has appeared in the world, but as a being that was expected, prefigured, called forth. In short, as a being that could . . . only come from a creator; and this idea of a creating hand that created me refers back to God."[10] At least by the time of the interview, Sartre himself had not achieved the stated goal of materialistic atheism. Against his own better judgment, the philosopher believed on what seems to be an intuitive, semi-conscious level that human beings were "set apart . . . by a divine consciousness that contemplates them and causes them to exist."[11] In Sartre's secularized theological account, the human being is made sacred by a nonexistent God.

I argue that Sartre's theological anthropology is based not only on God's absence, as other scholars have argued, but on Sartre's secularized theological belief that humanity bears the *imago Dei*, the sacred image of God. Sartre's decisionist metaphysics—his belief that human choice is the ontological origin of morality—authorizes an ethical paradigm that privileges human identity as "sacred," or as metaphysically superior to the rest of nature. But this theological view of ethics is complicated by the fact that sacred human identity, in Sartre's view, is not determined by God, who expressly does not exist, but by moral decision makers themselves, who have taken God's place as the ontological origin of moral value. Morality is thus determined by the *lawmaker* who, after supplanting God as divine creator of the universe, carves out the relative boundaries of sacred human identity. The *imago Dei* is, in effect, the image of God *without God*, the exceptional status afforded to human identity even after the divine creator of mankind has been removed from the picture. As Sartre writes in the *War Diaries*, "I imagine everyone freely determines a kind of moral affect for himself, on the basis of which he grasps, values, and conceives his own progress. For example, from the outset I undoubtedly had a morality without a God—without sin, but not without evil."[12] Sartre recognizes that he cognitively separates moral authority from its theological source, transferring God's creative power to the individual decision maker.

To unpack these claims, I bring Sartre into conversation with Agamben. The two thinkers are not often associated and, at first glance, they may even appear worlds apart, but Agamben's notions of secularized theism, anthropogenesis, and the sovereign production of *bare life* illuminate

Sartre's work in profound and even troubling ways. This is because Sartre's failed atheism can be framed as the target of Agamben's political critique, which seeks to correct authoritarian paradigms through a so-called *profanation* of secularized theological views by purging them of their tacit metaphysical presuppositions.

Agamben's work is particularly helpful in diagnosing Sartrean existentialism as a form of secularized theism. That being said, a full account of Agamben's philosophical solution to this problem exceeds the scope of this book. For this reason, I limit my analysis to those aspects of Agamben's thought that best illuminate the theological character of Sartre's atheism. My purpose is not to provide a solution to what I call secularized theism, but to diagnose the problem as an essential component of Sartre's existentialist philosophy. It would appear that Sartre himself attempted to correct his secularized theological view of morality by achieving the philosophical aims of materialistic atheism, but, as he explains to de Beauvoir, he was never entirely able to do so. Sartre retained a secularized theological belief in moral absolutes, which grew out of his deeply felt, semi-conscious intuition that human beings were "set apart" by God, whose existence Sartre paradoxically denied.[13] In due course, I will show how Sartre's secularized theological views illuminate those of Hemingway, whose own tacit belief in the *imago Dei*—or human exceptionalism, as I refer to it—is inseparable from his masculine ideals.

The Biographical Origins of Sartre's Failed Atheism

Tracing the exact origins of Sartre's failed atheism may not be possible in the end, but there are at least a few passages in his autobiographical works that shed light on the philosopher's peculiar situation. He recounts in *The Words*, for example, that "his whole family believed in God, as a matter of discretion" because atheism, in the political climate of Sartre's childhood, was closely associated with moral fanaticism.[14] He writes in the *War Diaries* that "[m]y mother made me take my first communion, but I think it was more out of respect for my future freedom than from true conviction. Rather as certain people have their children circumcised for reasons of hygiene," Sartre's family had him baptized to meet social expectations.[15] Unlike the nominal Christians he grew up around, the typical atheist was a "God-obsessed crank" who "refused the right to kneel in church, . . . to give his daughters a religious wedding, [and] who took it upon himself to prove the truth of his doctrine by the purity of his morals."[16] The atheist was someone who attempted to vindicate their radical worldview by demonstrating its moral value to a skeptical public, whose own morals appeared superficial by contrast, as customary behavior not genuinely felt. "For two thousand years, Christian certainties had had time to prove their worth," Sartre observes. "They belonged to everyone. . . . They were common to the heritage. Good society believed in God in order to not speak of Him."[17] Such was the nature of Sartre's religious upbringing. To believe in God was a matter of social decorum, and, likewise, to feel moral conviction was a matter of etiquette. "My grandfather was Protestant, my grandmother was Catholic. But so far as I could see, their religious feelings if decent were frigid."[18] For the religious believer, morality was a social nicety not ordinarily accompanied by feelings of genuine conviction. The atheist, by contrast, felt moral conviction without believing in God and sought to vindicate his unpopular worldview on the basis of moral authority.

Yet, despite the hyper-moralism of the "God-obsessed" atheist as well as the superficial moralism of polite Christian society, the young Sartre first experienced the pressures of moral contrition under the semblance of religious belief. Sartre tells us in the *War Diaries* that "I can still see myself at the age of seven or eight, in Rue Le Goff, burning the lace curtains on the window with a match. . . . this incendiary act had no witness and yet I was thinking: 'The Good Lord can see me.'"[19] Sartre echoes this sentiment in *The Words* while recounting a similar event: "I had been playing with matches and burned a small rug," he says. "I was in the process of covering up my crime when suddenly God saw me. I felt His gaze inside my head and on my hands. I whirled about in the bathroom, horribly visible, a live target."[20] Sartre says that he "flew into a rage" against this "crude indiscretion" and then blasphemed the judgmental deity who, in response, "never looked at him again."[21] Thus, unlike the "God-obsessed crank" of Sartre's youth who sought to vindicate atheism through a demonstration of its moral value, Sartre escaped the authoritarian reaches of morality by turning his back on religion. In this regard, Sartre was a different kind of atheist and so, too, a different kind of moralist in French society. The death of God relativized morality, as human behavior, under this paradigm, could no longer be surveilled by the moral authority upstairs. These biographical accounts corroborate Sartre's broader philosophical claim, argued elsewhere,[22] that moral authority originates with God.

But another passage from the philosopher's autobiography shows that Sartre's atheism—rather than being an outright rejection of transcendental moral authority—was self-divided from the beginning: on the one hand, Sartre wanted to escape the restrictions imposed on his behavior by Christianity's sovereign moral code, but, on the other hand, Sartre longed for a creator to give his life purpose and moral value. He admits that

> God would have managed things for me. I would have been a signed masterpiece. Assured of playing my part in the universal concert, I would have patiently waited for Him to reveal His purposes and my necessity. I reached

out for religion. I longed for it, it was the remedy. Had it been denied me, I would have invented it myself. It was not denied me. Raised in the Catholic faith, I learned that the Almighty had made me for His glory. That was more than I dared dream. But later, I did not recognize in the fashionable God in whom I was taught to believe the one whom my soul was awaiting. I needed a Creator; I was given a Big Boss. The two were one and the same, but I didn't realize it. I was serving, without zeal, the Idol of the Pharisees, and the official doctrine put me off seeking my own faith.[23]

In his early youth, Sartre felt that he was created for divine glory and was certain he played an essential role in the deity's cosmic design. As we have already seen, Sartre would continue to feel this way despite his atheism, confessing at a much older age that he felt "expected, prefigured, [and] called forth . . . as a being that could . . . only come from a creator."[24]

According to the Roman Catholic tradition, mankind was made in the image of God as superior to the rest of creation. Although this was more than Sartre dared to dream for at the time, Catholic teachings of the *imago Dei* validated his religious suspicion that he was created by God with a moral purpose. But Sartre was unwilling to reconcile his belief in sacred human identity with the moral dictates of the "Big Boss" upstairs. Instead, he jettisoned the "official doctrine" of the Church and replaced institutional morality with moral values of his own choosing. "I am affected by moralism," Sartre admits, and "moralism often has its source in religion. But with me it was nothing of the kind. Besides, the truth is I was brought up and educated by relatives and teachers most of whom were champions of secular morality and everywhere sought to replace religious morality by it."[25] Sartre followed in the footsteps of his teachers and relatives as a champion of secular morality, but, without God, he was confronted with the same question facing all secularists: how does one authorize moral precepts as *inherently* valuable? He says to de Beauvoir that killing a man is "absolutely wrong," but Sartre cannot take an absolutist stance on murder if ethical values are, by his own account, relative to the choices of each individual decision maker.[26] The atheist philosopher may certainly have turned his back on religion, but, driven by a peculiar need for moral certitude, Sartre retained his belief in sacred human identity, the metaphysical absolute by which the philosopher would authorize his moral choices.

Sartre himself claims to have replaced religion with a life of literary devotion. He says in *The Words* that he hoped to achieve immortality by writing texts that would carry his reputation beyond the grave. At the end of this work, Sartre admits that he finally gave up on these comforting illusions after realizing that everyone, no matter their celebrity, is forgotten with time; even if your reputation lives on without you, you still are not consciously present to experience the memories that other people may have of you. He writes that

> In order to assure myself that the human race would remember me forever, it was agreed in my head that the species would never end. For me to expire in humanity's bosom was to be born and become infinite, but if anyone put forward, in my presence, the hypothesis that a cataclysm might some day destroy the planet, even in fifty thousand years, I would be panic stricken. Though I am now disillusioned, I cannot think about the cooling of the sun without fear.[27]

Sartre recognizes at some point before 1963, when *The Words* was first published, that he secularized religion as the study of literature to preserve his semi-conscious belief in immortality. But Sartre, much like Agamben after him, was a critic of secularized theological views. As I have already shown, Sartre envisioned materialistic atheism as a remedy that would cure inferior, idealist forms of atheism of their unconscious theological errors. Sartre describes his personal progression from theist to secularized theist in the following passage, but present in these reflections is a tacit theological belief in the *imago Dei* that persists beyond his ostensible disillusionment and finally gives shape to his belief in sovereign decision making, as I will show:

> I was taught Sacred History, the Gospel, and the catechism without being given the means for believing. The result was a disorder which became my particular order. There were twists and turns, a considerable transfer; removed from Catholicism, the sacred was deposited in belles-lettres and the penman appeared, an *ersatz* of the Christian that I was unable to be ... After a while, not knowing what else to do to occupy my mind, I decided to think of the Almighty. Immediately He tumbled into the blue and disappeared without giving any explanation. He doesn't exist, I said to myself with polite surprise, and I thought the matter was settled. In a way, it was, since never have I had the slightest temptation to bring Him back to life. But the Other One remained, the Invisible One, the Holy Ghost, the one who guaranteed my mandate and who ran my life with his great anonymous and sacred powers. I had all the more difficulty getting rid of him in that he had installed himself at the back of my head in the doctored notions which I used in my effort to understand, to situate, and to justify myself.[28]

Sartre argues in *Being and Nothingness* that God cannot exist because no being is, at once, ontologically fixed and yet totally free. What Sartre calls God—being-in-itself-for-itself—is logically impossible.[29] Nevertheless, Sartre retains a belief in the Holy Ghost while rejecting God the Father and God the Son. Raised in the Catholic Church, Sartre undoubtedly knew that all three persons of the trinity were regarded by the Augustinian tradition as consubstantial, so it was impossible to reject one member of the godhead without rejecting all three members. But this is precisely what Sartre does, describing the Holy Ghost as an anonymous force in "the back of [his] head" who plays a godlike role in the philosopher's life after being severed from the trinity.

Especially pertinent to our study is the role attributed to the Holy Ghost by the Roman Catholic tradition. Concerning the *imago Dei*, the *Catechism of the Catholic Church* says that humanity was made "'in the image and likeness' of the Creator. It is in Christ, Redeemer and Savior, that the divine image, disfigured in man by the first sin, has been restored to its original beauty and ennobled by the grace of God."[30] Concerning the Holy Ghost, the Catechism says that "By his Passion, Christ delivered us from Satan and from sin. He merited for us new life in the Holy Spirit. His grace restores what sin had damaged in us."[31] One may deduce from these passages, first, that the *imago Dei* was corrupted by sin, and second, that the Holy Ghost restores the image of God in humanity. According to the New Testament, mankind is set apart as image bearers "by the sanctifying work of the Spirit."[32] For Christian believers, being created in the image of God sets humanity apart as exceptional beings with superior moral value, beings whose self-worth affords them particular rights and special treatment as God's primary concern. Paradoxically, Sartre retains a belief in the Holy Ghost, who restores the image of God in humanity, but he rejects God the Father and God the Son. This secularized theological view guides the logic of Sartre's philosophical theories, to be illuminated in the following pages by Agamben's critique of *anthropogenesis*, what he describes as the sovereign construction of human and nonhuman life.

Agamben and the Creation of Mankind

Central to Agamben's critique of sovereignty is the claim that our representational constructs are, by nature, divisive, hierarchical, and self-authorizing. Following the poststructural theory that linguistic concepts generate their meaning through opposition—what the linguist Ferdinand de Saussure referred to as a system of differences—Agamben argues that our notions of humanity entail representational exclusions of the *nonhuman other*. In a very literal sense, then, language distinguishes mankind from the rest of creation, but it does so at the expense of nonhumans, which are conceptually distinguished from humanity as inferior. What legitimizes these representational constructs as metaphysically authoritative is not, as one might think, the ability of language to describe the world accurately (as in a correspondence theory of language), but, rather, the performative nature of speech, which conjures into existence the world it describes.

Building on J. L. Austin's well-known argument that certain utterances perform the actions they describe (two people commit themselves to marriage, for example, by uttering the words "I do"), Agamben argues in *The Sacrament of Language* that all utterances, being differential in nature, imply the larger linguistic structures that, in turn, provide the context that gives these utterances their meaning. In the act of being spoken, the overarching linguistic structures implied by specific utterances enforce themselves upon nature as veridical by presupposing their own truthfulness. In his discussion of the oath—which, for the ancient Greeks, Romans, and Christians, represented the whole of language in and of itself—Agamben writes that "[e]very naming, every act of speech is, in this sense, an oath, in which the *logos* (the speaker in the *logos*) pledges to fulfill his word, swears on its truthfulness, on the correspondence between words and things that is realized in it."[33] In this way, a simple statement like "the grass is green" implies the larger linguistic structures that inform the meaning of both "grass" and "green," but the statement also performs the larger linguistic structures—and so conjures their meanings into existence—through the utterance "is," a word that asserts its truthfulness by pointing to the mere fact of existence. "The grass is green," in effect, claims to describe the nature of reality.

For Agamben and other poststructuralists, however, our representational constructs do not actually succeed in reaching outside of themselves to coincide with the natural world because language, the poststructuralist will argue, generates its meaning through the dual process of differentiation and deferral, as Jacques Derrida famously articulated. Because language endlessly defers meaning through differentiation it should therefore be understood as a self-enclosed system that never makes contact with the outside world. While today, poststructuralists recognize linguistic speech acts as arbitrary constructs that fail to embody the metaphysical nature they purport to describe, the classical world operated under a theological view of language that made it "impossible to separate name and being, words and things" because, as Agamben is careful to explain, the "verbal act br[ought] being into truth" by performing as veridical the meaning it articulated.[34] In the following passage, Agamben describes the dual function of language in the classical world as denotative and constitutive, the latter of which is also referred to below as *veridiction*, thus reflecting both a correspondence theory of language and its actualizing performance, respectively:

> While assertion has an essentially denotative value, meaning that its truth, in the moment of its formulation, is independent of the subject and is measured with logical and objective parameters (conditions of truth, non-contradiction, adequation between words and things), in veridiction the subject constitutes itself and puts itself in play as such by linking itself performatively to the truth of its own affirmation. For this reason the truth and consistency of the oath coincide with its performance, and for this reason the calling of the god as witness does not imply a factual testimony but is actualized performatively by the very utterance

of the name. What we today call a performative in the strict sense (the speech acts "I swear," "I promise," "I declare," etc., which must, significantly, always be pronounced in the first person) are the relics in language of this constitutive experience of speech—veridiction—that exhausts itself with its utterance, since the speaking subject neither preexists it nor is subsequently linked to it but coincides integrally with the act of speech.[35]

The act of speech constitutes subjecthood, and what the subject believes to be true—i.e., what constitutes the subject's world—is brought into existence by its verbal performance. This, of course, coincides with the lessons of poststructuralists who, following Louis Althusser, argue that subjects are *hailed* into being by discourse, and who, with Jean Baudrillard, argue that discourse is not a true or false representation of reality but the *simulation* of reality, which is always already experienced as true. The difference is that, in the classical world, the vast multitude of contradictory simulations were not regarded as equally valid, as they would be under a poststructuralist worldview, because, for the ancient Greeks, Romans, and Christians, only one of these narratives actually aligned with reality, which was spoken into existence by God.

As Agamben notes, the name of God in the Judaic and Christian traditions as well as among the ancient Greeks and Romans referred to a correspondence theory of language, or the language through which God spoke reality into being. "Language is the word of God, and the word of God is . . . an oath," writes Agamben; "it is God insofar as he reveals himself in the *logos* as the 'faithful one' (*pistos*) par excellence. God is the oath-taker in the language of which man is only the speaker, but in the oath on the name of God the language of men communicates with divine language."[36] To take an oath, according to Agamben, is to put your faith in the ability of language to account for the world accurately; it is to put your faith in the God who first spoke reality into being, thus ensuring the connection between words and things. But when people lie or fail to repeat the divine narrative verbatim, "the connection that unites language and the world is broken," and, consequently, "the name of God, which expressed and guaranteed this connection based in blessing [*bene-dicente*], becomes the name of the curse [*male-dizione*], that is, of a word that has broken its truthful relation to things."[37] But there is an even greater consequence at play here: the misuse of language discloses the impotence of its performative aspect—it reveals that language is not in fact capable of conjuring metaphysical reality into being, for, if it were truly capable of doing this, so-called liars could speak new realities into being at will, thereby dividing reality against itself, the world of one person against the world of another, the worlds created by mankind against the world created by God. Law and religion were formulated in part, Agamben says, to mitigate this unwanted effect by exercising control over liars, dissenters, and perjurers of the oath.

Stated somewhat differently, speech loses its performative power after being divorced from the sovereign, metaphysical narrative first spoken by God, who created and sustains the nature of reality. For this reason, "one could say that the existence of language" was for the ancients "the performative expression of the existence of the world. In this sense metaphysics, the science of pure being, is itself historical and coincides with the experience of the event of language to which man devotes himself in the oath"—i.e., the belief that what a person articulates as true does in fact correspond with reality.[38] But "[i]f the oath is declining, [and] the name of God is withdrawing from language," then speakers have no way to authorize their truth claims as veridical, "and this is what has happened," Agamben observes, with the "'death of God' or, as one should put it more exactly, 'of the name of God'—[where] metaphysics also reaches [its] completion."[39]

By stating that God has withdrawn from language, Agamben means to say that language is not able to conjure reality into being through its performance; the death of God should bring with it the end of metaphysics and the possibility of a univocal master-narrative. And yet, in the modern age, the death of God gives way to God-surrogates who, claiming to have sovereign ownership over exclusionary truth, assert their point of view with theological authority. The God-surrogate at the center of Sartrean existentialism is the sovereign subject, who, in keeping with Agamben's analysis, believes they are capable of conjuring reality into being through performative significations.

To state this plainly, Agamben makes a series of observations pertaining to the oath, the language through which God was thought to speak reality into being, thereby ensuring the connection between words and things. The first observation is that God alone determines the nature of reality, so whenever people speak the truth, they are repeating utterances already spoken by God. They are uniting their voices with God's voice and, through these utterances, giving life to a divine, truth-bearing narrative. However, perjury, or lying under oath, as it were, reveals that not all utterances are veridical, despite the fact that all utterances presuppose their veracity by virtue of their performative nature. Following Aristotle's law of non-contradiction, moreover, we find that disagreement among people is further proof that not all utterances are truthful. The logical conclusion, following these observations, is that spoken words do not conjure reality into being. For Agamben, however, it is not only that language fails to create reality through performative speech acts, but, more to the point, it is that language is a system of differentiation and deferral that even fails to describe the world beyond it. Recognizing this, the poststructuralist regards all significations as arbitrary, differential constructs lacking metaphysical authority. But the object of Agamben's political-theological critique—the sovereign subject—continues to wield language as a lawmaking force that conjures reality into existence. "The model of truth here is not that of the adequation between words and things but the performative one in which speech unfailingly actualizes its meaning. Just as, in the state of exception, the law suspends its own application only to found, in this way, its being in force, so in the performative," Agamben writes, "language suspends its denotation precisely and solely to found its existential connection with things."[40] The sovereign decision maker falsely believes they can speak reality into being, creating meaningful narrative discourse through self-authorizing significations. In similar fashion, society writ large continually reproduces violence against certain people groups through recurring acts of exclusionary signification, dividing the human from the nonhuman, the privileged from the marginalized.

What Agamben terms *anthropogenesis*—referring to mankind's origin, or the emergence of the human species as such—first took place, he says, when certain primates developed language and, in so doing, recognized themselves as superior to other animals. It just so happens that the characteristic humanity recognized as its defining quality—the ability to communicate with each other through speech—is also the very tool it utilizes to mark out and authorize distinctions between superior and inferior beings. Agamben applies a microscopic view to this important moment in our anthropological history. He reports that, for the nineteenth-century biologist Ernst Haeckel, language marked the evolutionary transition from *Pithecanthropus alalus* to *Homo sapien*, but, shortly after, the linguist Heymann Steinthal observed a significant aporia in Haeckel's claim: if speech is the characteristic that distinguishes mankind from the apes, then a *speechless man* or, for that matter, a *talking animal* can never logically exist, as both would violate Haeckel's assertion that language is the unique practice of human beings.

In Haeckel's view, human identity and the capacity to utilize speech are inextricable; one cannot exist without the other. But if language is humanity's defining characteristic then Steinthal is right: both *speechless man* and *talking animal* are logical contradictions; the first animalizes man by taking away his speech, the second humanizes animals by giving them a voice. Therefore, to make the evolutionary transition from animal to human there must be an intermediary stage between speechless animal and talking man that bridges—only by violating—their categorical separation. In the following passage, Agamben elaborates on the significance of this missing evolutionary link:

> What distinguishes man from animal is language, but this is not a natural given already inherent in the psychophysical structure of man; it is, rather, a historical production which, as such, can be properly assigned neither to man nor to animal. If this element is taken away, the difference between man and animal vanishes, unless we imagine a nonspeaking man—*Homo alalus*, precisely—who would function as a bridge that passes from the animal to the human. But all evidence suggests that this is only a shadow cast by language, a presupposition of speaking man, by which we always obtain only an animalization of man (an animal-man, like Haeckel's ape-man) or a humanization of the animal (a man-ape). The animal-man and the man-animal are the two sides of a single fracture, which cannot be mended from either side.[41]

No matter how gradual the psychophysical transition or incremental the development of language, at some point in its evolutionary history the animal *becomes* human through its acquisition of language proper. But defining humans by their use of language merely passes the buck, forcing us to define the exact nature of language. The logic at play here is clearly circular: animal life becomes human the moment we call it human, the moment it can demonstrate a mastery of language, which we ourselves define. For this reason, *Homo alalus*—the intermediary species identified above—should be thought of as an empty place holder, or *zone of indifference*, who signals the need to distinguish between man and animal through an interpretive decision. This zone of indifference is the place of pure decision because it stands at the crossroads between humanity and its structural opposites. Agamben calls this place of pure decision the *anthropological machine*.

The boundaries of human identity, he argues, must be arbitrarily decided upon through exclusionary representations of the nonhuman. In this sense, our every decision is a representational division, and all such divisions, by their very nature, must be decided upon—i.e., the representational divisions must be drawn. "Insofar as the production of man through the opposition man/animal, human/inhuman, is at stake here, the machine necessarily functions by means of an exclusion (which is also always already a capturing) and an inclusion (which is also always already an exclusion)."[42] Unfettered decisionism, or *the power to decide*, therefore marks the transition from non-speaking animal to humanity proper through the divisive operations of language itself—a decision that includes particular lifeforms under the privileged title of "mankind," and a decision that excludes its structural opposites in an act of sovereign domination. As Agamben explains:

> Both machines are able to function only by establishing a zone of indifference at their centers, within which—like a "missing link" which is always lacking because it is already virtually present—the articulation between human and animal, man and non-man, speaking being and living being, must take place. Like every space of exception, this zone is, in truth, perfectly empty, and the truly human being who should occur there is only the place of a ceaselessly updated

decision in which the caesurae and their rearticulation are always dislocated and displaced anew. What would thus be obtained, however, is neither an animal life nor a human life, but only a life that is separated and excluded from itself—only a *bare life*.[43]

Agamben believes with Sartre that existence precedes essence, that the "ceaselessly updated decision" of being-for-itself determines the boundaries of human identity, which are "always dislocated and displaced anew." Because humanity lacks being-in-itself, anthropogenesis can only take place through a sovereign decision that separates the human from the animal by presenting both lifeforms, in bad faith, as fixed ontological entities. In truth, however, the decision merely separates humanity from *bare life*, or its structural opposites, none of which are fixed ontic realities but rather arbitrary, differential constructs. So it is not biological difference, superior intelligence, or language acquisition per se that separates mankind from animal life, but the sovereign decision alone. The distinguishing characteristic of humanity is that it chooses to represent itself as a superior lifeform; man is the animal that distinguishes itself from all other animals as superior. "[T]o define the human not through any *nota characteristica*," Agamben states, "but rather through his self-knowledge, means that man is the being which recognizes itself as such, that *man is the animal that must recognize itself as human to be human*."[44] Joseph Slaughter echoes this phrase in his discussion of human rights: "Although human rights are presupposed to be self-evident, they must be publicly and officially articulated as such, named as self-evident to be made self-evident."[45] Human rights achieve their legally authorized status through self-insistence, sovereign choice, or the act of declaring oneself metaphysically superior to nonhumans.

Lynn Hunt observes this logic at play in the US Declaration of Independence and the French Declaration of the Rights of

Man and Citizen in her 2007 monograph *Inventing Human Rights: A History*: "This claim of self-evidence, crucial to human rights even now, gives rise to a paradox: if equality of rights is so self-evident, then why did this assertion have to be made and why was it only made in specific times and places?"[46] Were human rights truly self-evident they would be found in every human society throughout history, and they would not be argued over, questioned, or insisted upon because all people everywhere would already recognize human rights as an essential part of nature, such as our biological need to sleep, eat, and drink in order to survive (which itself is not a *right* but a biological truism). As Hunt observes, "[a]n assertion that requires argument is not self-evident."[47] Our commitment to human rights requires logical justification.

But logical justification cannot be found, I maintain, without incorporating a religious element into the explanation. To argue in concert with modern Western society that human rights are self-evident because human beings are inherently valuable is merely to pass the buck, for there is no way to justify our belief that human beings are inherently valuable without first introducing a religious belief in objective moral value. One could argue, for example, that human life was given inherent value by a divine creator who determines the metaphysical nature of being. Deprived of this theological explanation, however, inherent moral value must be insisted upon without logical justification. There is no good reason to believe that human life is more valuable than the rest of the natural world, and, likewise, there is no good reason to believe that our superior value is built into the metaphysical nature of being—at least not without God. Indeed, the belief that human life is inherently valuable grows out of the anthropocentric presupposition that human beings were created with moral purpose by a God who values them over the rest of creation.

As Agamben, Slaughter, and Hunt point out, it is the declarative act alone—the use of language to identify oneself as superior within nature—that distinguishes humanity from nonhuman existence as exceptionally valuable and rights bearing. This decisionist metaphysic—which divides humanity from the nonhuman other—represents, in Agamben's view, the prevailing ideology of modern state power. Even current democratic leaders have the legal right to suspend constitutional law in times of an emergency, he explains. When the sovereign makes use of these emergency powers, the moral authority of the constitution is transferred to the lawmaking decisions of whoever is in charge. In this manner, a sovereign democratic leader is afforded total command over the legal system just as, in Sartre's existentialist worldview, the sovereign individual is afforded total command over moral law after the death of God. This transvaluation of values, as Nietzsche called it, represents an emergency state where the fixed moral principles of, say, the Decalogue are suspended through the lawmaking authority of the free individual, whose every decision now operates, according to Sartre, as the ontological origin of moral law.

Ostensibly, then, Sartrean existentialism outlines the tacit philosophical logic of modern state power and can be framed, in this light, as the indirect target of Agamben's political-theological critique. Agamben agrees with John Gillespie that God's death and, concomitantly, the suspension of fixed moral laws result in "the secularisation of God in the person of the absolute free individual,"[48] but Agamben, in contrast with Gillespie, extends his critique beyond the sovereign individual to the sovereign leader of the state, whose lawmaking decisions produce *bare life*, or life that has been set apart as nonhuman, by drawing arbitrary divisions between citizen and non-citizen, humanity and the dehumanized other. This, I argue, is where Agamben's ontotheological critique of the Nazi legal theorist Carl Schmitt becomes especially helpful to our analysis of Sartre. For Schmitt's political theology is blatantly self-aware where

Sartre's materialistic atheism has failed him: the former is knowingly based on secularized theological views while the latter unwittingly conceals its theological origins (the *imago Dei*) within a secular form (human rights). For Schmitt, sacred human identity is determined by the sovereign decision maker alone, who, imitating the divine creator of mankind, endows the legal citizen with inherent rights or what I am calling the *imago Dei*—that which separates mankind from the rest of creation as superior. In a theological context, this refers to a divine being who literally creates human beings with superior moral value; in a secular context, however, where objective value has been severed from its theological origins, this refers to the dogmatic insistence that human exceptionalism is self-evident.

Looking at Sartre through Agamben's Eyes

Sartre's atheistic views are identical in this regard to Schmitt's political theology, but Sartre does not acknowledge their theological origin until very late in his philosophical career when he confesses to de Beauvoir that he feels like he was created by a deity. This, of course, directly contradicts his 1946 assertion in *Existentialism Is a Humanism* that "there is no human nature since there is no God to conceive of it."[49] According to Sartre, materialistic atheism "bear[s out] the full consequences of" God's nonexistence, so there can be no *human nature* to dictate the value, meaning, and significance of mankind; consequently, there is no fixed standard upon which to base a system of transcendental moral laws.[50] The problem, which I think Sartre does well to underscore, is that in order to standardize moral justice and thereby elude the consequences of cultural relativism people must base their juridical divisions of good and evil on God's moral character but also—*and just as importantly*—on mankind's moral value, which is itself determined by God. For it is only by standardizing human identity and thereby ascribing to all people an identical set of inherent rights that one may conceive of something like equal treatment and, with it, a universalist conception of morality. Under this metaphysical view, "[m]an possesses a human nature," Sartre writes, but "this 'human nature' . . . is found in all men, which means that each man is a particular example of a universal concept."[51] This is why the *imago Dei* is an essential part of any moralist paradigm; without it, the moral value of human identity is indeterminate, and this indeterminacy prevents us from standardizing a universal concept of morality. "[M]an as existentialists conceive of him cannot be defined," Sartre states. "He will not be anything until later, and then he will be what he makes of himself . . . since he conceives of himself only after he exists, just as he wills himself to be after being thrown into existence."[52]

In Sartre's view, the *natureless* nature of being-for-itself is the logical consequence of God's nonexistence. "That is what I mean when I say that man is condemned to be free: condemned, because he did not create himself, yet nonetheless free, because once cast into the world, he is responsible for everything he does."[53] Human life is therefore "perfectly empty," as Agamben says, for it is "the place of a ceaselessly updated decision in which the caesurae and their rearticulation are always dislocated and displaced anew."[54] But Sartre conflates the indeterminacy of being-for-itself with the transvaluation of moral law because "along with [God's] disappearance goes the possibility of finding values in an intelligible heaven. There could no longer be any *a priori* good, since there would be no infinite and perfect consciousness to conceive of it."[55] Sartre again references Dostoevsky's claim that, without God, everything is permissible. Moreover, he argues that morality and human nature are interdependent concepts because, if "God does not exist, we will encounter no values or orders that can legitimize our conduct," meaning that "we can never explain our actions by reference to a given and immutable human nature."⁵⁶

Without God, there is no human nature, and without human nature, there is no basis for moral conduct. Presumably, then, what ties all three elements of this moral-theological nexus together is the *imago Dei*, the secularized theological belief that mankind is more valuable than the rest of creation, that human beings as image bearers are superior to the nonhuman creatures—or *bare life*, in Agamben's terms— who lack the divine image, and that each of us bears inalienable rights only because we have declared those rights to be self-evident. As we have already seen, Sartre admits to de Beauvoir, against his better judgment and in spite of his atheism, that he believes in some version of the *imago Dei*. It "is doubtless not wrong for an eagle or a lion" to kill a human being, he states, but it is "directly, absolutely wrong" for human beings to kill one another.⁵⁷ Sartre affords mankind a unique moral station in life, asserting that human beings— who are not animals—must be held to a moral standard.

But Sartre also makes clear in his late interviews with de Beauvoir what he made explicit decades earlier in *Being and Nothingness* and *Existentialism Is a Humanism*: "secular morality" inherently lacks the a priori legitimacy that accompanies the theological.⁵⁸ He accuses so-called French radicals of secularizing the absolutist morality that can only exist in relationship with the *imago Dei*. But this is what makes Sartre's metaphysical reading of the sovereign decision all the more peculiar. He condemns the failed atheism of French radicals who sublimate a theological view of morality, but then, in what appears to be a blatant contradiction of this view, he depicts the freely made choices of being-for-itself as the ontological origin of moral law. Like the divine creator of the universe, the existential subject makes self-ratifying choices *ex nihilo*, but these choices combine the nothingness, or pure potentiality, of being-for-itself with the autonomous self-presence, or pure actuality, of being-in-itself to form universally binding laws—what Sartre calls being-in-itself-for-itself and Agamben calls the oath. In this manner, the sovereign individual unwittingly regards his decisions as reality-making, just as, in *The Sacrament of Language*, the oath names God's ability to speak reality into being. The following passage from *Existentialism Is a Humanism* reveals the illogic of Sartre's thought:

> the first effect of existentialism is to make every man conscious of what he is, and to make him solely responsible for his own existence. And when we say that man is responsible for himself, we do not mean that he is responsible only for his own individuality, but that he is responsible for all men. . . . When we say that man chooses himself, not only do we mean that each of us must choose himself, but also that in choosing himself, he is choosing for all men. In fact, in creating the man each of us wills ourselves to be, there is not a single one of our actions that does not at the same time create an image of man as we think he ought to be.[59]

The free individual as being-for-itself is forever condemned to carve out the boundaries of human identity, but one should never in bad faith regard those boundaries as immutable laws, in Sartre's opinion. To become in-itself-for-itself is impossible because nothing can be at once absolutely free and ontologically fixed, as he argues in *Being and Nothingness*. Every choice signifies the human being as a universal concept in ways that exclude opposing representations of humanity, but these choices can never authorize one representation of humanity over competing representations of humanity as veridical. For this reason, materialistic atheism ought to result in decisions that inherently lack the metaphysical authority of law. Yet Sartre describes the existential subject as a "legislator" who chooses "what humanity as a whole should be."[60] Under this view, the subject's decisions are not regarded as arbitrary representations lacking the metaphysical force of law but as instances of being-in-itself-for-itself, legally binding ontic realities that force the legislator to recognize "his own full and profound responsibility."[61] Thus, following God's death, the existential subject becomes the metaphysical origin of law; in choosing himself, he chooses the ontic nature of mankind and its structural opposite, the nonhuman. Subsequently, the *imago Dei* is ascribed to human beings in the secularized form of inherent rights, around which the sovereign subject then constructs moral precepts geared toward the preservation and protection of those rights.

According to Agamben, the sovereign decision is that "through which Being founds itself *sovereignly*, without anything preceding or determining it (*superiorem non recognoscens*) other than its own ability not to be."[62] But the metaphysical authority of sovereign decisionism relies not only on the absolute freedom of being-for-itself, but on the ontological impossibility of being-in-itself-for-itself, a "zone of indistinction" where "pure potentiality and pure actuality" become "indistinguishable."[63] When the pure potentiality of being-for-itself and the pure actuality of being-in-itself are combined as being-in-itself-for-itself, the sovereign subject becomes equipped with the absolute freedom to dictate, at will, the ontic nature of human identity. Under this secularized theological view, each and every intervention divides the human from the nonhuman, the *imago Dei* from *bare life*, and ratifies sovereign decision making with the moral authority of divine transcendence. According to Agamben, sovereign political leaders adopt this metaphysical paradigm during so-called emergencies to justify their suspension of constitutional law, claiming these legislative powers as their own. Sartre's existentialism mirrors the secularized theological view of state power described by Agamben in what appears to be an outright betrayal of materialistic atheism. He says that "[c]hoosing to be this or that is to affirm at the same time the value of what we choose, because we can never choose evil. We always choose the good."[64]

In the face of God's death, which Carl Schmitt frames as the deauthorization of constitutional law, both Sartre and Schmitt transfer divine authority to the sovereign individual, who now dictates the boundaries of human nature at the expense of lesser, nonhuman beings. Agamben, of course, dismisses sovereign decisionism as a secularized theological view bereft of true metaphysical authority while Sartre, by contrast, acknowledges the impossibility of being-in-itself-for-itself at the same time that he imagines a decisionist philosophy based entirely on its logic. "I've retained one single thing to do with the existence of God," Sartre admits near the end of a long philosophical career, "and that is Good and Evil as absolutes."[65] But these are not moral precepts based on the transcendental will of God; they are absolutes "in the midst of the relative," according to Sartre, freely chosen moral laws based on his personal construction of human identity.[66] Thus, failing to achieve the philosophical aims of materialistic atheism, Sartre transfers the moral authority of being-in-itself-for-itself to mankind. On the one hand, he lambastes those who, in bad faith, essentialize themselves to become like God, but, on the other hand, he unwittingly regards the free decisions of being-for-itself as lawmaking instantiations of being-in-itself-for-itself, where pure potentiality and pure actuality combine as relative absolutes, or individually chosen laws. In other words, Sartre disavows being-in-itself-for-itself as an impossible fantasy, but he then commits himself to premises that logically result in the fantastic. How Sartre misses the logical consequences of his combined philosophical assertions is unclear, but he unwittingly adopts the precise notion that he set out to critique, correct, and eliminate. Sartre announces the death of God with philosophical flourish and then transfers divine authority to the sovereign subject.

The theological force of sovereign decisionism is made explicit in Sartre's 1961 preface to Frantz Fanon's *The Wretched of the Earth*. According to Ronald Aronson, "[t]his stunning essay ... is one of Sartre's most vivid and brutal pieces of writing, both in its argument and its worldview"; it begins by "denouncing colonial violence, asserts that its damage was being undone by the natives' own violence, and then celebrates that violence being turned against Europeans."[67] As Sartre himself writes in *The Wretched of the Earth*, "no one can rob, enslave, or kill their fellow human beings without committing a crime," so European colonizers "establish the principle that the colonized are not fellow human beings. Our strike force has been ... given orders to reduce the inhabitants of the annexed territory to the level of superior monkey."[68] The colonizer establishes political sovereignty in captured territories by animalizing the natives, drawing a division between the human and nonhuman, the *imago Dei* and *bare life* under a zone of indistinction that endows the sovereign decision with metaphysical, lawmaking force. "I am not claiming that it is impossible to change human beings into animals,"[69] Sartre assures his audience. Because representational constructs bear out the same real-world application as ontic reality under the decisionist philosophy of Sartre's existentialist worldview, the transformation of human being into animal is only too plausible; as we have already seen, moral laws are relative absolutes, for Sartre, freely made decisions endowed with the secularized theological force of the *imago Dei*.

According to this view, every subject is captive to sovereign decision making, a zero-sum game of being-for-others that necessarily produces human identity at the expense of the nonhuman. Sartre asserts in *Being and Nothingness* that to be free is to limit another person's freedom, that being-for-itself seeks to preserve its personhood by "making an object out of the Other."[70] The other "puts me out of play and strips me of my transcendences by refusing to '*join in*,'"[71] Sartre writes, and so they reject his personal account of human identity in favor of their own account. As representational exclusions, the animalized victims of anthropogenesis can only ever reclaim their humanity by inflicting violence against their oppressors. This is why, in his famous dispute with Albert Camus over the ethico-political value of revolutionary violence, Sartre argues that "the limit of one right (that is, of one freedom) is another right (that is, another freedom) and not some 'human nature,'" or unchanging essence, that exists apart from the choices of being-for-itself.[72] Defending your humanity, Sartre insists, will have dehumanizing effects.

Sartre makes this point in response to Camus's assertion that communist concentration camps—and Sartre's loyal support of the Soviet Union—are morally unjustifiable. "Absolute freedom," Camus writes in his 1951 essay *The Rebel*, which prompted the initial conflict with Sartre and resulted in their eventual falling out, "is the right of the strongest to dominate. Therefore it prolongs the conflicts that profit by injustice. Absolute justice," by contrast, "destroys freedom."[73] Sartre believed that murder was morally justifiable in the context of political revolution if the revolutionary act liberates the oppressed person from their animalization under a hegemonic regime. Against Sartre's agonistic view of intersubjectivity, Camus wrote that "we have to live and let live,"[74] asserting that our lives can be carried out independently without directly impacting our neighbor's wellbeing. As we have already seen, however, Sartre did not believe there was any such middle ground. "If you are not victims," he asserts, "then you are unquestionably executioners."[75] For Sartre, humanity only ever exists at the expense of the nonhuman, and, likewise, the dehumanized are only able to recover their humanity at the expense of their oppressor. At the center of this zero-sum conflict are competing representations of the *imago Dei*, relative valuations of human identity that legitimize moral precepts through self-authorized decision making.

This is why Sartre can declare "that killing a man is wrong. Is directly, absolutely wrong,"[76] and at the same time declare, in what appears to be a blatant contradiction of this statement, that we "can never choose evil. We always choose the good."[77] People are unable to murder fellow human beings because the very act automatically reduces their victim to a nonhuman status. As Cary Wolfe puts it, "the full transcendence of the 'human' requires the sacrifice of the 'animal' and the animalistic, which in turn makes possible a symbolic economy in which we can engage in a 'non-criminal putting to death' . . . of other *humans* as well by marking *them* as animal."[78] Stated differently, being killed is literally dehumanizing, so murder is always already committed against the nonhuman. Sartre replaces God with mankind as the moral center of the universe; because every decision is literally man-making, the sovereign subject can do no wrong.

Sartre condemns this authoritarian behavior in *Being and Nothingness* as an impossible fantasy conducted in bad faith, but as he later confesses to de Beauvoir, "[i]n *Being and Nothingness* I set out reasons for my denial of God's existence that were not actually the real reasons."[79] So it may be that Sartre secretly envied the moral authority that comes with being-in-itself-for-itself. This would explain the contradictions that emerge from a close examination of his work. In fairness to Sartre, entirely ridding oneself of moral commitments is no easy task and, as Sartre admits to de Beauvoir, fully realizing the aims of materialistic atheism is "a very long-term affair."[80] It requires considerable work to recognize the full effect of God's absence on the world. That Sartre failed to realize its fullness is evident from the metaphysical authority he attributes to sovereign choice. It appears that Sartre was not entirely able to abandon his belief in sacred human identity, but without a God in heaven to uphold the *imago Dei*, sacred human identity had to be severed from its divine source. For this reason, human rights could no longer be understood on theological grounds, but had to be seen, by contrast, as self-originating, a priori realities that have no source of authorization outside of the sovereign subject. Sartrean existentialism weaves itself into a tangled web of contradiction, preserving the *imago Dei* while eliminating God. The result of this operation is a secularized theological view of moral decision making. Thus, at the center of Sartrean existentialism is a God-surrogate—the sovereign subject—who, in keeping with Agamben's critique, believes themselves to be capable of conjuring reality into being.

Hemingway's Youth as an Oak Park Congregationalist

Having conducted a philosophical reading of Sartre's life and work to explain the theoretical logic behind sovereign moral choices, I change direction with these building blocks in place to conduct a biographical study of Hemingway, whose childhood influences led him down a similar path of secularization. Like Sartre, Hemingway was born into a Christian environment, and the spiritual influence of Hemingway's youth spanned multiple generations of his family. Grandfather Hemingway, Anson Tyler, for example, was a Civil War veteran who converted to Christianity in 1859 and later attended Wheaton Academy, an Illinois college founded by Wesleyan abolitionists. Anson met his wife Adelaide, the only grandmother Hemingway knew, during a campus prayer meeting, and the two raised as devout Protestants six children that included Hemingway's father, Clarence. Strongly "opposed to such habits as smoking, drinking, dancing, and card playing," Anson would become general secretary of the Chicago YMCA whose evangelical focus "confirmed his deeply felt spirituality," as Hemingway biographer Mary Dearborn writes.[81]

Hemingway's maternal grandfather, Ernest Hall, another Civil War veteran, was a pillar of Grace Episcopal Church in Oak Park, Illinois, who assembled the family and household servants every morning to kneel in communal prayer. The Halls lived across the street from the Hemingways, so Ernest's parents, Grace Hall and Clarence Hemingway, would grow up in close quarters before eventually uniting in holy matrimony as devout members of the First Congregational Church. Ernest himself was baptized and confirmed in the church and would even become a member of the Plymouth League, a Christian organization that met every Sunday evening to organize community outreach programs. Steeped in a religious environment first carved out by his grandparents, Ernest was well primed for a life of spiritual devotion. Larry Grimes declares that "Family and church marched young Ernest double time into the army of Christ."[82]

He was baptized Ernest Miller Hemingway by Dr. William E. Barton of the First Congregational Church of Oak Park on October 1, 1899. As Hemingway biographer Carlos Baker records, both of these names were taken from Grace's side of the family—"Ernest for his grandfather Hall, and Miller for his great-uncle, the bedstead manufacturer. After the ceremony Grace wrote piously that the child had been carried 'as an offering unto the Lord, to receive his name and hence forth be counted as one of God's little lambs.'"[83] Shortly after, the family would start attending an affiliated church led by pastor William J. Norton so that Grace, a former New York City opera singer, could serve as the choirmistress. It was here at the Third Congregational Church of Oak Park that Hemingway and his sister Marcelline received their first communion. The two would also participate in a Bible-reading competition hosted by the youth group, and though neither of them would win the competition, Marcelline later wrote in her memoir that she and Ernest "passed a detailed test on the Bible reading and [they] both learned a lot."[84]

Ernest and Marcelline transferred back to the First Congregational Church in 1915, where they attended the sermons of Reverend Barton throughout their junior and senior years of high school. Barton was part of an accomplished family; his sister was Red Cross founder Clara Barton, and his son, Bruce Barton, would author a controversial bestseller titled *The Man Nobody Knows* (1925). Presenting Jesus as the ancient founder of modern business practices, the book promoted what Grimes calls the "Masculine Christianity" preached by Bruce's father.[85] Barton himself enjoyed a considerable renown and was even invited to speak to President Woodrow Wilson in 1917. Not surprisingly, Oak Park committed itself to the theological teachings of this religious powerhouse, whose sermons were often reprinted in the local newspaper, *Oak Leaves*.[86] There seems to be little question, in fact, that Reverend Barton was the spiritual lifeblood of Oak Park. If Hemingway believed in Christianity — and we certainly have reason to believe that he did — it was first presented to him in the form of Barton's Christianity. As Hemingway biographer Michael Reynolds explains, "it was not possible in Oak Park to be properly baptized, graduated, married or buried unless Rev. Barton conducted the ceremony."[87]

As to the exact nature of Barton's theological influence, Grimes asserts that the "hell-fire Protestantism associated with the Midwest" was abandoned by the citizens of Oak Park in pursuit of Barton's "forward-thinking" approach to religion, which sought to establish the kingdom of heaven on earth in the form of an otherwise secular medium known plainly as social progress.[88] The Oak Park community lacked the theological burden of original sin and, as a direct consequence of this view, they understood Christian salvation as a practice in self-mastery — which is to say, the responsible application of free will — not the redemptive intervention of a deity. According to Grimes, Barton's particular strand of Protestantism was

> a lumpy mix of liberal theology, Victorian morality, and sentimental piety. These terms describe the religious ethos of Oak Park during Hemingway's formative years and, taken together, they constitute a "civil religion." Between the years 1899 and 1920, neither religion nor the social order in Oak Park were static. During these two decades of rapid growth and change, Oak Park grew from a small town of 10,000 in 1900 to a city of 35,000 in 1917. As it grew, it tried hard to maintain the myth of its Edenic origins and perpetuate itself as a Covenant community of the early New England order. Essential to the myth were the notions of human innocence, healthy-mindedness, social progress, and optimism, all hallmarks of liberal theology. Blended with Victorian morality, sentimental piety, and expanded into a civil religion, this progressive Protestantism provided just the formula required to maintain the myth. For those who could affirm it, and they seem to have been a majority, this religio-mythic perspective on life in Oak Park had great power.[89]

Among the fundamental tenets of Barton's liberal theology was the belief that human nature is not yet completed at birth. We become fully human through morally righteous decisions that build up our ethical character in the image of Christ. When everyone in Christian society behaves like the risen lord, they "bring the kingdom of God ever closer to existence on this earth. Nothing but human weakness" — what Grimes qualifies as "a failure of the will" — "can prevent the triumph of goodness in private lives or in the public domain."[90] Because the residents of Oak Park likened themselves to John Winthrop's famous *city on a hill*, their sense of pride and community obligation drove the parents of this tightly knit congregation to indoctrinate their children with the theological teachings of Reverend Barton, their spiritual leader.

Self-mastery, for Barton and his followers, was a deeply gendered concept. Making morally righteous decisions was considered a masculine virtue, while immoral decision making was considered a feminine, or *effeminate*, vice. Under this theological rubric—where freedom was a sign of virility and masculinity a practice in sovereign decisionism—Reverend Barton fostered a "muscular" Christianity that measured moral character on a "masculine-feminine scale."[91] It is only through the sheer force of will that one develops Christian character, so the community pressure to live righteously was bound up with traditional gender expectations. Grimes tells us that, for the residents of Oak Park,

> Masculine Christianity was moral Christianity. It presupposed a God who had provided humans with the capacity to do good if they will it in fellowship with that God . . . No doctrine of special election sorts anyone out for eternal life, and no doctrine of total depravity condemns the rest to hellfire. Sin (an ontological state) is gone from the emergent modernist church; only sins (matters of morality) remain.[92]

Grimes distinguishes between competing theological worldviews: one that frames sin as the depraved ontological state of mankind, and one that frames sin as an isolated free choice in no way determined by humanity's fallen nature. Under the first theological system, a person overcomes their sinful nature by way of divine intervention. Under the second theological system, people are absolutely free to determine their own moral character without divine interference. To become the man he wanted to be, Hemingway would have to take possession of his identity, a moral pursuit that framed masculinity as the sovereign exercise of free will. For Hemingway and the other residents of Oak Park, the morally upright citizen was someone who exhibited total control over his destiny, so to be found lacking in this quality cast a shadow of doubt over that person's purported manhood. This might explain why Hemingway had such a vexed relationship with his mother. Biographers tell us that Grace was head of the household, the breadwinner of the family, and that she emasculated Clarence with her domineering personality. "Hemingway affected an exaggerated bravado" as a result of this, "and pursued activities that would exhibit male prowess" to compensate for the "early insecurity" he felt around his gender identity, a feeling that developed, J. Gerald Kennedy writes, from viewing "his father's passivity and 'cowardice.'"[93]

But this characterization of Clarence only gives a partial depiction of the man, for Hemingway's father was otherwise well practiced in the art of masculinity, traditionally conceived. He trained the young Ernest in so-called manly activities like camping, fishing, and hunting, but also, and most importantly, he trained Ernest in the practice of upright moral behavior. According to Dearborn, "Dr. Hemingway taught his children about life outdoors. . . . Ernest learned how to survive in the wilderness, how to walk like an Indian, how to preserve and stuff animals after they were dead, how to tie flies to catch trout, and countless other lessons about the out-of-doors."[94] Clarence also "forbade all recreational activity on the Lord's Day," Baker tells us; "attendance at church and Sunday school was compulsory. Major infractions of the rules were swiftly punished with a razor strop . . . followed by injunctions to kneel and ask [for] God's forgiveness."[95] According to Dearborn, Clarence was by far "the more rigid and serious about his faith."[96] He was also a stricter disciplinarian than Grace and regularly brought Ernest to tears for failing to live up to his moral expectations. This is not to say, however, that Grace was uninterested in Ernest's spiritual upbringing. On the contrary, "Grace called Hemingway back into step with true soldiers of the cross" after his moral failures "by reminding him of his heritage and urging him to measure up to . . . the standards set for him by his ancestors, particularly Reverend William Edward Miller and Ernest Hall."[97] It would seem that Grace, as much as Clarence, raised the boy to emulate the masculine ideals of his spiritual forebears, ideals that in Oak Park took the form of self-determination, self-mastery, and moral rectitude.[98] Grimes says that "Oak Park took quite literally the biblical injunction to raise up children in the way they should go. And in the case of Ernest Hemingway, the community was shocked, angered, and hurt when it seemed in later years that in spite of its best efforts he had chosen another way."[99]

A Change in Hemingway's Religious Temperament

The young Ernest would feel morally conflicted when River Forest High School nearly expelled him for authoring an underground publication titled *The Jazz Journal*, which attributed salacious jokes to various members of the teaching staff. Not surprisingly, Grace and Clarence chose to let Ernest face the consequences of this poorly made decision. He would not actually be expelled from school for circulating the publication, but Ernest seriously resented his parents for failing to intervene in the matter. Their inaction exacerbated his growing distaste for what Grimes calls the stifling "Victorian morality" of Oak Park Congregationalism and ignited a kind of rebellious streak in Ernest that he directed toward institutional authority.[100]

Ernest was urged by his father to attend Oberlin College with his sister, Marcelline, but he would reject his father's recommendation on principle and skip higher education altogether. Clarence was nevertheless invested in his son's future, so he reached out to his brother Tyler Hemingway, who wrangled Ernest a summer apprenticeship at *The Kansas City Star*. Ernest was hired by Henry J. Haskell, one of

Tyler's old school mates who was now editor-in-chief at the *Star*, to start a full-time position in the fall. During his time at the *Star*, Hemingway's adolescent rebellion matured into an egotistical battle for his parents' respect. "Kansas City represented the first time he had lived away from home," Dearborn writes, "and it was a liberation. He would begin a lifetime habit of serious drinking, he would write every day except Sunday and be paid for it, and he would fall in love for the first time."[101] But Hemingway still felt the lingering expectations of his former Oak Park community. It would seem that friends and family clung to an image of the boy that Hemingway rebelled against in his search for masculine independence.

For the young newspaper man—who was now fornicating, abusing alcohol, and working late into the early morning—establishing autonomy as an adult also meant sloughing off the religion of his youth. In January 1918, Hemingway wrote home to his mother from Kansas City in a letter that would poorly mask his growing skepticism about religion. Apparently, some time had passed since their previous correspondence, so Hemingway complains that they "were cut off for a while" because the "coal shortage [wa]s still pretty bad."[102] Whether or not Hemingway's excuse was legitimate, he clearly felt resentment toward his mother for criticizing his lack of religious devotion. He writes to her in an almost mocking tone:

> Now dry those tears Mother and cheer up. You will have to find something better than that to worry about. Don't worry or cry or fret about my not being a good Christian. I am just as much as ever and pray every night and believe just as hard so cheer up! Just because I'm a *cheerful* Christian ought not to bother you. The reason I don't go to church on Sunday is because always I have to work till 1 a.m. getting out the Sunday Star and every once in a while till 3 and 4 a.m. And I never open my eyes Sunday morning

until 12:30 noon anyway. So you see it isn't because I don't want to. You know I don't rave about religion but am as sincere a Christian as I can be. Sunday is the one day in the week that I can get my sleep out. Also Aunt Arabell's church is a very well dressed stylish one with a not to be loved preacher and I feel out of place.[103]

On the one hand, the passage feels self-assuring, as if Ernest were losing faith in his childhood religion but is too afraid to admit the fact to himself. It may have been that Ernest was not quite ready to take ownership of his budding atheism by confronting the matter head on. He writes to his mother that he prays "every night" and believes "just as hard," that he's "sincere" and wants to go to church but is not able to because of his schedule. It would also appear that Ernest genuinely missed the First Congregational Church of Oak Park; he feels "out of place" at Aunt Arabell's church and bemoans the fact that they dress differently and have a "not to be loved preacher" who clearly, in the young man's opinion, failed to live up to Reverend Barton.

On the other hand, the passage comes across as defensive. Ernest condescends to his mother and trivializes her moral concerns ostensibly because she discourages his sinful desires to skip church, fornicate, and abuse alcohol—desires that Ernest describes with the euphemism "*cheerful*" to justify his immoral choices. He distinguishes those who "rave about religion" from level-headed Christians like himself who pray to God with sincerity but also have the good sense to live their own lives. To master one's destiny is among the primary theological lessons of Hemingway's youth. He genuinely seems to miss the spiritual leadership of Reverend Barton, but the moral strictures of Oak Park Congregationalism were too closely associated with parental control for a young man in search of his independence. With Hemingway's transition into adulthood—which he hoped to realize in the form of masculine self-determination—came reasons to eschew his childhood Christianity, which embodied a host of community and parental expectations.

To complicate matters further were theological notions of masculinity that conflated self-mastery, or the sovereign demonstration of free will, with moral goodness. You become a man, according to Reverend Barton, by taking control of your will in the service of God. But simply conforming to the "Victorian morality" of Oak Park Congregationalism was no different, for Ernest, than submitting to his mother's control, an emasculating practice that the nineteen-year-old was trying his best to avoid. Ernest was therefore faced with a catch-22: he could either take ownership of his manhood by rejecting the moral expectations of his parents, or he could conform to the masculine ideals of Oak Park morality and, in the process of doing so, abandon his quest for masculine autonomy. Because of the unique structuring of Oak Park theology—which combined moral imperatives with the contradictory imperative to choose your own way—Hemingway was forced to side with one of two extremes. But as the young professional now living on his own discovered, mastering your will, in the theology of Reverend Barton, apparently did not mean taking control of your life; it meant choosing the path that best fulfills God's will, which, for Hemingway, meant conforming to the life already mapped out for him by his parents. The 1918 letter to his mother reveals a strong, if passive-aggressive, desire to break free from the bondage of parental authority, a masculine proclivity that prompted Ernest to reconsider his religious commitments. But, in his quest for manhood, Ernest was faced with a dilemma: how does he forgo the religious duty to perform upright moral behavior and, at the same time, retain his masculine identity? The mixed messages of Hemingway's theological upbringing instilled him with conflicting impulses. How he eventually overcame this conflict would be decided years later during the war, where a brief but very serious encounter with death forced the young man to acknowledge his diminishing faith.

Grimes concludes that the atrocities Hemingway witnessed as a Red Cross ambulance driver in the First World War turned him away from Oak Park Congregationalism but not away from Christianity as a whole. "When the liberal theology, sentimental piety, and Victorian morality of Hemingway's childhood were forced to do battle against the irrational forces and terrible realities of World War I and its aftermath, they failed Hemingway in the fray"; rather than "turn to atheism when Protestantism fails him," however, "Hemingway converts to Catholicism . . . and continues to attend mass and say prayers until his death."[104] Grimes admits that Hemingway experienced "a profound crisis of faith" during the war, but "Hemingway's descent into darkness" does not result in the loss of religious belief.[105] Disillusioned by the war, Hemingway turns from the optimism of Barton's liberal theology to the timeworn traditions of Roman Catholicism, whose doctrine of original sin, H. R. Stoneback and Matthew Nickel contend, helps to make sense of the death and destruction Hemingway witnessed during the war. Nickel agrees with Grimes that "Hemingway never rejected certain fundamental principles of Christianity; he rejected Oak Park's theologically liberal version" in favor of Catholic orthodoxy.[106] "[W]itnessing the dead bodies, hearing the injured soldiers and the gun-fire, and then being blown up" himself was simply too much for Hemingway to reconcile with Barton's theological teaching that spiritual perfection is achieved through self-mastery, or the sovereign exercise of free will.[107] "[W]hen he moved to Paris in 1921, [Hemingway] was immersed in a place very familiar with the imperfectibility of human life, with the acceptance of evil and original sin, and he was surrounded by the presence of a Church that allowed for a ritualistic and disciplined redemption."[108]

Like Grimes and Nickel, Stoneback accuses biographers of misrepresenting Hemingway's Catholic allegiance as strictly nominal and asserts that before "his twenty-eighth birthday (in 1927)," Hemingway had already "accepted the tradition, the authority, and the discipline of Rome and formalized his conversion" to Roman Catholicism.[109] But Hemingway was wounded in war at just eighteen years of age; this leaves nearly a decade between his spiritual disillusionment in 1918 and his Catholic conversion in 1927. Both Stoneback and Nickel point to a canonical inquest of the Parisian Archbishopric in 1927 that formally recognized Hemingway as a Catholic in good standing just one month prior to his second marriage. According to Nickel, the "inquest should resolve any doubt the biographers may have had regarding Hemingway's status as a Catholic up until his marriage to Pauline."[110] But this is a dubious claim; the inquest only accounts for the month prior to their marriage and leaves open the convenience of its motivation, telling us nothing about the preceding nine years. Nickel assigns "the moment of [Hemingway's] conversion" to 1918, writing that "until his marriage to the devoutly Catholic Pauline Pfeiffer in 1927, Hemingway read and learned about the Catholic Church and its rituals, travelled to sacred places, and incorporated this knowledge, emotional experience, and spiritual understanding into his writing."[111]

Nickel would have us believe that Hemingway was a Catholic believer throughout this entire period, as if he had directly swapped Oak Park Congregationalism for Roman Catholicism in one fell swoop. Stoneback, however, describes Hemingway's conversion as a gradual process, writing that after Hemingway's "near-death experience on an Italian battlefield in 1918, and continuing with increasing intensity through the early and mid-1920s, Hemingway's personal religious pilgrimage takes him ... far beyond the social-gospel" of Oak Park Congregationalism and "into the ever-deepening discovery of Catholicism."[112] At no point did Hemingway doubt the truthfulness of Christianity; as Stoneback, Nickel, and even Grimes contend, he simply doubted whether his theology—be it Protestant or Catholic—best explained his religious orientation.

These claims challenge the popular view that Hemingway lost his faith after a brush with death during the war. Scott Donaldson, for example, writes that Hemingway's "upbringing had provided him with a rosy picture of existence that did not square with the brutality of modern life he found everywhere about him."[113] The war "served as a catalyst in crystallizing Ernest's disillusionment with Oak Park religion," so the young man, Donaldson writes, "rebelled against his religious heritage."[114] Biographer Jeffrey Meyers likewise argues that while Hemingway's sisters "remained religious throughout their lives," Ernest "attempted to eradicate in himself every vestige of Oak Park" after leaving it.[115] Of course, the evidence would show that Hemingway was baptized by a Catholic priest who walked between the aisles of wounded soldiers at the field hospital in Fornaci, Italy. But, as Carlos Baker notes, the baptism failed to result in a genuine conversion for Hemingway, and, following the war, the young man would show evidence of religious doubt. In support of this claim, Baker records a conversation Hemingway had with a British infantry officer who, while contemplating the consequences of war, quoted Shakespeare's *The Second Part of Henry the Fourth*: "By my troth, I care not; a man can die but once; we owe God a death . . . and let it go which way it will, he that dies this year is quit for the next."[116] According to Baker, the line resonated with Hemingway, who, in a letter written home to his parents, had recently espoused a similar, fatalistic view of dying.

Personally, I agree with critics and biographers who cast Hemingway's near-death experience during the war as a catalyst that forces his religious doubts to surface. It appears that when people confront the end of life as a palpable, immediate threat to their existence rather than, say, as a distant, abstract possibility that will no doubt happen—they are persuaded—to a much older, significantly altered version of themselves, comforting narratives of immortality crack under the pressure. Even devout religious believers will sometimes experience moments of panic when death approaches, as if the promise of a spiritual afterlife is finally weighed against the uncertainty of the moment by someone who, until that very instance, never *really* believed they were going to die, separated, as they were, by time and the pacifying hypothesis that someone else—someone older and better prepared, perhaps—would take their place on the chopping block. Hemingway was a mere eighteen years old when death first confronted him as an inevitable fact of life. Italian soldiers were dying all around him, and, after just weeks as a Red Cross ambulance driver, Ernest was struck by a mortar shell that punctured his lower body in over two hundred places. One man lay next to him dead, and another man lay just beyond him who was "badly hurt and crying piteously."[117] After carrying the wounded soldier to safety, Hemingway was so "thickly soaked with Italian blood that they thought at first he had been shot through the chest" but no chest wounds were found.[118] Still, the "mortar shell that killed the man standing next to him," Michael Reynolds notes, "nearly crippled Ernest for life."[119]

Hemingway was treated for his leg injuries and moved to a hospital in Milan. There, he was visited by friend and fellow reporter at *The Kansas City Star* Ted Brumback, who had also volunteered to drive ambulances during the war. Brumback wrote a letter to Hemingway's parents after the visit that reported on their son's injuries and heroics. It would seem that Hemingway's adolescent bravado had matured into real confidence. Commenting on this transformation, Baker writes that "experience in being blown up, in rescuing a wounded companion, [and] in courageously enduring the pain of his wounds . . . had enlarged [Ernest's] confidence. Without loss of his endearing boyish qualities, he had suddenly taken on some of the qualities of manhood."[120] It would seem that moving away from home, working long hours as a newspaper man, and saving another human life during the war gave Hemingway a sense of ownership over his masculine identity, but it was his personal brush with death, I believe, that finally prompted the young man to let go of his religion and spurn the moral expectations of Oak Park. Hemingway writes home to his parents approximately three months after being hospitalized:

> There is nothing for you to worry about, because it has been fairly conclusively proved that I can't be bumped off. And wounds don't matter. I wouldn't mind being wounded again so much because I know just what it is like. And you can only suffer so much, you know, and it does give you an awfully satisfactory feeling to be wounded. It's getting beaten up in a good cause. . . . All the heroes are dead. And the real heroes are the parents. Dying is a very simple thing. I've looked at death and really I know. If I should have died it would have been very easy for me. Quite the easiest thing I ever did. But the people at home do not realize that. They suffer a thousand times more. . . . And how much better to die in all the happy period of undisillusioned youth, to go out in a blaze of light, than to have your body worn out and old and illusions shattered. So, dear old family, don't ever worry about me! It isn't bad to be wounded: I know, because I've experienced it. And if I die, I'm lucky. Does all that sound like the crazy, wild kid you sent out to learn about the world a year ago? It is a great old world, though, and I've always had a good time and the odds are all in favor of coming back to the old place.[121]

To be sure, much of what Ernest says here still smacks of youthful immaturity, for, yet again, the young man feels a need to posture. He calls his former self a "crazy, wild kid," as if adopting a condescending attitude toward his past self will demonstrate to his parents that he has grown more mature. At the same time, however, his tone strikes me as somewhat tongue-in-cheek, like someone who uses humor to cushion an otherwise serious comment. Perhaps Ernest knew his observations about personal growth would come across as needy to his parents, revealing that he was in fact desperate for their approval, so he engages in self-mockery to mask what is really a genuine comment. He refers to his earlier self as an "undisillusioned youth" who, protected by a lack of worldly experience, has not yet had his "illusions shattered," but we know from the context of his letter that this is not the case. Ernest stared death in the eyes and breathed in its stench; his ironic self-awareness is meant only to appease his parents, who make use of a hackneyed platitude—namely, that maturity comes with age—to maintain their parental authority over the young man. Obviously, Ernest knew that his parents were partial to an ageist view of maturity, so, feeling insecure about their response but still desiring to assert the value of his personal growth, he deploys a set of rhetorical strategies to persuade them to his side.

"Dying is a very simple thing," Hemingway observes. Death itself is never actually experienced because, at the moment you die, you have already ceased to exist. Our illusions of immortality—which is to say, the sense of metaphysical permanence that so many of us cling to in a futile effort to make meaning of our existence—only serve to mask the meaninglessness of our lives. Whether we die today or fifty years from now, a young Hemingway seems to observe, really makes no difference because each of us, regardless of how long we exist in the world, spends the rest of eternity in oblivion. A person's death might be unexpected or it may be anticipated and drawn out, preceded by fear and agony, but in both instances the light goes out; each person's fate is ultimately the same. What differences do exist are only encountered by the living and, even then, a longer life, stripped of its illusions, is not to be preferred. Significantly, the young man takes no solace in the possibility of an afterlife but instead confronts meaninglessness head on.

Writing to his parents that death "is a very simple thing," Hemingway appears to renounce his religious beliefs at a time when no one, not even Reverend Barton himself, would question the young man's masculinity. As Baker reports, Reverend Barton sent a letter to Hemingway after his injury saying that "the bell on the First Congregational Church was rung every day at noon for the boys who were at war," and Hemingway among them had proven himself to be a hero.[122] This was Hemingway's opportunity: he could assert his independence and abandon Oak Park Congregationalism without casting a shadow of doubt over his masculine identity. With a certain degree of leverage under his belt and, tactfully, without being too direct, that is, Hemingway asserts his masculine independence at the opportune moment, and he does so from what is ostensibly an atheistic perspective. It is only after establishing his masculine identity in a non-religious setting that Hemingway is able to take ownership over his atheism.

Hemingway the Existentialist

That being said, I take Nickel's point. To "presume that because Hemingway rejected Oak Park's Congregationalism, Hemingway must have rejected all Christianity" is a logical misstep; "these interpretations," he writes, "assume that one cause of Hemingway's World War I trauma was an inevitable abandonment of a traditionally religious faith . . . as if no man had ever been wounded in war before."[123] To reject Congregationalism is not to reject Christianity per se, and, likewise, to reject Christianity is not to reject theism.

Moreover, to assume that the brutalities of war or even a near-death experience would necessarily result in a loss of faith is to exclude a range of reasonable human responses to death and bloody warfare. Over the centuries, religion has been used incessantly to justify war, and, indeed, a person may very well find logical justification for military killings in various Christian theodicies. When confronted with their own mortality, a great many more will be comforted by the promise of an afterlife. So there is good reason to believe that Hemingway's confrontation with death would have strengthened rather than weakened his belief in God. As Nickel writes, the "possibility of evil," death, and destruction in Hemingway's fiction is not presented as a reason to "deny belief, but as an affirmation of the need to believe."[124] And yet, as the letter written home to his parents after being injured during the war indicates, Hemingway does appear to have lost his faith. "I've looked at death and really I know. If I should have died it would have been very easy for me,"[125] not because Hemingway had full confidence that he would be entering the Christian afterlife, but because, in his confrontation with death, he saw that life does not possess lasting significance. He realized that slipping into nonexistence is not something he would actually experience, and that letting go of life would be easy enough, as it was not really his to keep in the first place. "But the people at home do not realize that,"[126] he observes, for as we have already discovered, the people at home were deeply religious and therefore blind to the inherent meaninglessness of their mortal existence. Hemingway looks death square in the eyes and what he sees there shatters the illusion of immortality.

There is reason to believe, in light of this, that Hemingway's religious disillusionment during the war—which is to say, the deeply felt atheism he experienced after a confrontation with death and his own mortality—led him to develop an existentialist point of view. Killinger convincingly argues that throughout the 1920s and 1930s Hemingway produced work revolving around Sartrean themes. Like his own fictional heroes, Hemingway confronted mortality on the battlefield and, thereafter, death arguably became the central theme of his writing. "The Hemingway hero," Killinger observes, is "very much alone in this world, because he has no God and no real brother."[127] Confronted with the secular implications of death, these *code heroes*, as they are often called, take control of their identities and, in true Sartrean fashion, assert mastery over their will, lest they relapse, Killinger writes, "into ordinary childishness."[128] With these assertions, Killinger paves the way for future scholarship on Hemingway as a Sartrean thinker, a theme that in later years is taken up most deliberately by the literary critic Ben Stoltzfus, who writes in his 2010 *Hemingway and French Writers*:

> The tragedy of life and death is a dominant Hemingway theme, be it in the bullring, on the battlefield, or in daily life, and this is one of the reasons why Sartre incorporates Hemingway's writing into his thinking. . . . Death is a leitmotif that haunts Hemingway's oeuvre, and titles such as *Death in the Afternoon* and "A Natural History of the Dead" are symptomatic of artistic, epistemological, and ontological affinities with the author of *L'Être et le néant* (1943; *Being and Nothingness*). Nowhere is this nada—the void, emptiness, meaninglessness—more insistent than in the two African stories that Hemingway wrote in 1936: "The Short Happy Life of Francis Macomber" and "The Snows of Kilimanjaro."[129]

Significantly, the two works that Stoltzfus highlights, "The Short Happy Life of Francis Macomber" and "The Snows of Kilimanjaro," were composed well after Hemingway's Catholic marriage to Pauline in 1927 and well before their divorce in 1940. Like Killinger, Stoltzfus provides considerable evidence that Hemingway's work in the 1920s and 1930s reflected a Sartrean point of view, where the death of God in conjunction with one's own mortality rendered life inherently meaningless. Admittedly, it might be a mistake to confuse Hemingway's personal worldview with the worldviews exhibited by his characters, but even *Death in the Afternoon*, Hemingway's nonfictional commentary on Spanish bullfighting, reflects an atheistic view of death. Certainly, the author's personal comments in this work of nonfiction should be trusted as his own. In the following excerpt, Hemingway contrasts the Spaniard's attitude toward death with those held by the citizens of both England and America:

> In Castille the peasant . . . has food, wine, his wife and children, or he has had them, but he has no comfort, nor much capital and these possessions are not ends in themselves; they are only a part of life and life is something that comes before death. Some one with English blood has written: "Life is real; life is earnest, and the grave is not its goal." And where did they bury him? and what became of the reality and the earnestness? The people of Castille have great common sense. They could not produce a poet who would write a line like that. They know death is the unescapable reality, the one thing any man may be sure of; the only security; that it transcends all modern comforts and that with it you do not need a bathtub in every American home, nor, when you have it, do you need the radio. They think a great deal about death and when they have a religion they have one which believes that life is much shorter than death.[130]

Hemingway admires the Spaniards because they live in full view of their mortality. The American, by contrast, is not conscious of death, so he regards his belongings as something he truly possesses, as if they were not merely his to use before the grave swallows him up. The "one thing any man may be sure of," Hemingway writes, is not the eternal life of the soul, but the sobering truth that life will come to an end. Despite growing up as a Protestant believer, and despite having purportedly converted to Catholicism during the war, Hemingway expresses an atheistic view of death that spans from the 1918 letter written home to his parents all the way to his 1932 reflections in *Death in the Afternoon*. This, no less, was five years into his marriage with Pauline Pfeiffer—a time when Hemingway, according to Stoneback and Nickel, was a practicing Catholic in good standing. Without question, Ernest was affiliated with the Church during this time, and we know that his conversion to Catholicism was at least nominal, but we see articulated in his nonfiction writings throughout the period an atheistic view of death that for Killinger, Stoltzfus, and others conveys a Sartrean understanding of nothingness.

Hemingway the Catholic

As we have already covered at some length, Nickel believes that Hemingway made a direct transition from Protestantism to Catholicism, while Stoneback advances the more cautious thesis that Hemingway's Catholic conversion took place gradually between the years of 1918 and 1927, when Hemingway's marriage to Pauline required that he officially convert to Roman Catholicism. In both accounts, Hemingway's reported baptism during his hospitalization in Fornaci, Italy, his growing interest in the rituals and practices of Roman Catholicism, and his formal recognition in 1927 as a Catholic in good standing by the Parisian Archbishopric are cited as evidence that the writer experienced a genuine religious conversion. But as we have just seen, Hemingway expressed an atheistic view of death as early as 1918, and this view was elaborated in *Death in the Afternoon* five years after his marriage to Pauline in 1927, which was eight years before their divorce in 1940. In Chapter 3 of this book,

I will show that Hemingway portrayed an atheistic view of death in his short stories and novels throughout this period as well. That Hemingway expressed atheistic views during his years as a practicing Catholic is perhaps evidence that his conversion truly was nominal, but the writer's personal correspondences with family, friends, and priests throughout this period reveal a more complicated picture. My task is to square the atheistic view of death portrayed in Hemingway's writings throughout the 1920s and 1930s with his decision to self-identify as a Catholic believer.

In a letter written on November 17, 1929 to the modernist painter and American expatriate Waldo Peirce, Hemingway says that their mutual acquaintance, Charley Sweeney, used to join him at the Sunday bike races but then stopped after learning that the races were rigged. Hemingway claims not to mind the fixed races himself as long as he does not lose any money. He then writes: "It's Sunday morning and got to go to church—Dimanch C'est l'Eglise et le Vel D'Hiv—Thank God not forced to choose between them—They are wise not to compete—Imagine the priests derriere grosse motos at St. Sulpice."[131] The first part of the quote translates as "Sunday it's church and the Velodrome d'Hiver," an indoor bike racing track near the Eiffel Tower that Hemingway regularly attended; the end of the quote translates as "Imagine the priests behind big motorcycles at St. Sulpice," the second-largest church in Paris, which Hemingway regularly attended with Pauline. Given his irreverent tone, it seems obvious that Hemingway would choose to attend the bike races over church, if not for Pauline's expectation that he would join her in the pews. Because the Sunday bike races—which Hemingway liked to gamble on—would clearly be less important to an ardent believer than attending church, it seems plausible that Hemingway is mocking the Sunday Mass in this letter. "Thank God not forced to choose between them," he writes. "Imagine the priests behind big motorcycles."

Compare this with a letter that Hemingway wrote on July 15, 1931 to Guy Hickok, a Paris correspondent for *The Brooklyn Daily Eagle*, a newspaper published in Brooklyn, New York, from 1841 to 1955, and you get the sense that Hemingway was an irked and even resentful critic of the Church. Pauline was pregnant with their second child, Gregory, at the time, and doctors were recommending a Cesarean section. Gregory's predicted birth date was November 15, and Pauline was planning a trip to the U.S. in August. Hemingway explains to Guy that they hoped to make their way from Paris to Kansas City to Piggott, Arkansas, and finally to Key West:

> Original plan was for Pauline to go back to U.S in August—But she has gotten spooked on being caught in Piggott at mercy of Doc Cone—Ex German army pharmacist 2nd class—No hospital in Key West—Damn if we could only have it in K.W. Catholic church if it insists on production of more Catholics by all Catholics ought to make some provision for rolling hospital kitchens for members who have to risk death to conform to Papal encyclicals—I wish they'd have <u>one</u> married <u>Pape</u>—you'd see how long he'd put out those encyclicals.[132]

Hemingway and Pauline do not trust the family doctor in Piggott, and there are, in Hemingway's opinion, no suitable hospitals in Key West.[133] Frustrated that his wife is facing a life-threatening procedure as the result of her pregnancy, Hemingway voices his disapproval of the Church's stance on birth control. Were the Catholic Church to sanction the use of contraceptives, Pauline would not be pregnant again, and her life would not be at risk. In Hemingway's opinion, the Church is responsible for Pauline's pregnancy, so they should either create a makeshift hospital in the church kitchen for his and Pauline's convenience or the Papacy should change its stance on birth control. Hemingway questions the moral authority of the Pope and he again addresses the Church in an irreverent and mocking tone. Speaking to a friend and fellow news reporter, Hemingway does not want to lose face and risk coming across to the reading public as the willing dupe of papal authority, so the writer creates critical distance between himself and the Church to show Hickok and his readers at *The Brooklyn Daily Eagle* that, in keeping with his masculine reputation, he makes his own decisions (Hemingway insists that Hickok not publicly report the affair, but he certainly would not have to insist upon his personal privacy if Hickok was a trustworthy journalist).

It would be easy, in light of these letters, to cast Hemingway as an unbeliever who begrudgingly attends church to satisfy the moral expectations of his devout wife, but we can also frame Hemingway as a sincere Catholic believer who feels embittered by the Church's impossible moral standards, which he continually fails to live up to. Hemingway voices a similar sentiment about the Church's stance on contraceptives four months later in a letter to Pauline's parents. He writes that "at 10 minutes to Seven Dr. Guffy decided a caeserian was the only thing as 7 hours of labour had not moved it down a half an inch . . . He wanted to be sure a normal labor was impossible since the caeserian is dangerous of course and only justifiable if altogether necessary."[134] He then states more pointedly: "If the Church insists that I must put Pauline through what I have just seen her through am afraid must consider myself an outlyer from now on—'a lesser breed without the law' If a sovereign Pontiff bore children when not built for it he might write a bull of exceptions."[135] Hemingway again voices his disapproval of Catholic morality, asserting that the Papacy would change its stance on birth control if Church leaders had to undergo childbirth themselves. Again we encounter a hint of mockery in Hemingway's voice, but he seems to be genuinely disappointed with himself, uttering these words under a distinct air of sadness. It is as if Hemingway gives up hope after witnessing the pain and suffering of Pauline's labor. He wants to believe, he wants to be as devoutly Catholic as Pauline, he wants to live up to the moral standards of the Church, but he is unable to square these desires with his lived experience.

During a moment of self-realization, Hemingway somewhat defensively admits that he is an outlier and "lesser breed without the law." I doubt that Hemingway would feel compelled to make such an admission were his faith really just a matter of lip service. He solemnly refers to himself as a *lesser* Catholic who is unable to endorse the encyclicals surrounding birth control, which would likely be changed if a sovereign pontiff were to undergo childbirth himself, according to the writer. Were Hemingway really just an unbelieving critic of the Pope who falsely converted to Catholicism for the sake of marriage, he would probably reject the Church outright if he felt this strongly opposed to its stance on birth control. Instead of rejecting the Church, however, Hemingway draws a nuanced distinction between faith and obedience, between the devout believer who, like Job,[136] struggles to accept the ways of God, which he does not agree with and cannot understand, and the obedient Catholic, who blindly submits to papal authority. Hemingway is frustrated with the Church, and he struggles to embrace the pontiff's stance on birth control, but he does not renounce the faith. And yet, there are other ways to interpret the letter. If Hemingway were truly an unbelieving critic of the Church, he might be trying to jab the Pope without seriously injuring his relationship to Pauline's parents, who would likely question the legitimacy of his and their daughter's marriage were they to find out that their son-in-law was actually an atheist. So Hemingway's statements of faith may be rhetorical gestures. Both interpretations are possible.

The same is true of a letter Hemingway wrote to Father Vincent C. Donovan where he describes himself as a genuine but inferior Catholic:

> I have always had more faith than intelligence or knowledge and I have never wanted to be known as a Catholic writer because I know the importance of setting an example—and I have never set a good example. . . . Also I am a very dumb Catholic and I have so much faith that I hate to examine into it.[137]

Again, Hemingway identifies as a Catholic believer who is unable to live up to the moral expectations of the Church. Given the atheistic content of Hemingway's writings throughout the 1920s and 1930s, it makes sense that he would resist publicly identifying as a religious believer, either because he did not wish to tarnish the reputation of the Church, as he indicates above, or because he wanted to protect his reputation as a modernist writer, which could be minimized by his affiliation with Catholicism, a longstanding institutional force in the West. Hemingway explains in a letter to a Mr. Hall on October 16, 1933 that "no one writing as I write can be or has any . . . right to be a member of any religious organization. Especially would I not wish to embarrass the church with my presense [sic]. You may state, if there is any necessity to state, that Ernest Hemingway, the writer, is a man of no religion."[138] Hemingway's willingness to identify publicly as an atheist would reinforce the identity he was constructing for himself as a modernist author. That he continually identifies as a Catholic, however, shows that he was either genuinely faithful or he wished, for Pauline's sake and for the sake of their marriage, to remain in good standing with the Church. The documentary evidence fails to provide a definitive account. Hemingway publicly identified as an atheist and privately identified as a Catholic.

Hemingway the Un/Believer

So what are critics to make of this interpretive deadlock? On the one hand, the vast majority of Hemingway scholarship presents the writer as "Hemingway-the-Nihilist, Hemingway-the-Non-believer, Hemingway-the-amoral Existentialist, etc. ad infinitum."[139] On the other hand, Grimes, Stoneback, and Nickel argue that Hemingway was a Catholic believer. Both sides of the debate supply biographical evidence in addition to literary critical readings of Hemingway's fiction to substantiate their claims. I have focused on biographical evidence in Chapter 2 of this book to show that Hemingway's Congregationalism gave way to an atheistic view of death; Chapters 3 and 4 will provide additional evidence by way of literary criticism. To be sure, Stoneback and Nickel present persuasive arguments that Hemingway showed a spiritual interest in Catholicism before, during, and after his marriage to Pauline, but Hemingway's letter home after the war and his reflections in *Death in the Afternoon* present someone who clearly did not believe in an afterlife from the years 1918 to 1932. More will be said on *Death in the Afternoon* in Chapters 3 and 4 to illustrate the full extent of Hemingway's anti-Christian sentiments. Though it might be tempting to assert the authority of Hemingway's nonfictional statements over religious interpretations of his fiction, I do not wish to fall back on binary, either/or assertions concerning Hemingway's religious status. Instead, I am suggesting a third option that ties together the Oak Park Congregationalism of Hemingway's youth, the secular existentialism of his early adult life, and his ostensible conversion to Roman Catholicism years later.

Like Sartre, Hemingway knew that, without a God in heaven, he was free to be the master of his own life. But he was also taught from a very young age that self-determination was an essential part of his Christian identity. Add in the fact that masculinity, under both theistic and atheistic worldviews, was a matter of self-determination for Hemingway, and you have, in effect, an existential atheist whose masculinity carried with it implicit theological baggage. It may be that Hemingway genuinely believed in Catholicism, which existed paradoxically alongside his atheism; it may be that Hemingway's religious commitments were racked with existential doubt; it may even be that Hemingway's faith was nominal, but that his writings were informed by Catholicism, to which he remained sympathetic and in which he would consistently demonstrate genuine interest, despite his lack of faith. All three options are compatible with Hemingway's personal correspondences and works of nonfiction, which sometimes confess religious belief and at other times reveal an atheistic understanding of death. The common denominator in this binary struggle between religious belief and disbelief is Hemingway's internalized view of masculinity, which itself became a sort of religion for him. As Harvey Mansfield helped to illustrate in Chapter 1 of this book, masculine self-assertion was theologically significant for the author because it "is through manliness that humans insist that they are worthy of the attention of the gods or have an honored place in the scheme of things."[140] Comparing Hemingway with Sartre, we can see how a Roman Catholic view of human ontology as nothingness, or *nada*, complements Hemingway's existentialist view of sovereign freedom, which itself was informed by his masculine training under Reverend Barton as an Oak Park Congregationalist.

Ultimately, the writer's exact religious affiliation will likely remain ambiguous, but one thing can be regarded as certain: despite the vicissitudes of his religious odyssey, Hemingway retains a belief in sovereign moral choice and, with it, a belief in sacred human identity. This means that Hemingway's atheism, whatever its extent, is a failure; he secularizes divine morality through his masculine volition and commissions the *imago Dei*, or a secularized version of it, to authorize his choices (over against the Church at times). In Chapters 3 and 4 of this book, I trace how this secularized theological belief in masculine volition plays out in the context of Hemingway's fiction. The author's Sartrean view of nothingness overlays the atheistic tenor of his stories with divine elements, and, as I will show, many of his characters model the kind of failed atheism, or secularized theism, that has been explained at length in the previous pages.

Notes

1. Simone de Beauvoir, *Adieux*, trans. Patrick O'Brian (New York: Pantheon Books, 1984), 433.
2. Ibid.
3. Ibid.
4. Ibid., 439.
5. Ibid., 438.
6. Ibid., 439.
7. Ibid.
8. Ibid.
9. Ibid., 438.
10. Ibid.
11. Ibid.
12. Jean-Paul Sartre, *War Diaries: Notebooks from a Phony War 1939–40*, trans. Quintin Hoare (New York: Verso, 1984), 70.
13. Ibid.
14. Jean-Paul Sartre, *The Words: The Autobiography of Jean-Paul Sartre*, trans. Bernard Frechtman (New York: Vintage Books, 1964), 98.
15. Sartre, *War Diaries*, 70.
16. Sartre, *The Words*, 98.
17. Ibid.
18. Sartre, *War Diaries*, 70.
19. Ibid.

20. Sartre, *The Words*, 102.
21. Ibid.
22. See Jean-Paul Sartre, *Existentialism Is a Humanism*, ed. John Kulka, trans. Carol Macomber (New Haven, CT: Yale University Press, 2007), 28.
23. Sartre, *The Words*, 97.
24. Ibid.
25. Sartre, *War Diaries*, 72.
26. De Beauvoir, *Adieux*, 439.
27. Sartre, *The Words*, 249.
28. Ibid., 249–51.
29. Jean-Paul Sartre, *Being and Nothingness*, trans. Hazel E. Barnes (New York: Washington Square Press, 1953), 723–4.
30. Catholic Church, "The Dignity of the Human Person," in the *Catechism of the Catholic Church*, 2nd edn (Vatican: Libreria Editrice Vaticana, 2012).
31. Ibid.
32. 1 Peter 1:2 (NIV).
33. Giorgio Agamben, *The Omnibus Homo Sacer* (Stanford, CA: Stanford University Press, 2017), 335.
34. Ibid., 340, 342.
35. Ibid., 344.
36. Ibid., 338.
37. Ibid., 333.
38. Ibid., 343.
39. Ibid.
40. Ibid., 342–3.
41. Giorgio Agamben, *The Open: Man and Animal*, trans. Kevin Attell (Stanford, CA: Stanford University Press, 2004), 36.
42. Ibid., 37.
43. Ibid., 37–8.
44. Ibid., 26.
45. Joseph Slaughter, *Human Rights, Inc.: The World Novel, Narrative Form, and International Law* (New York: Fordham University Press, 2007), 14.
46. Lynn Hunt, *Inventing Human Rights: A History* (New York: W. W. Norton & Company, 2007), 19–20.

47. Ibid., 20.
48. John Gillespie, "Sartre and the Death of God," *Sartre Studies International* 22.1 (2016): 48.
49. Sartre, *Existentialism Is a Humanism*, 22.
50. Ibid., 27.
51. Ibid., 22.
52. Ibid.
53. Ibid., 29.
54. Agamben, *The Open*, 37–8.
55. Sartre, *Existentialism Is a Humanism*, 28.
56. Ibid., 29.
57. De Beauvoir, *Adieux*, 439.
58. Sartre, *Existentialism Is a Humanism*, 28.
59. Ibid., 23–4.
60. Ibid., 25.
61. Ibid.
62. Agamben, *The Omnibus Homo Sacer*, 42.
63. Ibid.
64. Sartre, *Existentialism Is a Humanism*, 24.
65. De Beauvoir, *Adieux*, 439.
66. Ibid.
67. Ronald Aronson, "Camus versus Sartre: The Unresolved Conflict," *Sartre Studies International* 11.1/2 (2005): 309.
68. Jean-Paul Sartre, "The Wretched of the Earth," in *We Have Only This Life to Live: The Selected Essays of Jean-Paul Sartre 1939–1975*, ed. Ronald Aronson and Adrian Van Den Hoven (New York: New York Review Books, 2013), 390.
69. Ibid.
70. Sartre, *Being and Nothingness*, 382.
71. Ibid.
72. Jean-Paul Sartre, "Reply to Albert Camus," in *We Have Only This Life to Live: The Selected Essays of Jean-Paul Sartre 1939–1975*, ed. Ronald Aronson and Adrian Van Den Hoven (New York: New York Review Books, 2013), 224.
73. Albert Camus, *The Rebel: An Essay on Man in Revolt*, trans. Anthony Bower (New York: Vintage International, 1991), 541.

74. Ibid., 476.
75. Sartre, "The Wretched of the Earth," 397.
76. De Beauvoir, *Adieux*, 439.
77. Sartre, *Existentialism Is a Humanism*, 24.
78. Cary Wolfe, "Fathers, Lovers, and Friend Killers: Rearticulating Gender and Race via Species in Hemingway," *boundary 2* 29.1 (2002): 228.
79. De Beauvoir, *Adieux*, 438.
80. Ibid.
81. Mary V. Dearborn, *Ernest Hemingway: A Biography* (New York: Vintage Books, 2017), 13.
82. Larry Grimes, "Hemingway's Religious Odyssey: The Oak Park Years," in *Ernest Hemingway: The Oak Park Legacy*, ed. James Nagel (Tuscaloosa, AL: University of Alabama Press, 1996), 49.
83. Carlos Baker, *Ernest Hemingway: A Life Story* (New York: Avon Books, 1968), 9.
84. Marcelline Sanford, *At the Hemingways, Centennial Edition* (Moscow, ID: University of Idaho Press, 1999), 133.
85. Grimes, "Hemingway's Religious Odyssey," 40.
86. As Grimes notes, Hemingway was present for one such sermon on April 15, 1917 entitled "Our Fight for the Heritage of Humanity." In the sermon, Barton insists that Germany's military tactics were inspired by a handful of noted German philosophers, including Friedrich Nietzsche, whose *Übermensch* was a symbol of the nation's desired political sovereignty. Ironically, Hemingway would later internalize similar notions of sovereignty, despite Barton's searing criticism of Germany. See Larry Grimes, "Things They Carried: Nick, Hemingway, and Oak Park Connections to the Western Front," *Midwestern Miscellany* 47 (2019): 16–28.
87. Michael Reynolds, *The Young Hemingway* (New York: Norton, 1986), 10.
88. Grimes, "Hemingway's Religious Odyssey," 38.
89. Ibid., 37.
90. Ibid., 40.
91. Ibid.

92. Ibid.
93. J. Gerald Kennedy, "Hemingway's Gender Trouble," *American Literature* 63.2 (1991): 192.
94. Dearborn, *Ernest Hemingway*, 21.
95. Baker, *Ernest Hemingway*, 17.
96. Dearborn, *Ernest Hemingway*, 33.
97. Grimes, "Hemingway's Religious Odyssey," 49, 50.
98. The cultural trend toward boyhood training in masculinity was taking place locally in Oak Park, but it was also taking place nationally and internationally in various forms. In 1908, for example, a Lieutenant General of the British Army, Robert Baden-Powell, formed the Boy Scouts, an organization that by 1920 had grown into the World Organization of the Scout Movement, promoting scouting worldwide. Baden-Powell formed the Boy Scouts partly in reaction to the British Army's military failures in the early part of the Anglo-Boer War. To overcome what he perceived as a widespread failure in British manhood, Baden-Powell trained the boys in such things as mapping, tracking, signaling, knotting, first aid, nationalism, chivalry, and morality.
99. Grimes, "Hemingway's Religious Odyssey," 42.
100. Ibid., 37.
101. Dearborn, *Ernest Hemingway*, 45.
102. Sandra Spanier and Robert W. Trogdon, eds., *The Letters of Ernest Hemingway Volume 1, 1907–1922* (Cambridge, UK: Cambridge University Press, 2011), 76.
103. Ibid.
104. Larry Grimes, *The Religious Design of Hemingway's Early Fiction* (Ann Arbor, MI: UMI Research Press, 1985), 3.
105. Ibid.
106. Matthew Nickel, *Hemingway's Dark Night: Catholic Influences and Intertextualities in the Work of Ernest Hemingway* (Wickford, RI: New Street Communications, 2013), 9.
107. Ibid.
108. Ibid.

109. H. R. Stoneback, "Pilgrimage Variations: Hemingway's Sacred Landscapes," *Religion and Literature* 35.2/3 (2003): 50.
110. Nickel, *Hemingway's Dark Night*, 12.
111. Ibid.
112. Stoneback, "Pilgrimage Variations," 50.
113. Scott Donaldson, *By Force of Will: The Life and Art of Ernest Hemingway* (New York: Viking, 1977), 224.
114. Ibid.
115. Jeffrey Meyers, *Hemingway: A Biography* (New York: Harper & Row, 1985), 5.
116. Baker, *Ernest Hemingway*, 74. This same line would be quoted in Hemingway's 1936 short story "The Short Happy Life of Francis Macomber" by the hunting guide Robert Wilson, whom Hemingway presents as the model of masculinity.
117. Baker, *Ernest Hemingway*, 62.
118. Ibid.
119. Michael Reynolds, *Hemingway in the 1930s* (New York/London: W. W. Norton & Company, 1997), 21.
120. Baker, *Ernest Hemingway*, 68.
121. Spanier and Trogdon, *The Letters of Ernest Hemingway Volume 1*, 147.
122. Baker, *Ernest Hemingway*, 72.
123. Nickel, *Hemingway's Dark Night*, 8.
124. Ibid., 59.
125. Spanier and Trogdon, *The Letters of Ernest Hemingway Volume 1*, 147.
126. Ibid.
127. John Killinger, *Hemingway and the Dead Gods: A Study in Existentialism* (New York: Citadel Press, 1965), 98, 99.
128. Ibid., 25.
129. Ben Stoltzfus, *Hemingway and French Writers* (Kent, OH: Kent State University Press, 2010), 79.
130. Ernest Hemingway, *Death in the Afternoon* (London: Arrow Books, 2004), 226.

131. Sandra Spanier and Miriam B. Mandel, eds., *The Letters of Ernest Hemingway Volume 4, 1929–1931* (Cambridge, UK: Cambridge University Press, 2018), 149.
132. Ibid., 541.
133. In fact, there were numerous Key West hospitals in 1931 that could perform Pauline's Cesarean section, including the Marine Hospital, the privately owned Louise Maloney Hospital, and the Mercedes Hospital. It is not clear why Hemingway denies their existence or regards them as unsuitable.
134. Spanier and Mandel, *The Letters of Ernest Hemingway Volume 4*, 592–3.
135. Ibid., 593.
136. Job is the faithful and prosperous protagonist of *The Book of Job* in the Hebrew Bible. Satan wagers with God that Job would lose his faith if he were befallen with tragedy, so God allows Satan to take away Job's family, health, and property. Job questions God's decisions but ultimately keeps his faith.
137. Hemingway to Vincent C. Donovan, December 1927, in Rena Sanderson, Sandra Spanier, and Robert W. Trogdon, eds., *The Letters of Ernest Hemingway Volume 3, 1926–1929* (Cambridge, UK: Cambridge University Press, 2018), 337–8.
138. Sandra Spanier and Miriam B. Mandel, eds., *The Letters of Ernest Hemingway Volume 5, 1932–1934* (Cambridge, UK: Cambridge University Press, 2020), 512.
139. Stoneback, "Pilgrimage Variations," 49.
140. Harvey Mansfield, "Manly Assertion," in *Hemingway on Politics and Rebellion*, ed. Lauretta Conklin Frederking (New York: Routledge, 2010), 99.

CHAPTER 3

THE PROBLEM WITH HUMAN EXCEPTIONALISM

Approaching the Masculine in Hemingway's Fiction

As we have already seen, revisionary scholarship from feminist and queer studies has gone a long way to disrupt the so-called Hemingway myth. The author's love of big-game hunting, deep-sea fishing, bullfighting, and boxing contributed to an exaggerated image of the man that his unmatched celebrity as a writer surely compounded. Hemingway rose to fame amid a burgeoning culture of celebrity worship, and, in a manner that rivals the acumen of today's social media influencer, Hemingway leaned into his macho persona in order to capitalize on his growing reputation. In 1935, after *The Sun Also Rises* and *A Farewell to Arms* catapulted the author to fame, Hemingway would write an "absolutely true" account of his African safari with Pauline to see whether it could "compete with a work of the imagination."[1] But the narrative mostly serves to demonstrate, in general, that Hemingway's self-discipline makes him a superior writer and that, when applied to the hunt, his self-discipline results in a higher number of quality kills, allowing him to win favor with the white hunter and native trackers, all of whom are experts at their trade. In this sense, *Green Hills of Africa* can be framed as an adventure narrative that compares itself against works of the imagination to underscore the grandiose nature of the hunt. Hemingway boldly asserts the veracity of the tale to fortify his masculine public image. To a remarkable degree, it would seem that *Green Hills of Africa* is geared toward self-promotion.

But as revisionary critics have repeatedly pointed out, Hemingway's literary treatment of masculinity is far more nuanced than the cultural stereotype of masculinity, tending to focus on male vulnerability rather than male bravado. Even *Green Hills of Africa* betrays the Hemingway myth at times, presenting manhood as a burden with occasionally toxic effects. Throughout the narrative, the kills are presented as thinly veiled phallic symbols: sometimes Hemingway takes pride in the size of his beast, asserting its superiority over the smaller kills of his opponent Karl, and at other times he feels ashamed of its comparatively small stature.

Near the end of the book, and after a long, exhilarating day of hunting, Hemingway boasts that "no one could beat" the size of his kill, but then Karl enters with a fifty-seven-pound kudu.[2] Encountering the beast, Hemingway writes that "[t]hey were the biggest, widest, darkest, longest-curling, heaviest, most unbelievable pair of kudu horns in the world. Suddenly, poisoned with envy, I did not want to see mine again; never, never."[3] That Hemingway is willing even to suggest through symbolic representation that his phallus might be inferior—just as he does in *The Sun Also Rises* with his fictional stand-in, Jake Barnes, whose member was injured beyond repair during the war—complicates overblown stereotypes of the writer as a male chauvinist. Hemingway demonstrates an unexpected willingness to engage with male vulnerability, exploring feelings of inferiority, inadequacy, and emasculation in the face of sometimes crushing expectations, as represented by Karl's "unbelievable pair" in the passage above. Voicing this same sentiment, the white hunter says to Hemingway: "We have very primitive emotions . . . It's impossible not to be competitive. Spoils everything, though."⁴ So even an exercise in self-promotion like *Green Hills of Africa* that enlarges upon the Hemingway myth by glorifying masculine stereotypes offers moments of male vulnerability, thus exposing the cracks in Hemingway's macho persona.

But Hemingway's exploration of male vulnerability and the burden of manhood extends well beyond *Green Hills of Africa* to permeate the writer's entire oeuvre. In the short story "Ten Indians," for example, a pubescent Nick Adams is teased by his neighbors, the Garner family, for becoming infatuated with a young Indian girl, Prudence Mitchell. In spite of the racist overtones of the story (at one point the Garner family refers to Prudence as a skunk), their teasing is well-intentioned, for they seem to be charmed by Nick's coy disposition and take delight in the young man's romantic vulnerability. According to the story's masculine coding, which Hemingway bases on patriarchal depictions of manhood, becoming infatuated with a love interest is one possible sign of male weakness, for men are supposed to demonstrate their sexual prowess through detached promiscuity. Under Hemingway's treatment of gender stereotypes, men are immune to feelings of romantic attachment, which is a characteristically female defect, and this is precisely why a young man can be teased for falling in love—it shows that he is guilty of behaving like a girl. Matters are made worse by Nick's father, who reveals that he saw Prudence "having quite a time" with Frank Washburn, one of Nick's peers, in the forest that afternoon.⁵ Nick weeps in front of his father, who maintains a cold disposition and orders Nick to bed. By the story's end, Hemingway shatters the emotionless exterior of traditional masculinity modelled by Nick's father to reveal what really happens in the broken heart of a young man. He writes:

> After a while he heard his father blow out the lamp and go into his own room. He heard a wind come up in the trees outside and felt it come in cool through the screen. He lay for a long time with his face in the pillow, and after a while he forgot to think about Prudence and finally he went to sleep.... In the morning there was a big wind blowing and the waves were running high up on the beach and he was awake a long time before he remembered that his heart was broken.[6]

Nick lies face down in the pillow, suffocating with emotional strife. Benumbed by the pain, he focuses on the wind outside, the sound it makes in the trees, and its cooling effect, quietly agonizing over Prudence, whose name is a warning against rushing in, falling too hard, and having your heart ripped out by an untrustworthy girl—be cautious, have prudence, and never let the opposite sex hurt you like this again, her name seems to counsel.

Hemingway's 1925 short story collection *In Our Time*[7] depicts masculinity in an era when joining the military, going into battle, and sacrificing life for country were exclusively male responsibilities. War epitomized masculine heroism for the young men of Hemingway's generation, and Hemingway grew up idolizing his grandfathers, who, we have already seen, both fought courageously in the Civil War. *In Our Time*—a title that marks a distinction between Hemingway's generation and the generations leading up to it—is largely about the crushing weight of male responsibility, the false heroism of military service, the disillusionment experienced by an entire generation of young men at war, and the unexplored underbelly of the masculine experience. Graphic paragraph-length sketches of the war are interspersed between each story, and the stories themselves feature accounts of Nick Adams's postwar trauma, as in "Big Two-Hearted River," as well as his prewar training in masculinity, as in "The Doctor and the Doctor's Wife." Hemingway's careful ordering of the collection ostensibly gives voice to a basic overarching narrative: namely, that the little boys of Hemingway's generation were raised to be masculine heroes, but their masculinity culminated in loss, disconnection, and the inexplicable tragedies of war.

Two of its titles, "The End of Something" and "Three-Day Blow," are companion stories that, in concert with "Ten Indians," explore Nick Adams's struggle with romantic vulnerability. In the stories, a young Nick breaks up with his girlfriend Marjorie and sometime afterwards he mourns the loss of Marjorie with the support of his friend Bill. The two of them get drunk while discussing their fathers' shortcomings, baseball, and finally Marjorie herself. "The liquor had all died out of him and left him alone. . . . All he knew was that he had once had Marjorie and that he had lost her. She was gone and he had sent her away. That was all that mattered. He might never see her again."[8] Nick's unwillingness to get tied down at a young age, sacrificing both his masculine ambition and the opportunity to prove his manhood through an array of sexual conquests, results in the loss of loving companionship. Spurred on by his masculine duties, Nick abandons what he really wants and perhaps what he really needs. Hemingway questions the value of masculine ambition by focusing on its counterproductive effects.

And yet, Hemingway was nevertheless captive to a culture of masculinity. When the second American edition of *In Our Time* was published by Scribner's in 1930, "On the Quai at Smyrna," then titled "Introduction by the Author,"[9] replaced "Indian Camp" as the first story of the collection. The original title of the story is remarkably fitting because, as the introductory piece of Hemingway's first critically acclaimed publication, "On the Quai at Smyrna" outlines the stakes of Hemingway's lifelong project. As that project unfolded, the author's purpose would become more and more clear: he wanted to show that mastery over death is the true indicator of masculine heroism and that masculinity, defined in this way, is that which distinguishes man from the rest of nature as sacred. Hemingway develops this idea across multiple works in the years and decades following the publication of *In Our Time*, but its origins can be traced back to "On the Quai at Smyrna," a powerful vignette that, in spite of its brevity, introduces a range of elements that would eventually define the Hemingway project. The young writer was disabused of Reverend Barton's social gospel by the noxious ramifications of war, but he nevertheless retained a commitment to masculine self-determination and its corollary, the *imago Dei*. "On the Quai at Smyrna" internalizes this tension, exploring masculine stoicism in the face of death.

"On the Quai at Smyrna"

The story takes place in the port city of Smyrna at the close of the Greco-Turkish War. Exercising the minimalist technique that would come to define his experimental style, Hemingway begins the vignette *in medias res* with one character commenting on the peculiarity of a scene that, as readers, we do not yet know anything about. As a matter of esthetic principle, Hemingway reveals the tip of an iceberg that becomes more and more visible as we put in the interpretive work:

> The strange thing was, he said, how they screamed every night at midnight. I do not know why they screamed at that time. We were in the harbor and they were all on the pier and at midnight they started screaming. We used to turn the searchlight on them to quiet them. That always did the trick. We'd run the searchlight up and down over them two or three times and they stopped it.[10]

Readers not already familiar with the story are confronted with uncertainty—who or what is screaming? Is the timing inopportune or just unpredictable and senseless? Should they be sleeping, or dead, or bound and gagged? Why does the searchlight eventually silence them? And, perhaps the most compelling question of all, why does the speaker describe their screaming as "strange"? Readers are given some indication that the screaming lifeforms are animals, not people, for the speaker and his compatriots would surely move to help other human beings if they were found screaming on the pier in agony. And yet the speaker says that, rather than aiding the floundering creatures, the sailors remained in the harbor and "turn[ed] the searchlight on them," running it "up and down over them two or three times" because that "always did the trick." We can imagine screaming animals growing silent out of caution when flooded by a blinding light, suddenly aware that something else, maybe a predator, is present in the vicinity, but it is much harder to imagine human beings growing silent in the same situation.

This is because human beings would recognize the searchlight as man-made, and, if anything, their cries would intensify, becoming more purposeful when presented with other human beings. The only time humans would not call out for help in this or a similar situation is if they recognized the searchlight as the approach of an outside threat, or the possibility of an outside threat. But we know from the passage that this is a recurring event; the creatures have had this same light shined on them for multiple nights in a row, and its owners have neither helped nor harmed them. Rather, its owners shine their searchlight merely to silence the creatures, whose screaming, readers are safe to assume, keeps the sailors awake at night. As the speaker callously remarks, the searchlight "always did the trick." He does not care about the creatures; their cries fail to elicit a compassionate response from the sailors, and it would seem that he and his compatriots demonstrate no interest in the lifeforms beyond keeping their mouths shut. Were the animals in fact human beings, their recurring cries at midnight may very well qualify as "strange" behavior, but the speaker's choice to describe their actions as *strange* rather than as *heartbreaking* or *disturbing*, for example, reflects a low level of concern for the animals. The speaker regards their cries as inconvenient, unpleasant, and unwanted. The sailors need to sleep.

Reading further down the page, however, we discover that the screams at midnight do emanate from human beings—Greek refugees who have been left behind by the military and their more affluent countrymen. As Jeffrey Meyers describes in "Hemingway's Second War: The Greco-Turkish Conflict, 1920–1922," Hemingway based the story on the complicated political history between the Greeks and the Turks. "The Greek occupation of the city in May, 1919, followed by a massacre of the Turks, inspired the Turkish Nationalist Movement and was the immediate cause of the Greco-Turkish War," but as Meyers explains, "The Turks reoccupied Smyrna and completed the reconquest of Anatolia on 9 September. Order prevailed for only a brief period, and arrests began immediately of vast numbers of Greeks and Armenians suspected of being implicated in the massacre of Turks in May, 1919."[11] Turkish troops subsequently set fire to the Greek, Armenian, and European quarters of Smyrna. The surviving population flocked to the quay at the western end of the city.

Readers may be surprised to learn, however, that Hemingway was never actually present to witness the exodus of refugees; he arrived too late after spraining his ankle at home and then battling malaria in Constantinople. He nevertheless produced fourteen articles on the Greco-Turkish War for the *Toronto Star* and he was also conversant with an array of war-related media. Meyers suggests that Hemingway lifted the story from two London newspaper articles, one from *The Times* and one from the *Daily Mail*. Here is the September 16, 1922 report from *The Times*:

> A stream of refugees is still leaving Smyrna, and my informant describes the quay last night as packed with dense crowds herded together inside a cordon of Turkish regulars, while searchlights of foreign warships in the harbour played upon them. . . . The waters of the harbour were full of the dead bodies of persons drowned or shot by the Turks while trying to reach the ships, and some of the corpses were horribly mangled by the propellers.[12]

The second report by the *Daily Mail* was published on September 19, 1922:

> The crews of the British destroyers moored near the quay say that it was the ghastliest experience of their lives to be obliged to listen to the imploring screams of the Greek women and children on the quay close by. The women shrieked to the British, "You can't leave us to burn alive or to be raped or murdered by the Turks!"[13]

There are clear similarities in these reports and Hemingway's story. That Hemingway felt inspired by the reports to write "On the Quai at Smyrna" is certainly possible and even likely, but the writer—rather than *the reporter*—in Hemingway knew how to use imagery and dialogue to illicit a deeper meaning from the events depicted, saying something more complex and significant than what the reports themselves were able to convey.

Regarding his formal techniques, the young writer presents readers with four interacting images: screaming refugees, dead babies, mothers in the midst of childbirth, and drowning livestock. The first of these terrifying images has already been accounted for. The speaker, presumably a British naval officer, describes himself and the crew as shining a searchlight on the suffering refugees to quiet their screaming at midnight. The refugees are not their military enemies but the citizens of a displaced nation, so there is no reason to attack, torture, or kill the refugees, as we can see reflected in the British sailors' apathetic response. But men, women, children, their grandparents, and presumably entire families scream out in agony, calling for mercy and supplication just a short distance away, and yet the sailors do nothing. Their apathy extends beyond a lack of military duty to a complete lack of concern for human life. The searchlight is almost certainly intended as an ironic symbol, for the refugees are "discovered" by the light and sadly no one rushes to their aid (this can be contrasted with the aid supplied by a "search party"). But, in reality, searchlights were created as military weapons to produce artificial moonlight in the First World War, increasing the opportunity for night attacks against a military's political enemy. In this sense, the sailors essentially *turn their weapon* on the screaming refugees in order to silence them because, again, doing so "always did the trick," as the officer callously reports.[14] The refugees are citizens without a nation who have been deprived of their legal rights. Consequently, they huddle together in the dark like animals, screaming at midnight not because they expect to be rescued, not to awaken the sailors out of spite, and not in the service of another such strategy, but because they are tormented and feel moved to express their desperation, plain and simple.

This first image combines with the final image of the vignette to form thematic bookends. The officer sarcastically remarks in the closing paragraph that "The Greeks were nice chaps too," referring here to members of the Greek military who left after the reoccupation of Smyrna by the Turkish government. "When they evacuated they had all their baggage animals they couldn't take off with them so they just broke their forelegs and dumped them into the shallow water. All those mules with their forelegs broken pushed over into the shallow water. It was all a pleasant business," the officer decries. "My word yes a most pleasant business."[15] The disfigured animals floating in the harbor will surely remind readers of the 1922 *Times* report that floating corpses filled the harbor and were subsequently disfigured by the boats' propellors. Just as the cargo animals are shoved into shallow water after having their front legs broken, so too are the Greek refugees abandoned by their government and rendered defenseless, many of them drowning alongside of the cargo animals themselves, which are shown a complete lack of mercy. To be sure, the Greek military drowns the animals so that their Turkish enemies do not inherit valuable military assets, but their actions are nevertheless cruel by conventional standards, prioritizing military advantage over the livestock's wellbeing. The officer takes umbrage with animal cruelty, looking down on the Greeks for their seemingly ruthless behavior, but the layered imagery suggests that the refugees were animalized not only by their fellow countrymen, who metaphorically "broke their forelegs and dumped them into the shallow water," but by the British naval officer as well, who, in the opening scene, shines a searchlight on their screaming bodies. That the officer exhibits no sympathy for the animalized refugees is surprising given his concern for the drowned livestock, but this apparent inconsistency in the officer's thought should not eclipse the bigger picture: refugees are animalized to justify their mistreatment. In the officer's opinion, moreover, leaving your own people for dead is truly unconscionable behavior, so he regards the whole lot with disgust, casting them as morally inferior, inhumane, and as literally inhuman.

These combined images—screaming refugees and screaming mules, both of whom float side by side in the harbor after drowning—form thematic bookends which encase two other prominent images: dead babies and mothers in labor. "The worst part," says the officer, "were the women with dead babies. You couldn't get the women to give up their dead babies. They'd have babies dead for six days. Wouldn't give them up. Nothing you could do about it."[16] In his characteristic use of repetition, Hemingway reinforces the shock value of these lines by repeating "dead babies" in back-to-back sentences and then inverting the phrase as "babies dead" in the sentence that follows. He subsequently presents readers with a truly morbid visual:

> Then there was an old lady, most extraordinary case. I told it to a doctor and he said I was lying. We were clearing them off the pier, had to clear off the dead ones, and this old woman was lying on a sort of litter.... So I had a look at her and just then she died and went absolutely stiff. Her legs drew up and she drew up from the waist and went quite rigid. Exactly as though she had been dead over night. She was quite dead and absolutely rigid. I told a medical chap about it and he told me it was impossible.[17]

The scene is jarring. An elderly woman becomes suddenly stiff, her corpse folding in half. This truly grotesque image—a phrase I choose carefully[18]—anticipates what, over the next century, will become horror cinema's excessive depiction of ugly, mutilated bodies on screen and harkens back to a long tradition of grotesquerie in painting and literature. Anna Journey describes aspects of the grotesque tradition, writing that "[t]he grotesque style of painting interweaves human and animal forms, . . . violat[ing] proportion, scale, and symmetry" to cultivate "distortion and bizarre, hybrid figures. . . . As in the hybrid bodies of the chimera, sphynx, or centaur, the grotesque's power lies in its ability to defy borders."[19] And as Ani Kokobobo explains, "Grotesque ugliness can strip someone of his or her humanity, turning them into a monstrous other unworthy of active love."[20] Thus, according to tradition, the grotesque refers in part to animalized individuals whose monstrosity diminishes their human value. A doctor describes the account as "impossible," as something the officer must have surely lied about due to its "extraordinary" nature. The woman is clearly a medical anomaly and her ugly, inhuman form is beyond the pale of scientific explanation. In these passages, Hemingway questions the difference between human and animal suffering, pressuring readers to formulate a moral response to both.

Coupled with these grisly images of death—which claims the lives of young and old alike—are, by the officer's description, feral women in the midst of childbirth. "You didn't mind the women who were having babies as you did those with the dead ones. They had them all right. Surprising how few of them died. You just covered them over with something and let them go to it. They'd always pick out the darkest place in the hold to have them."[21] Again, the officer uses dehumanizing language to describe the refugees. Like animals, the women seek out dark places to bear their young, and rather than tend to the mothers in their time of need, the sailors throw blankets over them while they "go to it" and are surprised by how few of them die. The story's admixture of death and new life, elder and infant, animal and human aims to remind readers that everyone—no matter their station, their nationality, their age, gender, or even their animal species—eventually faces death. Conveying the same message, the title of Hemingway's 1940 novel *For Whom the Bell Tolls* quotes part XVII of John Donne's 1624 *Devotions upon Emergent Occasions*, which reads: "never send to know for whom the *bell* tolls; It tolls for *thee*."[22] Of course, Donne himself was a devout cleric of the Church of England, and part XVII of *Devotions* celebrates each individual believer's unity in the body of Christ, so when Donne writes the lines quoted above, he has in mind the shared destiny of all Christian believers. Putting an ironic twist on *For Whom the Bell Tolls*, in which the protagonist, Robert Jordan, dies for a political cause, Hemingway co-opts the lines written by

Donne, urging readers to reconsider them from an atheistic point of view. What unites all lifeforms is not their shared ontology in the body of Christ, as Donne maintains, but their inevitable, everlasting annihilation, as my discussion of the novel later will show. Consigning them to an identical fate, Hemingway blurs the distinctions among women, babies, animals, and military men, interrogating the boundaries of human identity and, concomitantly, the basis of sacred human rights, which have been violated in spades.

Death in the Afternoon

Hemingway's 1932 meditation on Spanish bullfighting, *Death in the Afternoon*, is part cultural commentary, part travel guide, part political satire, and part polemic (seemingly against his former mentor Gertrude Stein, whom he fictionalizes as the *Old lady*). Throughout this piece, Hemingway plays with generic boundaries, finding himself carried away at one point with a fictional exchange between himself and the *Old lady*. At the end of chapter 12—a detailed account of bull breeding reminiscent of Herman Melville's cetology chapter in *Moby Dick*—Hemingway abruptly changes direction, leaving off his studied appraisal of the Spanish bullfight to satisfy the *Old lady*'s readerly expectations, which have not been met by the author. The result is a short, stand-alone piece entitled "A Natural History of the Dead," which would be republished one year later in *Winner Take Nothing* as a short story. But, according to Lewis E. Weeks, Jr., the piece "can hardly be called a story," for it is "a skillful and terrifying parody and satire."[23] Ray B. West, Jr. refers to the piece as "a short and curious little essay,"[24] and Hemingway himself describes the work as "the Whittier's *Snow Bound* of our time,"[25] a long narrative poem that depicts a peaceful return to rural domesticity after the Civil War. Much like *Death in the Afternoon*, the story defies generic boundaries, but it is nevertheless laser-focused in its critique of natural theology. Popularized by the nineteenth-century Christian apologist William Paley, natural theology proposed that God's existence and benevolent nature could be logically deduced through a scientific study of nature. Hemingway challenges this claim in the most sardonic of ways.

I turn to "A Natural History of the Dead" as the logical next step in our study, for Hemingway alludes to "On the Quai at Smyrna" twice in *Death in the Afternoon*, once in the opening pages and again in chapter 12. On the very first page of the book, in fact, Hemingway recalls explaining to Stein his reasons for disliking the sport of bullfighting. "I had just come from the Near East," he writes, "where the Greeks broke the legs of their baggage and transport animals and ... shoved them off the quay into the shallow water when they abandoned the city of Smyrna, and I remember saying that I did not like the bullfights because of the poor horses."[26] Just as the British naval officer of *In Our Time* feels sympathy for the drowned mules at Smyrna, a young Hemingway not yet educated in the art of bullfighting feels sympathy for the horses killed in the ring, admitting that "I cannot see a horse down in the street without having it make me feel a necessity for helping the horse."[27] He references "On the Quai at Smyrna" again in chapter 12 while giving the *Old lady* an account of the horrors he witnessed during the war:

> In twenty years of observation in civil life I had never seen a dead mule and had begun to entertain doubts as to whether these animals were really mortal. . . . But in war these animals succumb in much the same manner as the more common and less hardy horse. . . . They seemed a fitting enough sight in the mountains where one was accustomed to their presence and looked less incongruous there than they did later, at Smyrna, where the Greeks broke the legs of all their baggage animals and pushed them off the quay into the shallow water to drown.[28]

Meyers may be correct that Hemingway never witnessed the drowning of the mules at Smyrna, but the secondhand reports clearly got under Hemingway's skin and grew into something bigger than the reports themselves. "You wrote about these mules before," the *Old lady* remarks, to which Hemingway replies, "I know it and I'm sorry. Stop interrupting. I won't write about them again. I promise."[29] There is something to be gleaned, Hemingway suggests, from watching an innocent mule have its bones shattered and be pushed off the quay, where it struggles to stand upright, its front legs inverted and its back legs fully functioning, in water just deep enough to drown it. Hemingway is unable to shake off this disturbing image and draws our attention to the fact perhaps to signal its rare importance to the writer.

The reason these images resonate, moving Hemingway and many of his readers to an emotional response, is because we identify with the animal as a thinking, feeling creature and, consequently, we empathize with the creature in its time of need. We understand feelings like fear, confusion, and helplessness, we understand physical pain, and, as mortal creatures ourselves, we can at least imagine the wild panic that boils up and takes hold of an animal in the face of its impending doom. Significantly, animal life resembles human life, but as Hemingway is careful to emphasize, the reverse is also true, as humans will sometimes resemble animals. "The first thing you found about the dead," he writes, "was that, hit badly enough, they died like animals."[30] But what does it mean to die like an animal? Hemingway answers:

> They died from little wounds as rabbits die sometimes from three or four small grains of shot that hardly seem to break the skin. Others would die like cats, a skull broken in and iron in the brain, they lie alive two days like cats that crawl into the coal bin with a bullet in the brain and will not die until you cut their heads off. Maybe cats do not die then,

they say they have nine lives, I do not know, but most men die like animals, not men. I'd never seen a natural death, so called, and so I blamed it on the war and like the persevering traveller, Mungo Park, knew that there was something else, that always absent something else, and then I saw one.[31]

According to Hemingway, the majority of men do not die like human beings but like animals. The difference, he seems to imply, is that human beings die with dignity, perhaps in the comfort of their home, where loved ones have gathered by their bedside to honor them and pay their respects as the departing pass into their eternal slumber. Such a depiction sanitizes death, making it appear domestic, peaceful, and even beautiful. How much easier to face death, a person may conclude, if we are surrounded by loved ones at home in the comfort of our beds. But this is not how most people die. The average person, Hemingway assures his readers, dies like an animal, their bodies brutalized, their psyches tormented, and their personhood robbed of all dignity. Again, Hemingway makes use of grotesque imagery—a broken skull, a severed head, and the walking dead corpse of a feline—to illustrate just how *dehumanizing* death can be. Death is undignified and aberrant, violating our human standards and expectations.

Hemingway entertains the possibility that a death resulting from natural causes, rather than from gunshot wound or the blast of a mortar shell, can in fact be dignified, reflecting the unparalleled value of human life. He writes that the natural theologian Mungo Park realized, on the brink of death while stranded in the desert, that God would never allow for one of his beloved children to perish in such an undignified manner. But even natural deaths, Hemingway replies, are often horrific. "The only natural death I've ever seen, outside of loss of blood, was death from Spanish influenza. In this you drown in mucus, choking, and how you know the patient's dead," Hemingway quips, is that "he shits the bed full. So now I want to see the death of any self-called Humanist because a persevering traveller like Mungo Park or me lives on and maybe yet will live to see the actual death of members of this literary sect and watch the noble exits that they make."[32] The thirty-two-year-old writer is grim and cruelly mocking. Humanists wrongly assume that our noble species is superior to the rest of nature and will exhibit deaths worthy of the dignified, exceptional creatures that we are, but Hemingway has seen deaths both natural and unnatural, on the battlefield and off, and so he lacks the anthropocentric presumptions of humanism. Human beings and animals die in like manner, he asserts; there is no hierarchy of value.

Alongside this already scathing critique of secular humanism is a more severe critique of Christian humanism in the form of natural theology. Beginning his polemic with a meditation on the eighteenth-century explorer Mungo Park, Hemingway underscores the illogic of natural theology to show, against Park's conclusion, that human beings lack the exceptional status afforded to them by the *imago Dei*, or sacred image of God.

> When the persevering traveler, Mungo Park, was at one period of his course fainting in the vast wilderness of an African desert, naked and alone, considering his days as numbered and nothing appearing to remain for him to do but to lie down and die, a small moss-flower of extraordinary beauty caught his eye. "Though the whole plant," says he, "was no longer than one of my fingers, I could not contemplate the delicate conformation of its roots, leaves and capsules without admiration. Can that Being who planted, watered and brought to perfection, in this obscure part of the world, a thing which appears of so small importance, look with unconcern upon the situation and suffering of creatures formed after his own image? Surely not. Reflections like these would not allow me to despair;

I started up and, disregarding both hunger and fatigue, travelled forward, assured that relief was at hand; and I was not disappointed." With a disposition to wonder and adore in like manner, as Bishop Stanley says, can no branch of Natural History be studied without increasing that faith, love and hope which we also, every one of us, need in our journey through the wilderness of life? Let us therefore see what inspiration we may derive from the dead.[33]

Park's logic runs as follows: the physical size of an organism does not determine its complexity, for the moss-flower is much smaller than a human being but extremely complex; complexity, in turn, is proof that an organism was intelligently designed, for surely no one would encounter an operating wristwatch in nature, as in the famous watchmaker analogy,[34] and assume that it was assembled through chance, natural selection, and other natural processes; finally, if God cares for a complex lifeform of seemingly "small importance" in an "obscure part of the world," as he does with the moss-flower, then he will surely care for more complex organisms like human beings; in conclusion, observing the natural world should increase a person's faith in God because its complexity is evidence that God designed it with a special purpose.

Readers of Hemingway discover, however, that if God exists, he actually neglects human beings, who die horrifically both on and off the battlefield, and whose "sacred" bodies are profaned, mutilated, and defiled, as Hemingway will demonstrate over the course of ten pages. "Until the dead are buried," Hemingway writes,

> they change somewhat in appearance each day. The color change in Caucasian races is from white to yellow, to yellow-green, to black. If left long enough in the heat the flesh comes to resemble coal-tar, especially where it has been broken or torn, and it has quite a visible tarlike

iridescence. The dead grow larger each day until sometimes they become quite too big for their uniforms, filling these until they seem blown tight enough to burst. The individual members may increase in girth to an unbelievable extent and faces fill as taut and globular as balloons.[35]

Again, Hemingway indulges in the grotesque, describing the bloated corpses of soldiers rotting on the battlefield. He writes about how ambulance drivers collected fragments of human scalp after the explosion of a munition factory; they knew the fragments belonged to women, he says, because they were attached to extra-long strands of hair. He writes about the "half-pint of maggots working where [people's] mouths" used to be and about "a man whose head was broken as a flower-pot may be broken."[36] This robust gallery of grotesque images comprises Hemingway's natural history of the dead. Contra the naïve conclusion made by Park and other natural theologians that God protects and honors those created in his divine image, Hemingway proposes that human beings are really no different from animals, who, in the Christian tradition, are believed to lack the *imago Dei*. This is because human beings *are* animals, in Hemingway's view, glorified beasts whose undignified deaths reflect, as would be the case with other animal species, a complete lack of divine interest in their survival and wellbeing. He writes that "few travellers would take a good full breath of that early summer air" filled with the stench of rotting flesh "and have any such thoughts as Mungo Park about those formed in [God's] own image."[37]

Hemingway's stance on the inherent value of human life—or, rather, its total lack of inherent value—is made explicit in the final three pages of "A Natural History of the Dead," where the writer finally delivers the story he had promised to the *Old lady* before getting distracted by his reflections on Mungo Park and the grotesqueries of war. This short sketch is about a conflict between an artillery officer and the Captain Doctor, a leading medical advisor with the army. Rather than lay a dying soldier among those recovering from their wounds, the Captain Doctor lays the soldier among the dead, for there is little hope the man will survive his injuries. Troubled by his groans, the stretcher-bearers implore the doctor to place the dying man among the other survivors, saying "We don't like to hear him in there with the dead."[38] When the doctor refuses, the artillery officer begs him to kill the soldier with a lethal dose of morphine, but morphine is a valuable resource that cannot be wasted, so the doctor says no, urging the artillery officer to handle the problem himself. The following interaction ensues:

> "I will shoot the poor fellow," the artillery officer said. "I am a humane man. I will not let him suffer."
> "Shoot him then," said the doctor. "Shoot him. Assume the responsibility. I will make a report. Wounded shot by lieutenant of artillery in first curing post. Shoot him. Go ahead shoot him."
> "You are not a human being."
> "My business is to care for the wounded, not to kill them. That is for gentlemen of the artillery."
> "Why don't you care for him then?"
> "I have done so. I have done all that can be done."[39]

There are two perspectives at war in this passage—one humanist, represented by the artillery officer, and the other anti-humanist, represented by the Captain Doctor, who has been disabused of the artillery officer's anthropocentric presuppositions. We can see from their interaction that the doctor maintains a clinical practice, carrying out his professional tasks with an austere and even robotic consistency. When their argument intensifies and the artillery officer attacks the doctor, the latter is forced to defend himself, blinding the artillery officer with iodine. Living up to his professional duty, the doctor then prepares the artillery officer for medical treatment.

The cold-hearted doctor is detached from his patients—he does not exhibit a sliver of sympathy for the dying soldier, and he is ready to administer medical treatment to the artillery officer in spite of their conflict—but it is nevertheless the artillery officer who should unsettle readers, especially those who share his humanistic urges. Certainly, the artillery officer demonstrates a genuine concern for the dying soldier, first imploring the doctor to save the soldier's life and then, after the doctor refuses, courageously offering to end the young man's suffering himself. But the artillery officer threatens to murder the doctor almost immediately afterwards, drawing his pistol as he rushes toward the doctor in a fit of rage. "I'll kill you!" he screams after having iodine splashed into his eyes. "I'll kill you as soon as I can see."[40] At first glance, the officer appears morally driven to protect human life, declaring himself "humane" and regarding the doctor as inhumane (indeed, as literally inhuman—"You are not a human being," he asserts), but the officer betrays his moral conviction at the drop of a hat, threatening to take the life of another human being himself. The officer's contradictory impulses both to destroy and to preserve human life, vowing either to harm or to protect an individual in the service of humanity, reveal what in Chapter 2 of this book was described as the problematic nature of humanitarian thought: namely, that affording humanity special treatment with protected rights and privileges comes at the expense of the nonhuman, which, by logical necessity, is conceptualized as inferior.

Without realizing it, the artillery officer has committed himself to a kind of game, where a negotiable boundary between human and nonhuman determines his moral convictions. Because the doctor's robotic medical practices strike the artillery officer as dehumanizing, he seeks to preserve the soldier's dignity first by relocating him and then by mercifully ending his life. Human beings should not have to suffer, and they should never be left for dead, the artillery officer reasons, because, unlike the rest of creation, human beings have intrinsic moral value and, as such, they deserve to be treated with morally upright behavior on the basis of their humanity alone. When presented with an individual who does not follow this humanitarian code, the artillery officer is quick to identify that person as nonhuman, for this is the only way to make sense of an individual who acts outside of our understanding of human behavior and, more importantly, this is the only way to justify harming an enemy without violating their human rights. The artillery officer dehumanizes the doctor precisely in order to harm him, for the doctor stands in the way of the artillery officer's humanitarian project. We saw this kind of behavior enacted before by the British naval officer at the quay of Smyrna. The Greek military's decision to abandon their own people violated the officer's understanding of normal human behavior, so he comes to view the Greeks not only as inhumane but as literally inhuman. Because of this, he treats the screaming refugees like animals, joining both the Greek and the Turkish militaries in their dehumanization of the Greek refugees. The irony is palpable, but, as Agamben makes clear, this is precisely how humanism works: humanity cannot exist as a meaningful concept without the nonhuman; consequently, the special rights afforded to humanity can only ever be realized at someone else's expense.

Hemingway begins "A Natural History of the Dead" by lambasting Mungo Park and the natural theologians for their belief that scientific observations of nature will increase a person's faith in God, so readers will recognize that, when taken in context, the doctor's perspective, which appears to be thoroughly atheistic, represents Hemingway's perspective as well. Human life, as with animal life, ends in death, or eternal nonexistence, so there is no reason to believe that human beings are intrinsically more valuable than animals; all living species end up in the ground. Moreover, to believe that God created human beings for everlasting glory simply because our physical bodies show evidence of intelligent design is naïve. Our bodies are designed to age, die, decay, and disintegrate. If God created us—a premise that Hemingway is clearly reluctant to accept—it is not for everlasting glory, but for a life that ends in brutality, horror, and eventually death. Just moments after the doctor blinds the artillery officer, the wounded soldier is announced dead, prompting the doctor to remark: "See, my poor lieutenant? We dispute about nothing. In time of war we dispute about nothing. . . . Your eyes will be all right. It is nothing. A dispute about nothing."[41] Readers of Hemingway hear pulsating in these lines the existential nothingness, or *nada*, that Hemingway will write about one year later in "A Clean, Well-Lighted Place." Not believing in God, the doctor sees no significant difference between human and nonhuman lifeforms, so he stands firmly against the officer's humanitarian code.

Hemingway's Stance on Animal Equality

On Hemingway's account, the war forced—*what are supposed to be*—morally superior creatures to commit heinous acts of violence against—again, *what are supposed to be*—creatures made in God's image, relegating an exceptional species of superior moral value to grotesque, undignified deaths. Hemingway entered the war as a young man who, until that point, had merely questioned the Christian faith, struggling, as he did at the time, to reconcile his newfound autonomy as a Kansas City newspaper man with the religious expectations of Oak Park. But he left the war disillusioned. This is why Frederic Henry, the protagonist of *A Farewell to Arms*—a novel inspired by Hemingway's service as an ambulance driver on the Italian front—says to the soldier Gino that "[a]bstract words such as glory, honor, courage, or hallow were obscene" to him, and that he was "always embarrassed by the words sacred, glorious, and sacrifice."[42] Frederic, as with Hemingway at the time, lost faith in the war and could no longer support the patriotic worship of so-called war heroes. Struggling to reconcile warfare's dehumanizing effects with its humanitarian goals, members of Frederic's platoon likewise confess that they "don't believe in the war" anymore.[43] "I had seen nothing sacred," Frederic confesses, "and the things that were glorious had no glory and the sacrifices were like the stockyards at Chicago if nothing was done with the meat except to bury it."[44] In the now infamous Chicago stockyard, animals were slaughtered, processed, and distributed at an unprecedented rate. "The sheer scale of the processing and slaughter of cattle, hogs, and sheep is mind boggling," Angela Pienkos writes. "In 1924, the peak year of its operations, the Stockyard took some 18.6 million head of livestock into its endless maze of holding pens."[45] Upton Sinclair's 1906 novel *The Jungle* memorialized the stockyard by drawing attention to its unsanitary labor practices. In the novel, careless accidents on the factory floor—like dismembered human body parts making their way into the meat grinders—resulted in the blending of animal product with human flesh. Remembering the dead bodies of soldiers scattered across the battlefield, Hemingway refers to the Chicago stockyard to depict the animalization of men at war.

But the takeaway here is not that Hemingway objected to the war for animalizing human beings, or for desecrating the *imago Dei* by violating their human rights; rather, the takeaway is that the war uncovered humanity's animal nature, disabusing Hemingway of the anthropocentric delusion that human life is inherently superior to the rest of the natural world. Hemingway again questions the ideological privileging of man over beast in his 1940 novel *For Whom the Bell Tolls* in a conversation between the protagonist Robert Jordan and Anselmo, one of Robert's guerilla comrades in the anti-fascist efforts of the Spanish Civil War. Fantasizing about life after the war, Anselmo invites Robert to hunt with him on a future date:

> "And after we have won [the war] you must come to hunt."
> "To hunt what?"
> "The boar, the bear, the wolf, the ibex—"
> "You like to hunt?"
> "Yes, man. More than anything. We all hunt in my village. You do not like to hunt?"
> "No," said Robert Jordan. "I do not like to kill animals."
> "With me it is the opposite," the old man said. "I do not like to kill men."
> "Nobody does except those who are disturbed in the head," Robert Jordan said. "But I feel nothing against it when it is necessary. When it is for the cause."
> "It is a different thing, though," Anselmo said. "In my house, when I had a house, and now I have no house, there were the tusks of boar I had shot in the lower forest. There were the hides of wolves I had shot. In the winter, hunting them in the snow. . . . It was a very beautiful thing and all of those things gave me great pleasure to contemplate."[46]

Just as the doctor and artillery officer in "A Natural History of the Dead" represent opposing perspectives on the matter of human rights, so too do Robert Jordan and Anselmo represent opposing perspectives on the matter of animal rights. Anselmo loves to kill animals, decorating his home with their corpses, but he does not like to kill men. He says, in fact, that decorating your home with animal corpses is a "very beautiful thing" and he contemplates it with "great pleasure." Robert Jordan, by contrast, likes to kill neither men nor animals, and, in his judgment, those who kill men out of pleasure rather than out of practical necessity are "disturbed in the head." The discussion continues:

> "On the door of the church of my village was nailed the paw of a bear that I killed in the spring, finding him on a hillside in the snow, overturning a log with this same paw."
> "When was this?"
> "Six years ago. And every time I saw that paw, like the hand of a man, but with those long claws, dried and nailed through the palm to the door of the church, I received pleasure."
> "Of pride?"
> "Of pride of remembrance of the encounter with the bear on that hillside in the early spring. But of the killing of a man, who is a man as we are, there is nothing good that remains."
> "You can't nail his paw to the church," Robert Jordan said.
> "No. Such a barbarity is unthinkable. Yet the hand of a man is like the paw of a bear."
> "So is the chest of a man like the chest of a bear," Robert Jordan said. "With the hide removed from the bear, there are many similarities in the muscles."
> "Yes," Anselmo said. "The gypsies believe the bear to be a brother of man."
> "So do the Indians in America," Robert Jordan said. "And when they kill a bear they apologize to him and ask his pardon. They put his skull in a tree and they ask him to forgive them before they leave it."
> "The gypsies believe the bear to be a brother to man because he has the same body beneath his hide, because he drinks beer, because he enjoys music and because he likes to dance."[47]

Robert Jordan and Anselmo agree that human beings and bears have similar skeletal structures in addition to other important similarities. This is why gypsies and American Indians regard the bear as their equal, ask for forgiveness whenever they kill a bear, and assume that bears have the power to grant them forgiveness in the first place. This egalitarian view of the animal kingdom—under which mankind is equally considered an animal species—runs up against Anselmo's belief that animals are inferior to human beings. It would be unthinkable, barbarous, and even sacrilegious in Anselmo's view to nail a human hand to the door of the church, ostensibly because human beings are superior creatures endowed with the sacred image of God. This is why he can remember killing a bear with pleasure but is sickened by his memory of killing men:

> "You have killed?" Robert Jordan asked in the intimacy of the dark and of their day together.
> "Yes. Several times. But not with pleasure. To me it is a sin to kill a man. Even Fascists whom we must kill. To me there is a great difference between the bear and the man and I do not believe the wizardry of the gypsies about the brotherhood with animals. No, I am against all killing of men."
> "Yet you have killed."
> "Yes. And will again. But if I live later, I will try to live in such a way, doing no harm to any one, that will be forgiven."
> "By whom?"
> "Who knows? Since we do not have God here anymore, neither His Son nor the Holy Ghost, who forgives? I do not know."
> "No. Man. Certainly not. If there were God, never would He have permitted what I have seen with my eyes. Let *them* have God."
> "They claim Him."
> "Clearly I miss Him, having been brought up in religion. But now a man must be responsible to himself."
> "Then it is thyself who will forgive thee for killing."
> "I believe so," Anselmo said. "Since you put it clearly in that way I believe that must be it. But with or without God, I think it is a sin to kill. To take the life of another is to me very grave."[48]

Anselmo models what Chapter 2 of this book describes as a secularized belief in the *imago Dei*. For him, it is not only *wrong* to kill another human being—in the sense that killing someone violates society's ethical standards—it is also a *sin*. The difference here between an ethical violation and a sin is that the former is *subjectively* wrong (in that it violates a communal agreement) while the latter is *objectively* wrong (in that it violates the will of God). Killing another human being breaks a metaphysical law because human beings, according to this view, were created in God's divine image with superior moral value. But just as Frederic Henry of *A Farewell to Arms* is unable to reconcile his belief in God with the brutal atrocities of war, so too is Anselmo unable to believe in a God who permits such atrocities to take place. For this reason, Anselmo embraces contradictory viewpoints: he loses faith in God but retains a belief in sacred human identity. After Robert Jordan underscores the contradiction in Anselmo's thought, Anselmo is forced to admit that, in his now secularized theological view, human identity, rather than some divine mandate, is the metaphysical basis of moral law. "[W]ith or without God, . . . it is a sin to kill," he says, because human beings are inherently valuable. But whereas the *imago Dei* is bestowed upon mankind by a deity who determines the metaphysical nature of being, "human identity," as we saw in Chapter 2, is a cultural construct that must, in essence, be *decided* upon by each individual meaning-maker. Anselmo must define "human identity" over against the gypsies and American Indians who, we have learned, have a different understanding of "human identity."

Thus, metaphysical authority is first transferred from God to "human identity," after Anselmo stops believing in God, and then from "human identity" to Anselmo himself, the lawmaking individual who realizes, with the help of Robert Jordan, that "human identity" is a cultural construct. Under this contradictory point of view—which conflates subjective morality with objective morality—each individual decision maker now operates as the ontological origin of moral law, for the individual alone, the Sartrean existentialist will argue, defines the boundaries of human identity. As with Sartre, Anselmo begins with the belief that mankind was created in God's image with inherent rights and privileges. After losing his faith, however, Anselmo continues to believe in the inherent value of human life against his better judgment, retaining a secularized view of the *imago Dei* in spite of God's absence. But just as Sartre realizes that all people must construct a notion of "human identity" for themselves, so too does Anselmo realize, in concert with Sartre, that the individual decides "what humanity as a whole should be."[49] As Robert Jordan adeptly observes, Anselmo is logically forced to adopt the role of a deity due to an irresolvable conflict in his thought. As a result, he must ask *himself* for forgiveness rather than God.

Robert Jordan, however, does not understand the pleasure of killing, whether the target is man or beast, for, in contrast with Anselmo, he does not view humanity as fundamentally different from the rest of the animal kingdom and, arguably, for this reason, he does not take any pleasure or pride in the act of killing, as Anselmo does. Rather, Robert Jordan kills out of necessity and believes that those who take pleasure in killing are mentally disturbed. He says that neither man nor beast bears the sacred image of God, and so it is perfectly acceptable to kill either species if the situation calls for it. But this does not mean that Robert Jordan will experience pride or pleasure in the act of killing, for such emotions grow out of a mental disturbance, he asserts—the belief that an individual's superiority is reinforced through repeated acts of sovereign domination.

Now, it is certainly the case that human beings are smarter than other animal species (granting, of course, that, when saying this, we adopt an anthropocentric view of what constitutes superior intelligence), but it should also be noted that some human beings are significantly smarter than other human beings, so superior intelligence does not necessarily indicate a difference in species. It is similarly the case that human beings can physically dominate other animals, but, in like manner, it should be noted that human beings can physically dominate each other as well, so neither does the ability to physically dominate your opponent necessarily indicate a difference in animal species. Nevertheless, when it comes to certain abilities, some species are superior to other species, just as some individuals are superior to other individuals. The dorcas gazelle, for instance, which can survive its entire life without drinking water, is much better than any human being at remaining hydrated in arid conditions. But this does not mean that the gazelle should be afforded sacred rights and privileges in light of its (hypothetical) superior metaphysical value, which has no logical relationship to its abilities whatsoever. So even if human beings are the most intelligent animals on earth, the most loving animals on earth, the most creative animals on earth, or what have you, this does not mean that they have superior metaphysical value. In short, differences in ability do not necessarily indicate a "great difference" between animal species, as Anselmo would seem to believe, and, moreover, a lifeform's inherent, metaphysical value has no logical relationship to its abilities whatsoever, no matter how "superior" that lifeform may appear.

    The problem is that human beings tend to overvalue their own abilities and, as a direct consequence of this, they mistakenly regard themselves as *inherently* more valuable than other lifeforms. But values are subjective by nature; they vary from person to person and from species to species. So *inherent value*, in principle, is a purely hypothetical notion—it does not actually exist for the atheist, or at least it shouldn't. Thus, when non-religious people use the phrase *inherent value*, they do so in bad faith, for, without logical justification to demonstrate its existence, *inherent value* is a mere rhetorical device—it authorizes the speaker's value system over competing value systems by simply calling itself authoritative. For Christians, by contrast, the phrase refers to anything valued by God, who determines the metaphysical nature of being. Christians therefore have logical justification for their belief in objective moral value: human beings are superior to other species because they bear the divine image. The atheist's belief in human superiority, however, reflects entirely subjective values that are mistakenly regarded as objective.

Not being captive to anthropocentric views himself, Robert Jordan, as with many of Hemingway's characters, disrupts the human/animal hierarchy. From the 1925 edition of *In Our Time* to *A Farewell to Arms* (1929), *Death in the Afternoon* (1932), *For Whom the Bell Tolls* (1940), and, looking some thirty years into the future, *The Old Man and the Sea* (1952)—a period of time when Hemingway is thought to have been a practicing Catholic by Grimes, Stoneback, and Nickel—the writer consistently undermines the notion that human beings are inherently superior to nonhuman lifeforms. "You are killing me, fish," reflects Santiago, the celebrated protagonist of Hemingway's Nobel-Prize-winning novella, "[b]ut you have a right to. Never have I seen a greater, or more beautiful, or a calmer or more noble thing than you, brother. Come on and kill me."[50] Not only is the marlin superior to Santiago in a variety of ways, but, according to Santiago, it is the marlin's *right* to kill him. This directly contradicts the Christian teaching that "[e]very moving thing . . . shall be food" for God's image bearers, that special creature of supreme importance at the center of his cosmic plan.[51] Santiago recognizes the fish as his "brother" just as the American Indians and gypsies in *For Whom the Bell Tolls* recognized the bear as their brother. Hemingway presents us with an egalitarian view of the animal kingdom that recognizes human beings as themselves an animal species. There is no *imago Dei*; human life is not sacred.

Readers of Hemingway scholarship will already be familiar with the often-cited passage of the lion's first-person perspective in "The Short Happy Life of Francis Macomber." According to Ryan Hediger, "Hemingway reverses conventional anthropocentric perspectives [in the short story by] literally making the 'man' in the scene an it, part of an 'object,' a mere scent on the wind. To do this, Hemingway has relied upon the subjectivity of the lion to make his own text."[52] Christopher McGill says that the lion "becomes a character," providing "an opportunity for the reader to think through the experience of a hunted animal."[53] The lion "eclipses the privileged perspective of the hunters," he writes, "and generates, in turn, a distinct and powerful nonhuman presence in the story."[54] The animal perspective introduces a shift in power, exposing readers to an interspecies dynamic that questions the value of human story-telling, which tends to be self-oriented and self-aggrandizing by nature. As Margot Macomber says to Francis and their hunting guide, Robert Wilson: "You're both talking rot . . . Just because you've chased some helpless animals in a motor car you talk like heroes."[55] One could extend Margot's sentiment a bit further and argue that most man-made stories are egotistical by nature insofar as they focus on human characters, human action, and human concerns from an all-too-human perspective. Not surprisingly, Francis and Wilson are the heroes of their own story, performing courageous, praiseworthy acts that result in the triumphant defeat of their antagonists (whom Margot identifies as innocent, unsuspecting animals). Hemingway's shift to the animal perspective is only a momentary blip in the narrative—it seems to appear without anticipation or forethought, as if the writer seized the opportunity, quite simply, to experiment with shifting perspectives—but the technique nevertheless decenters the story and, through this decentering, the shift to an animal perspective brings the value of anthropocentric story-telling and, alongside it, the superiority of human life into question.

Given the fact that many readers feel sympathy for the lion—take, for example, Nina Baym's article "Actually, I Felt Sorry for the Lion"[56]—Hemingway's critique of anthropocentrism may come across as a defense of animal rights. But Hemingway's egalitarian vision of the animal kingdom should not be interpreted as a defense of animal rights, in which he expressly does not believe. As Hemingway states in the opening pages of *Death in the Afternoon*, there are "two general groups" of people: those who do not identify with animals and those who do, "the almost professional lovers of dogs, and other beasts."[57] As we have already seen, Hemingway does not believe, as the first group does, that human beings are inherently superior to other animals, but he also fails to identify with the second group, who agree with his view that human beings are themselves an animal species. This is because, in contrast with Hemingway, the second group is opposed to animal cruelty (something that Hemingway defends at great length), and they base their defense of any nonhuman creature "on that fact that [said creature] is an animal and hence worthy of love."[58] The animal rights advocate would appear to defend animals on the basis of their animality alone just as the human rights advocate defends human beings on the basis of their humanity alone. As I explained in Chapter 2, however, the lifeforms in question are illogically attributed an inherent, metaphysical value which then serves as the basis of their inviolable rights. Hemingway admits that he loves certain animals on a personal basis in light of their individual qualities, but he does not love "dogs as dogs, horses as horses, or cats as cats."[59] He does not, in other words, love animals on the basis of their animality alone, and he does not, with the animal rights advocate, believe that animals have inherent, metaphysical value. Thus, Hemingway is actually part of a third group: he identifies with both animals and humans (themselves an animal species), but he does not believe that either group has inherent rights.

At stake here are contrasting forms of egalitarianism, one positive and one negative. The positive form seeks to elevate animals to the level of humans, granting animals the same rights and privileges traditionally afforded to humanity, while the negative form lowers humanity to the level of animals, stripping humans of the rights and privileges that have traditionally set them apart as superior. In both cases, humans are regarded as equal to animals, but in the former case humans and animals alike are afforded sacred rights, whereas in the latter case humans and animals are both stripped of their rights and denied a sacred status. It is my belief that Hemingway falls within this second camp of egalitarianism, stripping humanity of its sacred rights in order to identify as an animal, which is given no rights whatsoever. After all, the deep-sea fisherman and big-game hunter loved to kill animals, and, as a bullfight aficionado, he loved watching other people kill animals as well, so it is quite probable that Hemingway opposed the idea of animal rights.

That being said, critic Kevin Maier persuasively argues that, as Hemingway ages, he becomes more and more committed to wildlife conservation and the so-called "sportsman's ethic [that President Theodore] Roosevelt helped [to] make famous."[60] But Roosevelt—Hemingway's childhood hero—demonstrated an insatiable bloodlust in his lifetime, killing nearly 300 animals on safari in 1909 and famously leading the Rough Riders to victory at San Juan Hill during the Spanish-American War. Hemingway continued to idolize Roosevelt well into his adulthood and even hired Philip Percival, one of Roosevelt's hunting guides from the well-known and highly celebrated expedition of 1909, to lead his own safari with Pauline in 1933 and then again with Mary in 1953. Like Roosevelt, Hemingway was a lifelong hunter whose own "body-count" was, in the words of Glen Love, "startlingly high."[61] The "Hemingway kill record is astonishing," Love states. "Not only big-game animals (lions, leopards, buffalo, rhinoceros, kudu, etc.) in Africa and the American West, including a flying eagle and some of the last grizzly bears outside protected areas in America, but also shoals of marlin, tuna, dolphin, tarpon, kingfish, and sea turtles."[62] Like Roosevelt, Hemingway loved to kill, so he most likely adhered to a negative form of egalitarianism that animalizes humanity rather than to a positive form of egalitarianism that humanizes animals.

These contrasting forms of egalitarianism also mark the difference between animal rights activism and certain veins of posthumanist thought. Take, for example, Tom Regan's landmark study *The Case for Animal Rights* (1983). Regan argues that animals share certain qualities with human beings, among which include self-consciousness, the ability to experience pleasure or pain, and the instinctual desire to protect their own wellbeing; these qualities indicate, in turn, that animals have inherent, inviolable rights, just like the human beings whom they resemble. In other words, because human beings—the "genius and the retarded child [sic], the prince and the pauper, the brain surgeon and the fruit vendor, Mother Teresa and the most unscrupulous used-car salesman—all have inherent value," it follows, in Regan's view, that animals too have inherent value, for they consciously experience both pleasure and pain just as human beings do, and they wish to increase their pleasure and decrease their pain just as human beings wish to.[63] Regan wrongly conflates a creature's inherent value with their conscious desire to avoid pain, as if the two elements were somehow evidence of each other, but there is simply no reason to conflate the two, as neither claim logically requires that the other be true as well. Regan reverse engineers an argument for animal rights, first, by treating the desire to avoid pain as proof that animals resemble humans, and second, by treating the similarities between animals and humans as proof that animals too are inherently valuable. But Regan's argument rests on a religious presupposition for which he does not provide logical justification: namely, the belief that human beings are inherently valuable.

Regan models a positive form of egalitarianism that characterizes how the majority of animal rights activists approach the issue of animal equality. Beginning with Peter Singer's 1975 *Animal Liberation*, animal rights advocates have argued that sentient lifeforms should be given the same moral consideration as human beings because, like humans, they too are capable of suffering. Singer argues that speciesism, or discrimination against other (nonhuman) species, is comparable to racism and should therefore be abolished. Singer promotes a positive form of egalitarianism that strives toward a more inclusive, ever-widening scope of personhood. As Michael Pollan, a contemporary voice in the study of animal rights, describes in his reading of Singer's watershed contribution to the field, "the white man's circle of moral consideration was expanded to admit first blacks, then women, then homosexuals. In each case, a group once thought to be so different from the prevailing 'we' as to be undeserving of civil rights was, after a struggle, admitted to the club. Now it [i]s the animal's turn."[64] But, as Pollan indicates, there is a problem with Singer's egalitarian vision. "I asked Salatin," the owner of Polyface Farm, which specializes in sustainable agriculture, "how he could bring himself to kill a chicken," and Salatin replied: "People have a soul; animals don't . . . Unlike us, animals are not created in God's image, so when they die, they just die."[65] Under the positive form of egalitarianism, to be treated equally is to be treated like a human being, but, barring the *imago Dei*, there is simply no reason to believe that human life constitutes the metaphysical standard around which we should organize a moral code. Positive egalitarianism is the driving force behind animal rights advocacy; it strives to include animals, the dehumanized, and other nonhuman lifeforms within the fold of sacred human identity, a secularized theological standard whose true vacancy, when revealed to be vacant, unravels the entire system from within.

Certain veins of posthumanist thought offer in its place an alternate form of egalitarianism, a negative egalitarianism that, in keeping with Agamben's critique of anthropogenesis, eliminates the violent oppression of nonhuman lifeforms through the deconstruction of "human rights"—a point which I developed at length in Chapter 2 of this book. In works like *Homo Sacer: Sovereign Power and Bare Life* (1998) and "Beyond Human Rights" (1993), a short essay written five years earlier, Agamben argues that in modern nation-states human rights are only afforded to legal citizens. But citizenship can be revoked, as it often has been in the modern era, the consequence of which is the loss of one's legal rights and, alongside them, the loss of one's humanity. So-called human rights, then, as with legal citizenship, are not inherent qualities, and, as Agamben will argue a decade later in *The Open* (2003), the very concept of humanity is the problem here, not just the laws governing citizenship. This is because, as a differential construct, "human identity" must be distinguished from the nonhuman to appear intelligible, so the very notion of human rights, whether those rights are legally authorized or not, itself has dehumanizing effects, producing the nonhumans who, as a matter of principle, will not be afforded those same rights.

Agamben recognizes that humanism will only ever protect humanity at the expense of nonhuman life because positive forms of egalitarianism necessarily subsist of hierarchies. He offers in its place a negative egalitarianism that levels the playing field through a so-called *profanation* of transcendental forms. Agamben's project is posthumanist, in this sense, because it seeks to overcome the founding metaphysical divisions of humanistic thought. His goal, therefore, is not to reform humanism, but to deconstruct it. Humanism itself cannot be reformed, according to Agamben, because every humanitarian gesture toward a more inclusive society is also already exclusive by nature. In order to achieve true equality, then, we must overcome human exceptionalism. According to Agamben scholar Matthew Calarco, "humanism is founded on a separation of the *humanitas* and *animalitas* within the human," so "no genuinely posthumanist politics can emerge without grappling with the logic and consequences of this division," as we see in Agamben's assiduous examination of anthropogenesis and "human-based politics."[66] Agamben scholar Adam Kotsko seconds this notion, observing that Agamben's goal "is not to reform the system or return it to a more stable balance—for instance, to stop relying on exceptional emergency powers and return to the 'normal' rule of law—but to fully grasp it in order to understand how to dismantle it."[67] Agamben wants to deconstruct "human rights," which are based on human exceptionalism—or a secularized theological belief in the *imago Dei*—in order to make room for a new kind of equality, what he calls *absolute immanence*, or a world devoid of metaphysical hierarchies. This is the negative form of egalitarianism to which Agamben subscribes in his critique of the sovereign exception; it is also the model to which Hemingway subscribes in his own ostensible rejection of God, the afterlife, and the *imago Dei*.

Notes

1. Ernest Hemingway, *Green Hills of Africa* (New York: Charles Scribner's Sons, 1935), foreword.
2. Ibid., 291.

3. Ibid.
4. Ibid., 293.
5. Ernest Hemingway, *Men Without Women* (New York: Scribner Paperback Fiction, 1997), 115.
6. Ibid., 116–17.
7. The 1924 Paris edition was originally titled *in our time*. One year later, the collection was republished in the United States as *In Our Time* (with the first letter of each word capitalized). The second U.S. edition was published in 1930 under the same title.
8. Ernest Hemingway, *In Our Time* (New York: Scribner, 2003), 47.
9. "Introduction by the Author" was renamed "On the Quai at Smyrna" in the 1938 publication of *The Fifth Column and the First Forty-Nine Stories*.
10. Hemingway, *In Our Time*, 11.
11. Jeffrey Meyers, "Hemingway's Second War: The Greco-Turkish Conflict, 1920–1922," *Modern Fiction Studies* 30.1 (1984): 26, 28.
12. Quoted ibid., 29.
13. Ibid.
14. Hemingway, *In Our Time*, 11.
15. Ibid., 12.
16. Ibid., 11.
17. Ibid., 12.
18. At several points in "A Natural History of the Dead," Hemingway says that the grotesque images he describes could only properly be depicted on canvas by the Spanish painter Francisco de Goya, the topic of Kristin A. Durkin's 2012 monograph *Goya and the Grotesque: A Study of Themes of Witchcraft and Monstrous Bodies*.
19. Anna Journey, "Earn the Vomit: Employing the Grotesque in Contemporary Poetry," *The American Poetry Review* 43.5 (2014): 15.
20. Ani Kokobobo, *Russian Grotesque Realism* (Columbus, OH: Ohio State University Press, 2018), 118.
21. Hemingway, *In Our Time*, 12.

22. Ernest Hemingway, *For Whom the Bell Tolls* (New York: Scribner, 1940), epigraph.
23. Lewis E. Weeks, Jr., "Mark Twain and Hemingway: 'A Catastrophe' and 'A Natural History of the Dead,'" *Mark Twain Journal* 14.2 (1968): 15.
24. Ray B. West, Jr., "Ernest Hemingway: The Failure of Sensibility," *The Sewanee Review* 53.1 (1945): 120.
25. Ernest Hemingway, *Death in the Afternoon* (London: Arrow Books, 2004), 114.
26. Ibid., 1–2.
27. Ibid., 3–4.
28. Ibid., 115.
29. Ibid.
30. Ibid., 118.
31. Ibid.
32. Ibid., 119.
33. Ibid., 114–15.
34. Articulations of the watchmaker analogy have been issued over the centuries by Sir Isaac Newton, René Descartes, and William Paley, among others. The analogy played a prominent role in Paley's work and natural theology in general. The argument from design has been widely discredited and was famously criticized by evolutionary biologist Richard Dawkins in *The Blind Watchmaker: Why the Evidence of Evolution Reveals a Universe without Design* (New York/London: W. W. Norton & Company, 1986).
35. Hemingway, *Death in the Afternoon*, 117.
36. Ibid., 119, 120.
37. Ibid., 118.
38. Ibid., 121.
39. Ibid.
40. Ibid., 122.
41. Ibid., 122–3.
42. Ernest Hemingway, *A Farewell to Arms* (New York: Charles Scribner's Sons, 1929), 185, 184.
43. Ibid., 217.
44. Ibid., 185.

45. Angela T. Pienkos, "Slaughterhouse: Chicago's Union Stockyard and the World It Made," *Polish American Studies* 74.1 (2017): 94.
46. Hemingway, *For Whom the Bell Tolls*, 39.
47. Ibid., 39–40.
48. Ibid., 41.
49. Ibid., 25.
50. Ernest Hemingway, *The Old Man and the Sea* (London: Vintage Books, 2000), 71.
51. Genesis 9:3 (NASB).
52. Ryan Hediger, "Becoming with Animals: Sympoiesis and the Ecology of Meaning in London and Hemingway," *Studies in American Naturalism* 11.1 (2016): 12.
53. Christopher McGill, "A Reading of Zoomorphism in 'The Short Happy Life of Francis Macomber,'" *The Explicator* 70.1 (2012): 58, 59.
54. Ibid., 59.
55. Ernest Hemingway, *Winner Take Nothing* (London: Arrow Books, 1994), 29.
56. Nina Baym, "Actually, I Felt Sorry for the Lion," in *New Critical Approaches to the Short Stories of Ernest Hemingway*, ed. Jackson J. Benson (Durham, NC: Duke University Press, 1990), 112–20.
57. Hemingway, *Death in the Afternoon*, 4.
58. Ibid.
59. Ibid., 5.
60. Kevin Maier, "Hemingway's Hunting: An Ecological Reconsideration," *The Hemingway Review* 25.2 (2006): 120.
61. Glen A. Love, "Hemingway's Indian Virtues: An Ecological Reconsideration," *Western American Literature* 22.3 (1987): 203.
62. Ibid., 212.
63. Tom Regan, "The Case for Animal Rights," in *The Norton Reader: An Anthology of Nonfiction*, 14th edn, ed. Melissa A. Goldthwaite et al. (New York/London: W. W. Norton & Company, 2017), 676.

64. Michael Pollan, "An Animal's Place," in *The Norton Reader: An Anthology of Nonfiction*, 14th edn, ed. Melissa A. Goldthwaite et al. (New York/London: W. W. Norton & Company, 2017), 681.
65. Ibid., 694.
66. Matthew Calarco, *Zoographies: The Question of the Animal from Heidegger to Derrida* (New York: Columbia University Press, 2008), 88, 91.
67. Adam Kotsko, *Agamben's Philosophical Trajectory* (Edinburgh: Edinburgh University Press, 2020), 118.

CHAPTER 4

HEMINGWAY'S MASCULINE HERO

There Are No Happy Endings

Hemingway's animalization of human beings follows his war-time observations of dead and dying soldiers, none of whom exited the world in a dignified way. As a young ambulance driver, Hemingway was shaken by the grotesque manner in which both soldiers and civilians were killed; he was likewise disturbed by the process undergone by their decaying bodies. As discussed at length in Chapters 1 and 2 of this book, Hemingway was raised as a devout Congregationalist in the tight-knit community of Oak Park, so when he saw that God's beloved creatures, who were made in his image for a special purpose, could themselves rot above ground without proper ceremony, he realized that human beings are inherently no different from the cargo mules drowned at Smyrna. Both animals and humans (an animal species themselves) end up in the same place, and, in this sense, they are equals, he reasoned; there is no hierarchy of value. By the time Hemingway wrote *Death in the Afternoon*, the concept of negative equality had already taken hold of the writer, as we see in his sardonic appraisal of Mungo Park, the traveler and natural theologian. At some point in his discussion with the *old lady*, Hemingway tells her a story about a monogamous bull who is sent to the ring and deemed useless after he stops mating with the entire herd. The *old lady* calls it a "sad story," and Hemingway replies:

> Madame, all stories, if continued far enough, end in death, and he is no true-story teller who would keep that from you. Especially do all stories of monogamy end in death, and your man who is monogamous while he often lives most happily, dies in the most lonely fashion. There is no lonelier man in death, except the suicide, than that man who has lived many years with a good wife and then outlived her. If two people love each other there can be no happy end to it.[1]

Hemingway again draws a comparison between animals and human-animals. The *old lady* expresses sympathy for the bull, perhaps because she identifies with its seemingly romantic desire to be monogamous. But Hemingway implores the *old lady* to redirect that sympathy toward herself, for, in a manner of speaking, she too will be sent to the ring. Death is the true equalizer, Hemingway suggests; it proves that we are inherently no different from the animals we condescend to, as far as objective moral value is concerned, for, at the time of death, we slip into nonexistence and our bodies start to decay. As Salatin, the owner of Polyface Farm, had put it in his conversation with Michael Pollan, "when [animals] die, they just die."[2] The same is true of humans, so even the person who lives "most happily," basking in the pleasure of their day-to-day experience, should realize that their joy will soon come to an end. Just as monogamy—an archetypal site of the much-sought-after *fairytale ending*—eventually gives way to unfathomable loneliness, so too does every attempt to create lasting significance in our lives eventually give way to feelings of insignificance, the devastating realization that the life we live will soon be replaced by eternal nonexistence.

The passage alludes to the final pages of *A Farewell to Arms*, Hemingway's great love story published just three years earlier. After deserting the war, Frederic Henry and his lover, the nurse Catherine Barkley, abscond first to Montreux and then to Lausanne, Switzerland. Away from the war, Frederic and Catherine live happily in romantic bliss, awaiting the birth of their child. But tragedy looms on the horizon, and after many strenuous hours in the delivery room, Catherine and the baby die. Earlier in the novel, we learn that both Frederic and Catherine are atheists. Catherine, for instance, confesses that she "ha[s]n't any religion," though she carries a necklace of Saint Anthony with her "for luck," in keeping with the popular custom.[3] Frederic too observes that our earthly existence is "all and all and all" there is to life, a sad reality that keeps him awake at night.[4] After losing their baby boy, who was strangled to death by his umbilical cord, Frederic confesses that he has "no feeling" for the deceased child, but he wonders if the baby should have been baptized, given the Catholic teaching that unbaptized babies go into limbo.[5] Like Catherine, Frederic pays tribute to the Church out of respect for polite society, but, when it comes down to it, he simply "ha[s] no religion."[6] Frederic then reflects on the fact that both he and Catherine will die too. "That was what you did," Frederic thinks to himself. "You died. You did not know what it was about. You never had time to learn. They threw you in and told you the rules and the first time they caught you off base they killed you. . . . You could count on that. Stay around and they would kill you."[7] Life has no lasting significance and, even if you put your faith in the Church, there is still no hope of an afterlife, or so Hemingway appears to suggest.

As we have already seen, both Frederic and Catherine pay tribute to the Church, practicing aspects of religion without actually believing in their efficacy, as if out of respect for tradition and cultural custom. Frederic admits to an elderly priest, his friend Count Greffi, that his "religious feeling . . . comes only at night," though he expects to "become very devout" as he ages.⁸ Readers should note, however, that this "religious feeling" is not the same as religious belief, for Count Greffi compares it to romantic love, which can be experienced by anyone, regardless of their religious affiliation. From what I can gather, "religious feeling," in Hemingway's secularized theological view, is a natural inclination toward the core qualities of religion, an aspiration for something greater beyond ourselves, such as everlasting love. But Frederic is disabused of his religious feeling after God takes the life of Catherine, his one true love: "Don't let her die. Oh, God, please don't let her die. I'll do anything for you if you won't let her die. Please, please, please, dear God, don't let her die. . . . You took the baby, but don't let her die."⁹ Frederic does not believe in religion, but he genuinely wants to, befriending priests, observing Catholic doctrine, and sincerely begging God for help. But Frederic knows deep down that God will not help him. He sits in the hospital, awaiting Catherine's diagnosis, when a troubling memory comes to mind:

> Once in camp I put a log on top of the fire and it was full of ants. As it commenced to burn, the ants swarmed out and went first toward the centre where the fire was; then turned back and ran toward the end. When there were enough on the end they fell off into the fire. Some got out, their bodies burnt and flattened, and went off not knowing where they were going. But most of them went toward the fire and then back toward the end and swarmed on the cool end and finally fell off into the fire. I remember thinking at the time that it was the end of the world and a splendid chance to be a messiah and lift the log off the fire and throw it out where the ants could get off onto the ground. But I did not do anything but throw a tin cup of water on the log, so that I would have the cup empty to put whiskey in before I added water to it. I think the cup of water on the burning log only steamed the ants.¹⁰

The analogy runs as follows: God has the power to save every human being, those exceptional creatures of supreme importance at the center of his cosmic plan, and yet he chooses not to, allowing a great many of them to perish. Reconciling the two concepts—the first, that human life matters to God, the second, that God chooses to save some people and not others—is a difficult task, especially when you put yourself in the shoes of the deity, as Frederic does. The fact is, Frederic could have removed the log without any effort, saving the entire colony, just as an omnipotent deity can save the soul of every person, should he choose to. But Frederic watches the ants burn. The act is sadistic, at worst, and apathetic, at best, as we could say that Frederic simply lacked the motivation to rescue creatures of so little importance. But this is precisely Frederic's point: that an omnipotent deity would choose not to save every person is evidence that human life is not as significant as we think—Frederic suggests that we are mere "ants" in the cosmic scheme of things. Hemingway challenges Christianity's belief in the *imago Dei* by depicting human beings as mortal animals; he challenges anthropocentrism by advancing a negative view of equality that frames death as the shared destiny of every organism. Human exceptionalism is a religious fiction.

With this point in place, I draw my reader's attention back to Sartre, for the belief that human life is rendered insignificant by death is an important tenet of his existentialist philosophy. My thesis, of course, is that both writers secularize the *imago Dei* without realizing it, that both Hemingway and Sartre adopt a belief in human exceptionalism after first rejecting their belief in the *imago Dei*. Thus, throughout this project, it has been my task to delineate the logical (or perhaps illogical), step-by-step process that leads both Hemingway and Sartre down the path of secularized theism. Their shared belief in human insignificance—or *the meaninglessness of life*, as the phrase is often put—is the first of several parts, all of which are portrayed in the authors' fiction. As a point of comparison, I offer a brief analysis of Sartre's "The Wall," a short story on the Spanish Civil War written just one year prior to Hemingway's publication on the same topic in *For Whom the Bell Tolls*. Three prisoners of war are sentenced to death, the protagonist, Pablo Ibbieta, and two of his comrades, Tom and Juan. They spend the night in anticipation of their executions, which will take place against a firing wall, from which the story gets its name. Of course, the title also symbolizes the inevitable ending that each of us will someday face: insurmountable, impermeable, a dead stop—the wall is a passage into permanent nonexistence.

Readers should note that Pablo is a leftist revolutionary fighting against the fascist dictatorship of Francisco Franco. Pablo cares deeply about politics and refuses to give up their leader, Ramon Gris, when the fascists offer to spare his life in exchange for Gris's location. But, at some point during Pablo's long journey into the morning, at which time he will finally be executed, he undergoes a transformation. Sartre presents us with the changes that take place in a human being after they have accepted their mortality, a before-and-after look at an individual confronted with certain death. Finding himself on the other side of this transformation, Pablo is stricken by the absurd thoughts and behavior of his former self:

> A crowd of memories came back to me pell-mell. There were good and bad ones—or at least I called them that *before*. There were faces and incidents. I saw the face of a little *novillero* who was gored in Valencia during the *Feria*, the face of one of my uncles, the face of Ramon Gris. I remembered my whole life: how I was out of work for three months in 1926, how I almost starved to death. I remembered a night I spent on a bench in Granada: I hadn't eaten for three days. I was angry, I didn't want to die. That made

me smile. How madly I ran after happiness, after women, after liberty. Why? I wanted to free Spain, I admired Pi y Margall, I joined the anarchist movement, I spoke in public meetings: I took everything as seriously as if I were immortal. At that moment I felt that I had my whole life in front of me and I thought, "It's a damned lie." It was worth nothing because it was finished. I wondered how I'd been able to walk, to laugh with the girls: I wouldn't have moved so much as my little finger if I had only imagined I would die like this. My life was in front of me, shut, closed, like a bag and yet everything inside of it was unfinished. For an instant I tried to judge it. I wanted to tell myself, this is a beautiful life. But I couldn't pass judgment on it; it was only a sketch; I had spent my time counterfeiting eternity, I had understood nothing.... death had disenchanted everything.[11]

Pablo's thought process begins with the memory of a young bullfighter, a matador in training who was gored to death before his time. Pablo remembers the young man's face, as if perceiving the memento mori in his expression. He then remembers the face of his uncle, who presumably also died, and then the face of Ramon Gris, whose own death has been foreshadowed. Their deaths remind Pablo that he once battled to stay alive himself, still enchanted, as he was at the time, with the illusion of immortality. He strove after women, happiness, and liberty as if they were his human right, and he fought to secure these rights as if they had lasting significance. But the truth is that Pablo will die, just as every person dies, and whether or not he had women, happiness, or liberty will make no difference in the end. "I took everything as seriously as if I were immortal," Pablo states. "I had spent my time counterfeiting eternity." When confronted with the overwhelming promise of eternal nonexistence, our current lives appear relatively unimportant. Had someone "told me [while I was on death row that] I could go quietly," Pablo reflects, "it would have left me cold: several hours or several years of waiting is all the same when you have lost the illusion of being eternal."[12] People may experience pain or pleasure, despair or ecstasy, peace or even outright boredom in their lifetimes, but their quality of life will cease to matter after they die. Every one of us is on death row, waiting for the flame to burn out.

After reading "The Wall," one cannot help but wonder if Sartre, himself a reader of Hemingway, was inspired by "Chapter V" of Hemingway's *In Our Time*, which reads as follows:

> They shot the six cabinet ministers at half-past six in the morning against the wall of a hospital. There were pools of water in the courtyard. There were wet dead leaves on the paving of the courtyard. It rained hard. All the shutters of the hospital were nailed shut. One of the ministers was sick with typhoid. Two soldiers carried him downstairs and out into the rain. They tried to hold him up against the wall but he sat down in a puddle of water. The other five stood very quietly against the wall. Finally the officer told the soldiers it was no good trying to make him stand up. When they fired the first volley he was sitting down in the water with his head on his knees.[13]

Sartre's short story is reminiscent of Hemingway's sketch, in which "the wall" is mentioned three times.[14] Hemingway depicts a cabinet minister sick with typhoid who resembles Pablo's comrade, Juan Mirbal, "a sick man who defends himself against illness by fever."[15] In Sartre's story, "Two soldiers took [Juan] under the arms and set him on his feet. But he fell as soon as they released him."[16] Likewise, in Hemingway's sketch, "Two soldiers carried [one of the cabinet ministers] downstairs and out into the rain. They tried to hold him up against the wall but he sat down in a puddle of water." The striking similarities between the two works are perhaps evidence that Sartre was familiar with Hemingway's sketch, which appeared in the 1924 Paris edition of *in our time*. That Sartre wished to enlarge upon its themes, even borrowing specific images from the sketch, is debatable, but the similarities between the two works show that Hemingway and Sartre were operating on a shared wavelength: both understood the consequences of death's inevitability.

Similar comparisons can be made between "The Wall" and Hemingway's "In Another Country," which was published as part of the 1927 short story collection *Men Without Women*. The two stories exhibit important overlap in their portrayal of individuals who have come face-to-face with death, in their portrayal, that is, of the transformation undergone by people who have accepted their mortality. The story takes place in Milan, Italy, during the First World War. A band of injured soldiers make daily visits to a doctor who treats their ailments with new, experimental machinery. The narrator, for example, puts his leg into a contraption that "bend[s] the knee and make[s] it move as in riding a tricycle. . . . In the next machine was a major who had a little hand like a baby's."[17] The doctor encourages the patients to have high hopes, promising that the machinery will improve their conditions and even make them stronger. The doctor presents stunning before-and-after photos to prove the machinery's efficacy, but the narrator knows not to trust the photos, as he and the other soldiers are "the first ones to use the machines."[18]

Among the injured soldiers was the lieutenant of Arditi, a "tall boy with a very pale face" who "had lived a very long time with death and was a little detached. They were all a little detached" because, as soldiers formerly in battle, each of them had lived with death for a time.[19] Like Harold Krebs of "Soldier's Home," who struggles to find employment and appears totally unable to connect with friends and family after his return home from the war—stating at one point that he "do[es]n't love anybody"[20]—the injured soldiers appear indifferent to life and even lack enthusiasm for the machines that promise their recovery. Supposing they do recover, it will not be long before they die, for death is always just around the corner for people who recognize its inevitability. That being said, momentary gratification in the lived experience itself can certainly motivate a dying person to engage meaningfully in life, but even momentary joy, however ecstatic, loses its appeal when you know that certain death follows in its wake.

The same can be said of momentary rage and the gratification that one gets from causing harm to one's enemy. When Sartre's Pablo Ibbieta is shown false kindness by a fascist doctor on the night before his execution, Pablo begins to accost the doctor but quickly loses interest. "I was going to continue, but something surprising suddenly happened to me; the presence of this doctor no longer interested me. Generally when I'm on somebody I don't let go. But the desire to talk left me completely; I shrugged and turned my eyes away."[21] And then later: "I had been dripping [sweat] for an hour and hadn't felt it. But that swine of a [doctor] hadn't missed a thing; . . . I wanted to stand up and smash his face but no sooner had I made the slightest gesture than my rage and shame were wiped out; I fell back on the bench with indifference."[22] No longer beholden to a false sense of immortality, Pablo's rage wells up and very quickly fizzles out.

"In Another Country" ends with a heated exchange between the narrator and a fellow patient, the major, who asks the narrator what he plans to do after the war. When the narrator answers that he hopes to marry, the major castigates him: "'The more of a fool you are,' he said. He seemed very angry. 'A man must not marry. . . . If he is to lose everything, he should not place himself in a position to lose that. He should not place himself in a position to lose.'"[23]

The narrator asks the major why a man should necessarily lose his wife, and the major responds:

> "He'll lose it," the major said. He was looking at the wall. Then he looked down at the machine and jerked his little hand out from between the straps and slapped it hard against his thigh. "He'll lose it," he almost shouted. "Don't argue with me!" Then called to the attendant who ran the machines. "Come and turn this damned thing off." He went back into the other room for the light treatment and the massage. Then I heard him ask the doctor if he might use his telephone and he shut the door. When he came back into the room, I was sitting in another machine. He was wearing his cape and had his cap on, and he came directly toward my machine and put his arm on my shoulder. "I am so sorry," he said, and patted me on the shoulder with his good hand. "I would not be rude. My wife has just died. You must forgive me." ... The doctor told me that the major's wife, who was very young and whom he had not married until he was definitely invalided out of the war, had died of pneumonia. She had been sick only a few days.[24]

Ripping his hand away from the machine in a symbolic gesture, the major rejects the false hope that this new technology represents. It is technological advancement, after all, that led to automatic weaponry, his own injuries, and the unprecedented death toll of modern warfare. The major's hope of recovery is soured, in other words, by the fact that technological advancement is indirectly responsible for the soldiers' injuries. At the same time, he recognizes that—with or without technology, with or without debilitating injuries—he, his loved ones, and every soldier at the hospital is going to die; the unexpected loss of his young wife, moreover, reminds the major that youth is no protection against death, which is always imminent, regardless of one's age. The major castigates the narrator for investing too much hope in a temporary life, urging him to invest only in things that cannot be lost. As the reader discovers, however, both the major and the narrator well know that everything will eventually be lost. The major expresses a desire to kill himself but confesses that he is too afraid to go through with it. The narrator likewise states: "I was very much afraid to die, and often lay in bed at night by myself, afraid to die and wondering how I would be when I went back to the front again."[25] Both characters are confronted by *the wall*, certain that eternal nonexistence will overtake their lives, and it terrifies them.

On the Use of Ritual

Before we declare the Hemingway hero a full-blown atheist who rejects the *imago Dei*, the afterlife, and everything that religion entails, I will remind readers that Hemingway's characters often practice religion, just as the writer himself practiced religion, and they often demonstrate the "religious feeling," just as Frederic Henry does in *A Farewell to Arms*. In short, there is a marked ambiguity reflected in Hemingway's fiction: he lacks a sincere belief in the afterlife—an essential doctrine of Christianity—but he shows genuine interest in religious ritual and practice. "Now I Lay Me," the final story of the *Men Without Women* collection, embodies this ambiguity, as the narrator, Nick Adams, recites Catholic prayers but recognizes death as the final stop. The title of Hemingway's short story alludes to the famous child's prayer "Now I Lay Me Down to Sleep," the first four lines of which most often appear as follows, though there are other versions: "Now I lay me down to sleep / I pray the Lord my soul to keep / If I should die before I wake / I pray to God my soul to take." As even a cursory examination of Hemingway's short story reveals, however, the allusion does not suggest a Christian interpretation of the story's themes, which, to the contrary, are atheistic in nature. The title is clearly meant to be ironic.

Nick, a lieutenant, and John, a fellow soldier, lay injured in a hospital tent awake at night while the other soldiers sleep. Nick had a near-death experience on the battlefield and he desperately tries to stay awake at night for fear of dying in his sleep:

> I myself did not want to sleep because I had been living for a long time with the knowledge that if I ever shut my eyes in the dark and let myself go, my soul would go out of my body. I had been that way for a long time, ever since I had been blown up at night and felt it go out of me and go off and then come back. I tried never to think about it, but it had started to go since, in the nights, just at the moment of going off to sleep, and I could only stop it by very great effort. So while now I am fairly sure that it would not really have gone out, yet then, that summer, I was unwilling to make the experiment.[26]

Recounting the summer he was hospitalized in Milan during the war, Nick says he experienced an irrational fear of dying in his sleep. We learn from the passage that he was "blown up at night," during which time his soul left his body and then returned to it, so it may be the close association of night-time with dying that first caused his paranoia. "I knew my soul would only go out of me if it were dark," he says.[27] Readers of *A Farewell to Arms* will remember that Frederic Henry had a strikingly similar experience on the Italian front after being hit by an explosion: "I tried to breathe but my breath would not come and I felt myself rush bodily out of myself and out and out and out and all the time bodily in the wind. I went out swiftly, all of myself, and I knew I was dead," he narrates. "Then I floated, and instead of going on I felt myself slide back."[28] In both instances, the character's soul leaves his corporeal form, floats around, and then returns to the body. The accounts suggest that Hemingway believed in a human soul.

When we compare these excerpts against Hemingway's own near-death experience on the Italian front, however, it seems less likely that Hemingway believed in the human soul, or the continuation of life after death. We already discussed in Chapter 2 the letter that Hemingway wrote home to his parents after being hospitalized, in which he states that "[d]ying is a very simple thing. I've looked at death and really I know. If I should have died it would have been very easy for me. Quite the easiest thing I ever did. . . . And how much better to die in all the happy period of undisillusioned youth, to go out in a blaze of light."[29] On the one hand, dying would be *very easy* for a Christian believer if they could be certain of life after death. Like Frederic Henry and Nick Adams, they could simply float out of their bodies and return to God, confident that their next phase of existence will be blissful. But readers cannot in good faith adopt a Christian interpretation of Hemingway's letter. I would remind them that Hemingway was still very young at the time of writing, and while he had managed to break ties with the Congregationalist church of Oak Park, he was still beholden to parents who expected their son to be faithful. Were it, in fact, the case that Hemingway was a believing Congregationalist (or even a believing Catholic, for that matter), there would be no reason to tiptoe around the concept of death. He would undoubtedly reassure his parents that death is succeeded by everlasting life, stating the fact overtly, in celebration, as something that he and his parents can take solace in together. Instead, he writes that death is a "simple thing" that he alone understands, for, *unlike his parents*, he has "looked at death and really [he] know[s]." People do not transition from this life into the next as everlasting souls that survive their mortal bodies; they simply "go out," Hemingway writes, moving from existence to nonexistence in the blink of an eye. As Hemingway will write decades later in his posthumously published *Under Kilimanjaro*,[30] "I began to think if Miss Mary or G.C. or Ngui or Charo or I had been killed by the lion would our souls have flown off somewhere? I could not believe it and I thought that we would all just have been dead, deader than the lion perhaps."[31]

Matthew Nickel argues in his analysis of "Now I Lay Me" that Nick's relationship to "darkness and night is complicated, not only because it reminds him of the wound[s incurred on the battlefield], but because his wounding experience led him to the recognition of his soul. Thus, night and darkness are perpetual reminders that he has a soul and of the possibility [that] he may lose his soul again, permanently."[32] "Now I Lay Me" is proof of Hemingway's Catholic belief, in Nickel's opinion, but, according to Catholic doctrine, the human soul is eternal, so, if Nick really has a Catholic point of view, as Nickel says he does, he would not fear losing his soul permanently, as if it risked annihilation. The matter becomes even more confusing when Nickel writes that "many tribal cultures [still believe] that one's soul goes out of one in the night. Thus, in the night, Nick contemplates the existence of his soul in the dark" as something he risks temporarily losing.[33] Nickel equates Nick's anxiety over these matters with the Catholic mystic's *dark night of the soul*, a "moment of fatigue following joyous ecstasy."[34] But if we accept Nickel's rather complicated reading, Nick is afraid of nightfall for multiple, contradictory reasons: first, he fears that his soul will be permanently annihilated; second, he fears that his soul will escape his body to wander the earth until morning; and third, he fears descending into a *dark night of the soul*, a spiritual crisis described by Catholic mystics that, we learn, has nothing to do with the first two fears at all. Catholics do not believe that the human soul risks annihilation, after all, and neither do they believe that the human soul temporarily leaves the body at night. It is strange that Nickel presents these views in support of his interpretation, to say the very least.

Moreover, there is a glaring problem with the third item on this list, for Nick is not afraid of the darkness itself, which forces the narrator into a spiritual crisis, according to Nickel. Rather, Nick is afraid to *fall asleep* in the darkness. "I myself did not want to sleep," Nick states, "because I had been living for a long time with the knowledge that if I ever shut my eyes in the dark and let myself go, my soul would go out of my body."[35] The distinction here is important. By Nickel's account, "darkness itself" is the problem; it represents "an emptiness; [and] the struggle through darkness requires a leap of faith."[36] So Nick should actually *want* to sleep at night, as sleep is the only way to avoid the darkness of night and, with it, *the dark night of the soul*. Against Nickel's interpretation, we learn something very different from the story itself. Nick is not afraid of darkness per se and he is not afraid of the spiritual crisis brought on by darkness; he is afraid to fall asleep in the darkness, as Nick very clearly states, because the combination of sleep and darkness will result in death. He fears the possibility so much, in fact, that he spends long nights engaged in a kind of ritual performance designed specifically to keep himself awake. Nickel arrives at a Catholic interpretation of the story only by ignoring this important detail. Nick does not believe that there is an afterlife waiting for him, which is precisely why he dreads falling asleep at night.

"I had different ways of occupying myself while I lay awake. I would think of a trout stream I had fished along when I was a boy," Nick reflects, "and fish its whole length very carefully in my mind; fishing very carefully under all the logs, all the turns of the bank, the deep holes and the clear shallow stretches, sometimes catching trout and sometimes losing them."[37] Nick methodically recounts the details of his childhood fishing trips, walking the same paths, fishing the same spots, baiting his hook, and eating "lunch very slowly," just as he had done many times before.[38] When fishing failed to occupy his attention, Nick tried to remember every girl he had ever dated, and at other times still, he "tried to remember everything that had ever happened to [him], starting with just before . . . the war and remembering back from one thing to another."³⁹ For fear of dying in his sleep at night, Nick would try to remember things that demanded his attention, performing a kind of ritual to test his memory. On some nights, as well, Nick turned to prayer, for it was challenging to remember everyone on his prayer list, requiring significant time and effort. "But some nights I could not fish, and on those nights I was cold-awake and said my prayers over and over and tried to pray for all the people I had ever known," Nick says. "If you prayed for all of them, saying a Hail Mary and an Our Father for each one, it took a long time and finally it would be light."⁴⁰ It would be easy to dismiss Nick's recitation of Catholic prayer as the mechanical ramblings of a lapsed Catholic who, in fear of annihilation, or eternal nonbeing, will take any measure to stay awake at night, even resorting to the rote memorizations of his boyhood religion. But Hemingway paints a more complicated picture than this.

Scholars will note that "Big Two-Hearted River," one of the author's most anthologized short stories, has often been interpreted as a redemption story, the river symbolizing holy water that helps to restore Nick after the war.⁴¹ Moreover, repetition and recital are essential parts of the Catholic liturgy, so the fact that Nick engages in these practices lends further credence to a Catholic interpretation of "Now I Lay Me," which is, after all, the partial title of a well-known prayer. Obviously, it would be a mistake to dismiss the Catholic elements of the story, which are readily apparent. At the same time, it would be equally misguided to interpret Nick as a believing Catholic, for the reasons I have already discussed, but for additional reasons, as well. The incompleteness of the story's title, for one—presented by Hemingway as "Now

I Lay Me" rather than as "Now I Lay Me Down to Sleep" — mirrors the frequent partiality, or incompleteness, of Nick's prayers. "Some nights," Nick recalls that, while attempting to recite the paternoster, he "could only get as far as 'On earth as it is in heaven' and then have to start all over and be absolutely unable to get past that."[42] For readers unfamiliar with the paternoster, or Lord's Prayer, the first few lines are recited as follows: "Our Father, who art in heaven, hallowed be thy name; thy kingdom come; thy will be done on earth as it is in heaven." Nick is able to imagine a hallowed deity and he can even imagine the coming kingdom (or, if he cannot imagine them, he can at least utter this part of the prayer without choking on his words). What Nick cannot imagine, finding himself "absolutely unable to get past," is the notion that God's will is somehow performed on earth "as it is in heaven." Like Hemingway, Nick witnessed the dark realities of bloody war, and just as Hemingway is unable to believe in a God who allows for the brutal killing of his beloved creatures, so too is Nick unable to believe that God's benevolent will is present on earth.

Further evidence of Nick's atheism can be seen in the short story's treatment of the marriage motif, which is similarly handled by "In Another Country," the second title of the *Men Without Women* collection, to which I'd like to return. The major of "In Another Country" loses his young wife to pneumonia and then castigates the narrator for planning to get married. "A man must not marry," the major says to the narrator. "If he is to lose everything, he should not place himself in a position to lose that. He should not place himself in a position to lose.'"[43] The major is naïve to think that there is something — anything at all — that will not eventually be lost in life, but it is especially naïve to think that marriage will somehow mitigate that loss. Hemingway seems to suggest, in fact, that in order to commit oneself to marriage, an individual must first buy into the idea that family life, domestic partnership, and monogamous romance are worth their devastating loss. Ironically, Hemingway married four times, fathering three children, but he nevertheless seems opposed to the idea of marriage in principle. The major warns against it, and Hemingway himself writes in *Death in the Afternoon* that "all stories of monogamy end in death . . . There is no lonelier man in death, except the suicide, than that man who has lived many years with a good wife and then outlived her. If two people love each other there can be no happy end to it."[44] From one perspective, at least, institutional monogamy presents itself as a safeguard against death, for, as a Catholic sacrament, marriage implies the eternality of the soul; as an archetype of romantic love, moreover, it obscures death with the promise of everlasting companionship.

Romantic love ideology had grown into a cultural centerpiece by the time that Hemingway was writing in the 1920s and 1930s; the author contributed to society's idea of romantic monogamy through love stories like *A Farewell to Arms* and *For Whom the Bell Tolls*, both of which were great commercial successes. But the presence of death in Hemingway's novels overshadowed their romantic elements, even if the film adaptions of Hemingway's books often did the reverse, presenting romantic storylines that overwhelmed and eclipsed their treatment of death. In "Now I Lay Me," as elsewhere, Hemingway regards marriage with skepticism. Readers learn that John too stays awake at night, traumatized by the war, but he sleeps more often than Nick does, so he offers the following advice: "You ought to get married, Signor Tenente. Then you wouldn't worry."[45] Nick resists the idea, and they quarrel over the topic until John finally reasserts: "A man ought to be married. You'll never regret it. Every man ought to be married."[46] John takes comfort in his marriage, which, for symbolic reasons, tempers his fear of death. Seeing that Nick faces a similar challenge, John recommends marriage just as someone might recommend religion to an individual struggling to make meaning out of their life. Nick remarks at the end of the story that John "came to the hospital in Milan to see me several months after and was very disappointed that I had not yet married, and I know he would feel very badly if he knew that, so far, I have never married. . . . he was very certain about marriage and knew it would fix up everything."[47] For John, marriage is the end-all solution that, like religion, will finally help a person sleep at night. Nick, however, recognizes in John's religious certainty the over-confidence and naïvety of dogmatic thinking. He knows that marriage will not ward off death.

Critics generally adopt the view that Nick Adams and other Hemingway heroes are surrogates for the author himself, fictional alter-egos who convey Hemingway's point of view, re-enacting versions of his life in what is clearly autobiographical literature. Lesley M. M. Blume argues in *Everybody Behaves Badly: The True Story behind Hemingway's Masterpiece 'The Sun Also Rises'* (2016) that Hemingway's debut novel was a carbon-copy depiction of the real-life experiences of Hemingway and his closest friends.[48] That Nick's religious experience in "Now I Lay Me" mirrors Hemingway's real-life experiences is therefore plausible and even likely, given the atheistic tenor of Hemingway's writings and his nominal commitment to the Catholic Church (*Men Without Women* was released the same year that he married Pauline). We find that Nick recites Catholic prayers and engages in ritual practices — perhaps because, like Frederic Henry of *A Farewell to Arms*, he hopes to achieve the "religious feeling" — but we also find that Nick dreads dying for fear of permanent annihilation, a view that utterly contradicts the Catholic promise that there will be eternal life after death. Like his protagonists, Hemingway is not able to place his faith in God, but he strives after the "religious feeling" — a sense that we matter beyond our mortal existence — and attempts to replicate that feeling through a kind of ritual practice.

In anticipation of the next section, I highlight a final element of "Now I Lay Me"—Nick's relationship to animals. As we have already discussed at some length, Hemingway promoted a negative view of animal equality. As an avid hunter, he also loved to kill animals and went about the practice ritualistically. In the short story, Nick uses worms, insects, "white grubs with brown pinching heads," pieces of cut-up trout, grasshoppers, and a variety of additional nonhuman lifeforms as fishing bait.[49] He then tries a salamander, running a hook through its miniature body, and regrets doing so. "Once I used a salamander from under an old log. The salamander was very small and neat and agile and a lovely color. He had tiny feet," Nick reflects, "that tried to hold on to the hook, and after that one time I never used a salamander, although I found them very often. Nor did I use crickets, because of the way they acted about the hook."[50] One need only compare the feet of a salamander with the hands of a human baby to see that Hemingway is drawing a ghastly comparison: salamander feet wrapped around a fishing hook look like a baby's hand grasping at their parent's finger. Nick sympathizes with salamanders and crickets because their suffering reminds him of human suffering. But this does not mean, perforce, that Nick humanizes the creatures, elevating them to a human status. By drawing the comparison, Nick could just as easily be animalizing human beings, supplanting a positive egalitarianism with a negative egalitarianism that reduces humans to an animal status. Nick is himself a predator, after all, hooking live insects in order to catch fish, and he beams with pride when his father returns home from a hunting trip, hands Nick his gun, and orders the boy to carry his game-bags. In light of these details, it seems improbable that Nick stops hooking salamanders and crickets out of a concern for their animal rights.

More likely, in my opinion, is that Nick recognizes his own animal nature in the salamander. Lying injured in the hospital tent, he imagines the wriggling, writhing body of a dying creature and it reminds him of himself. Nick recognizes that the boundary separating humans and animals is alterable, that the *imago Dei* is therefore a fiction, and that, consequently, death is the beginning of eternal nonexistence for himself, the salamander, and every other living being. This is why he fights to stay awake at night—he realizes that death is the ultimate equalizer, and that there is hope for neither himself nor the salamander in the end. Nick refuses to use the salamander as bait because he does not want to be reminded of this unwelcome truth. He is like Catherine Barkley of *A Farewell to Arms* who says on her death bed that "I'm going to die . . . I hate it. . . . I just hate it."[51] Like Nick and Catherine, Hemingway hates it too, but, being unable to deny the truth, he puts significant effort toward dismantling human exceptionalism, both secular and religious, in spite of the dark reality it forces us to confront. Hemingway acknowledges that human beings share the same lot as their animal counterparts, but, at the same time, this is ultimately not something that he wants to embrace. In other words, he knows that human beings lack inherent value, but he wishes to overcome the fact. How the writer deals with this predicament will be addressed in the following sections: after explaining an important difference between nihilism and existentialism, the latter of which represents Hemingway's point of view, I argue that he reasserts human exceptionalism in the face of death through the ritualistic killing of animals. The act of killing, it would seem, fills Hemingway with the "religious feeling," a momentary glimpse of eternity that deludes the writer into reinstating a secular version of the *imago Dei*.

Suicide as Cowardice

"Death was Hemingway's great subject," Scott Donaldson writes, "and his great obsession. He wrote about it in his earliest stories, and his last ones. Of his seven completed novels, five end with the death of a male protagonist, and a sixth with the death of the heroine."[52] Death, it seems, was the author's foremost concern, and, like a prisoner condemned to the electric chair, he lived in anticipation of that final moment. Hemingway discovered that, when you are on death row, the size of your prison cell, your haircut, who said what about whom, the tear in the crotch of your pants, and what happens to be for dinner that night no longer seem as important. But, as he would make apparent at various points in his fiction, every one of us is on death row, and absolutely no one gets out alive. Considering this almost defeatist attitude toward death, readers might assume that Hemingway had given up on life, that there was no reason to engage with the world after realizing how meaningless our actions truly are. One might even ask why Hemingway did not simply kill himself sooner in life, echoing the existentialist Albert Camus's assertion that, when confronted with meaninglessness, we come "face to face" with "the problem of suicide."[53] But, like Camus's rebel, who revolts against suicide by positively affirming life, Hemingway lived passionately, tackling his pursuits, one could say, with the desperation of a dying man. The author was ambitious, competitive, earnest (and aptly named), he loved feverishly, and he wrote thoughtfully. This is not the disposition of someone who had checked out of life.

Yet Hemingway really did believe that life was ultimately meaningless, and, likewise, he really did believe, as a logical corollary, that human beings lack inherent moral value. How a person reaches these conclusions and then goes on to live with ardor and determination, as Hemingway did, may at first seem difficult to account for, as one might reasonably expect a hopeless person to give up on life. But this apparent conflict between Hemingway's thoughts and actions can be explained away if we note the difference between nihilism and existentialism, the latter of which represented Hemingway's philosophical worldview. For one to become an existentialist—or someone who, every moment, revolts against the inherent meaninglessness of life by creating their own personal meaning through (what they believe to be) sovereign acts of volition[54]—one must first become a nihilist. For nihilism is the logical first step toward existentialism, and one must move through the former to become the latter, first accepting that life has no inherent purpose in order to then manufacture a sense of purpose for oneself. Nihilism and existentialism can be thought of, in this sense, as opposing responses to death: the former completely denies the value of life while the latter reinstates its value through sovereign acts of volition (commonly referred to as existential choices). Much like Camus, Hemingway actually disparaged nihilism and judged those who, like Hemingway's father in 1928, succumbed to suicide. According to Donaldson, "Ernest always believed that the principal reason for his father's suicide was his emasculation" at the hands of Grace, but, nevertheless, Hemingway "could not condone what his father had done."[55] This is because Hemingway was an existentialist at his core, and though he would sometimes make use of fictional characters to express a nihilistic viewpoint, he believed that a person should always—vigorously and defiantly—choose life.

Of course, Hemingway too would eventually kill himself, as would three of his siblings, his granddaughter Margaux Hemingway, and his ex-wife Martha Gellhorn. Suicide haunted the Hemingway clan, and though Ernest believed that his father's suicide was a cowardly, emasculating act, the writer would himself go out with a bang, taking his own life with a 12-gauge shotgun in July of 1961. I describe the suicidal act as emasculating because—for Hemingway the existentialist, Hemingway the Oak Park Congregationalist, and Hemingway the Catholic—positively affirming life through sovereign acts of volition was a manly endeavor, as I demonstrated in Chapters 1 and 2. Much to Hemingway's chagrin, his father, Clarence Hemingway, was not the master of his life; he cowered under the iron fist of a domineering spouse, and it seems that, for Ernest, his father's suicide was *the* supreme act of submission.

The poet Dylan Thomas urged the men of Hemingway's generation to revolt against death, even in their old age, when he wrote: "Do not go gentle into that good night, / Old age should burn and rave at the close of day."[56] Published in 1951, ten years before Hemingway's suicide, the poem was addressed to wise men, good men, wild men, and grave men, and though the designation "man" was often universalized in Hemingway's era to include all people, regardless of their gender, the masculine coding of Thomas's poem is nevertheless obvious: real men don't go down without a fight. Like Thomas, Hemingway believed that a man should resist death, even when it seems inevitable. Readers of *For Whom the Bell Tolls* will remember that Robert Jordan, in the throes of his final moments, not only refuses to commit suicide but fights to remain conscious in order to get off a final round of bullets against the opposition. Like Robert Jordan, men should revolt against death through positive affirmations of life, or sovereign acts of volition—a force of will that originates its own legitimacy. Clarence may have been driven to kill himself by a domineering wife, but suicide was nevertheless a cowardly act in his son's opinion.

I quoted a line from Harvey Mansfield earlier in this book that yet again bears repeating: "Manliness is an assertion of man's worth because his worth does not go without saying. So too, because worth needs to be asserted it needs to be proved; in asserting, one must make good the assertion."[57] The positive affirmation of human life as ontologically valuable rests upon a kind of masculine presumption—lacking a clear metaphysical basis, human worth can only legitimize itself (unsuccessfully) through arrogant self-assertion. Hemingway's commitment to sovereign, existential choice would therefore seem to coincide with his masculinity. Bereft of the *imago Dei*, Hemingway had to make good on the assertion that mortal existence is worth living, so he conducted himself with a kind of masculine bravado, practicing autonomy, self-determination, and imperious self-insistence. Critics have offered various explanations for Hemingway's suicide, which appears to contradict the writer's masculine values, but, in my opinion, he very simply lost the will to live. At the time of his suicide, Hemingway was suffering from depression, dementia, and paranoia. To make matters worse, he could no longer write coherent sentences, for a lifetime of traumatic head injuries compounded by recent treatments of electroshock therapy had taken its toll. In short, there remained no more *quality* life to live.

But as Richard and Rena Sanderson write, suicide "seemed to violate Hemingway's own values."[58] During an interview on the way to his funeral, Hemingway's sister Ursula likewise insisted that "[s]uicide was against all [of her brother's] convictions and principles. Anyone who had read his works should know that."[59] And yet many readers have tried to preserve Hemingway's masculine reputation by casting the suicide as an act of heroism. Among Hemingway aficionados, in fact, this "reading of the suicide remains popular: Hemingway is portrayed as so dedicated to his story-telling art, and so personally identified with his own 'code-heroes,' that he cancelled his own life story when his control over it began to slip."[60] Refusing to give the Grim Reaper satisfaction, Hemingway took control of his life by ending it. In this sense, Hemingway's suicide was itself an act of rebellion, for he chose the inevitable, defiantly, as if to divest the grave of its power. And yet, if one adopts this view of Hemingway's suicide, one must still recognize that Hemingway chose to exit life rather than fight. The masculine writer may have landed a last-minute sucker punch, but death took home the championship belt. Like his father, Hemingway throws in the towel and is finally dominated by his opponent.

On the topic of suicide, Hemingway's fiction reinforces the bonds between existential choice and masculinity. In particular, both "Indian Camp" and *For Whom the Bell Tolls* depict suicide as a masculine failure. In the first story, a young Nick Adams travels late at night with his father, a medical doctor, to the Indian camp, where a woman is in desperate need of a Cesarean section. Nick's father heroically completes the procedure with a jack knife and fishing line, demonstrating his resourcefulness and unparalleled competence with masculine tools. Oddly, the doctor invites his prepubescent son to witness the bloody procedure, which is completed without anesthesia. The doctor refers to Nick as his "interne,"[61] walking his son through a barbaric performance that Doctor Adams will later boast about, even though Nick continually resists participation in the event, at one point begging his father to give the woman anesthesia and, toward the end of the procedure, turning his eyes away in horror. After delivering the baby and sewing up the woman's stomach, Doctor Adams attends to the "proud father" only to find that "his throat had been cut from ear to ear. The blood had flowed down into a pool where his body sagged the bunk. His head rested on his left arm. The open razor lay, edge up, in the blankets."[62]

Nick asks why the Indian killed himself and Doctor Adams replies: "I don't know, Nick. He couldn't stand things, I guess."[63] Then, when Nick asks if dying is hard, the doctor replies: "No, I think it's pretty easy, Nick. It all depends."[64] The doctor first models masculine heroism for his son, instructing Nick in medicine, his subject of mastery. After witnessing the suicide, the doctor draws a contrast between death, which is easy, and life, which can be hard to stand. Hearing your lover scream out in pain as a jack knife slices into her pregnant belly would certainly be extremely difficult to endure, but this does not seem like adequate reason to kill yourself, in the doctor's opinion. The Indian father could have simply left the room if the procedure was too much to witness. Instead, he chose a permanent solution to a temporary problem.[65] This is all part of Nick's masculine training: suicide, he learns, is for the weak.

Hemingway, of course, was a skilled practitioner of the short story, and much can be gleaned from "Indian Camp" through an examination of the author's formal techniques. There are a number of elements we can attend to on this front. For example, the narrative is structured around the binary opposition of young and old characters. In the span of just a few pages, the words "young" and "old" are used a total of ten times to emphasize generational differences, just as "younger" and "older" are used in "A Clean, Well-Lighted Place" to differentiate between the young, brash waiter and the older, emotionally defeated waiter, as readers of the story will no doubt recall. This careful use of repetition draws the reader's attention to the obvious age difference between Nick and his father. Readers quickly realize that the story is about a father mentoring his son, as well as the contrast between adult knowledge and youthful naïvety.

But Hemingway complicates this picture by drawing yet another contrast: "Nick lay back with his father's arm around him. It was cold on the water. The Indian who was rowing them"—the older Indian—"was working very hard, but the other boat moved further ahead in the mist all the time."[66] Nick and his father are compared against the two Indians, the younger of whom easily outpaces the older Indian, who was nevertheless "working very hard."[67] The contrast suggests that Nick too will eventually catch up to his father and overtake him, just as the younger Indian has supplanted his generational predecessor, figuratively speaking, as the more capable and physically dominant male of the tribe; it is not unusual, after all, for maturing children to rebel against parental authority in the attempt to carve out an autonomous space of their own. Hemingway uses repetition and imagery, first, to draw our attention to the generational gap between father and son, and then to complicate it. At this point, adept readers will recall the title of Hemingway's short story collection—*In Our Time*—which similarly emphasizes generational difference. This is a book about Hemingway's generation—the *lost* generation—postwar survivors whose traumatic experiences make them different from the generations that came before. The title draws attention to their unique place in history. This is relevant, I think, because "Indian Camp" is told from the perspective of an omniscient third person, but the narrative is very clearly focalized through Nick, Hemingway's fictional surrogate. If *our* time belongs to Hemingway's generation, as the title implies, then it is Nick's perspective, not his father's, that matters most. Nick will supplant Doctor Adams just as the younger Indian has supplanted the older Indian.

When it comes to the generic conventions of the short story form, it is generally agreed upon that a story's ending will force a reconsideration of everything that went before it, for the protagonist will usually undergo a final, revelatory experience that recasts the story in a new light. As a result, readers themselves often experience a kind of epiphany, understanding the story on a deeper level after having the narrative echoed back to them in reverse from a different perspective. "Consistent with Poe's 'Philosophy of Composition'—in which he emphasized beginning with the end of a work and then creating a formal pattern that inevitably leads up to that end—[B.M.] Ejxenbaum argues that the short story amasses all its weight on its conclusion," Charles E. May writes in his discussion of the short story genre. "This emphasis on 'closure' in the short story—also suggested by Chekhov's intuition that he must focus on the end of a short story and 'artfully' concentrate there an impression of the total work—becomes a central characteristic of the form."[68] Of course, there are variations on these formal conventions and, as with any genre, not every work is going to fit the pattern perfectly. When it comes to the formal conventions of the short story, however, I would say that "Indian Camp" is exemplary.

The final exchange between Nick and his father models the genre exactly. We know from the beginning of the story that Doctor Adams was trying to teach his son self-mastery and masculine stoicism. The Indian woman screams in pain, even before the doctor makes an incision, and Nick begs his father to give the woman anesthesia. "No, I haven't any anesthetic," the doctor replies. "But her screams are not important. I don't hear them because they are not important."[69] There is, however, a vital task to perform—Doctor Adams must save two human lives—and though it is a difficult, emotionally taxing procedure, Nick's father demonstrates discipline as a master of his craft and self-control as the model of masculinity. All seems to be going according to plan until Doctor Adams discovers the husband's dead body.

> "Take Nick out of the shanty, George," the doctor said.
> There was no need of that. Nick, standing in the door of the kitchen, had a good view of the upper bunk when his father, the lamp in one hand, tipped the Indian's head back.
> It was just beginning to be daylight when they walked along the logging road back toward the lake.
> "I'm terribly sorry I brought you along, Nickie," said his father, all his post-operative exhilaration gone. "It was an awful mess to put you through."
> "Do ladies always have such a hard time having babies?" Nick asked.
> "No, that was very, very exceptional."
> "Why did he kill himself, Daddy?"

"I don't know, Nick. He couldn't stand things, I guess."
"Do many men kill themselves, Daddy?"
"Not very many, Nick."
"Do many women?"
"Hardly ever."
"Don't they ever?"
"Oh, yes. They do sometimes."
"Daddy?"
"Yes."
"Where did Uncle George go?"
"He'll turn up all right."
"Is dying hard, Daddy?"
"No, I think it's pretty easy, Nick. It all depends."

They were seated in the boat, Nick in the stern, his father rowing. The sun was coming up over the hills. A bass jumped, making a circle in the water. Nick trailed his hand in the water. It felt warm in the sharp chill of the morning.

In the early morning on the lake sitting in the stern of the boat with his father rowing, he felt quite sure that he would never die.[70]

For Nick, the revelatory experience is the Indian's suicide. Not only do people die, but sometimes they do so voluntarily. This is shocking to Nick, who is still very young and has not yet learned about suicide, as the dialogue reveals. In general, this has been an educational experience for the child: he learned that women endure excruciating pain to bring life into the world, he learned how to perform a Cesarean with a jack knife and fishing line; he learned that human life is mortal and that some people end their lives voluntarily. Or at least this is what readers are led to believe, for, as the final line of the story reveals, Nick felt "quite sure that he would never die."

The final sentence forces readers to reconsider how the story has been developed up to this point, casting their glances backwards. At first, it seems as though a self-promoting father brings his son to witness something that Nick simply is not ready for. Then, as if the Cesarean were not itself traumatizing enough, Nick is confronted with a brutal suicide, which leaves the boy in shock. Attempting to pick up the pieces, Doctor Adams explains to Nick that not every childbirth is so difficult, that suicide is committed by the weak, and that dying will be easy enough when the time comes, so there is really nothing for Nick to worry about. In short, the doctor attempts to reassure his distressed son that none of the crushing realities he just witnessed are really as bad as they appear. But the doctor's feeble reassurances have most likely fallen on deaf ears, for Nick just discovered, through indisputable evidence, that human existence begins with pain, that life is sometimes too much to bear, and that people eventually die, the most startling truth of all. Until they reach the final sentence, readers assume that Hemingway's story is about a child's first confrontation with death. After reading the final sentence, however, readers discover that Nick somehow comes away from the experience assured against all reason that he alone will never die.

So how does Nick reach this inexplicable conclusion? It is worth noting that Nick's father never hints at the possibility of immortality, even in the form of a Christian afterlife. He does not say, for example, that only some people die, excluding himself and Nick from the fold. Nor does he neutralize death by describing it as a *passage* from this life to the next, though doing so would certainly help to comfort a child who just realized, in his great distress, that he and his family will someday die. By contrast, Doctor Adams tells Nick that dying is easy (just as Hemingway informed his parents after the mortar shell injury in 1918), and, in making this rather bold statement, he affirms not only that death is inevitable but that it comes for every one of us. The only reasonable conclusion, in light of this reading, is that Nick is so terrified by his father's response that he represses its dark implications into his unconscious mind and manufactures in their place a kind of salvation narrative—in particular, the unwarranted belief that he will live on forever. In keeping with the short story genre, the final line of "Indian Camp" enjoins readers to repackage Nick's epiphany as an outright denial. Consequently, the reader's developing understanding of Nick is replaced by a more complex understanding that infects the rest of the narrative. Ultimately, the story is not about a father mentoring his son; it is about a disquieted boy silently rejecting his father's wisdom; the story is not about childhood disillusionment but about the power of illusory thinking. Confronting his readers with this final, unexpected revelation, Hemingway causes us to look back at the story with a different set of conclusions in mind.

Three competing perspectives on the value of mortal existence emerge from the narrative as a direct consequence of this final, epiphanic moment: helping to bring life into the world, Doctor Adams affirms the value of mortal existence; running a blade across his neck, the Indian father denies the value of mortal existence; and refusing to accept these two paths as viable options, Nick denies his own mortality and perhaps the possibility of natural death altogether. To understand Nick's perspective, readers should notice how the first two perspectives are symbolized by parallel images: the doctor runs his blade across the pregnant woman's belly just as the Indian father runs a blade from ear to ear across his neck. Both incisions are undoubtedly very painful, but one cut brings life into the world while the other brings life to an end. Moreover, both incisions are equally gruesome in their physical appearance, but Nick looks directly at the suicide and looks away from the Cesarean. One could argue, in light of these contrasting symbols, that, in looking away, Nick rejects his father's teaching that mortal existence is worth living, and that by looking directly at the suicide, Nick accepts the Indian's teaching that mortal existence lacks inherent value. For fear of death, however, Nick is unable to recognize suicide as a viable option, and, resorting to a kind of survival mode,[71] he denies the possibility of natural death to preserve the value of life. Not yet ready to become a masculine hero, who, like his father, affirms the value of mortal existence, Nick takes refuge in a sort of religious illusion, for he is also not ready to accept death as the inevitable outcome of life.

While the individual stories of the *In Our Time* collection can be read as autonomous works, they can also be read in relationship to each other as essential parts of a unified whole. Readers of "On the Quai at Smyrna," for example, will hear the screams of the pregnant refugees echoed in "Indian Camp" and beyond. Take, for instance, the following quote from "Chapter II," which directly follows "Indian Camp" and appears just three stories after "On the Quai at Smyrna": "There was a woman having a kid with a young girl holding a blanket over her and crying."[72] The pregnancy motif runs through the first number of stories just as various other themes and motifs run through the entire collection, threading the stories together into a single, cohesive unit. Foremost among these themes are the relationship between father and son, masculinity in the face of death, and suicide as an act of cowardice. But, as I have already shown, these topics bleed beyond *In Our Time* to permeate every corner of the Hemingway canon.

The most overt instance of this can be found in the pages of *For Whom the Bell Tolls*. The protagonist, Robert Jordan, is one of Hemingway's code heroes, though I prefer to use the term *existential hero*, as elements of Sartre's worldview are clearly mirrored in Robert's existential reflections. Indeed, some of his lines appear to be taken straight from Sartre's short story "The Wall," which was published one year prior to *For Whom the Bell Tolls*, just as certain sections of "The Wall" seem to have been lifted from "Chapter V" of *In Our Time*, as we discussed earlier. Whether the authors actually borrowed from each other is ultimately beside the point, as they clearly shared a lot of the same ideas. Concerning the nature of mortal human existence, Robert Jordan makes the following observations:

> I suppose it is possible to live as full a life in seventy hours as in seventy years; granted that your life has been full up to the time that the seventy hours start and that you have reached a certain age. . . . So if your life trades its seventy years for seventy hours I have that value now and I am lucky enough to know it. And if there is not any such thing as a long time, nor the rest of your lives, nor from now on, but there is only now, why then now is the thing to praise and I am very happy with it.[73]

He states later while reflecting on his love for Maria:

> I would like to have it for my whole life. You will, the other part of him said. You will. You have it *now* and that is all your whole life is; now. There is nothing else than now. There is neither yesterday, certainly, nor is there any tomorrow. How old must you be before you know that? There is only now, and if now is only two days, then two days is your life and everything in it will be in proportion. This is how you live a life in two days. And if you stop complaining and asking for what you never will get, you will have a good life. A good life is not measured by any biblical span. So now do not worry, take what you have, and do your work and you will have a long life and a very merry one."[74]

Robert Jordan agrees with Pablo Ibbieta, protagonist of "The Wall," that "several hours or several years of waiting is all the same when you have lost the illusion of being eternal."[75] According to Christianity, the human soul is immortal, so Christians believe that every person has lasting, metaphysical value. Past, present, and future all matter for the Christian because human beings have an essential nature (i.e., the *imago Dei*) that remains intact throughout the span of their existence, even beyond the grave. When we escape the illusion of immortality, however, removing God from the picture, death appears as the final frontier and permanently separates the individual from their essential nature, whatever that may be. As a result, the present, existential moment emerges as a site of radical freedom, an originary choice that sets the standards of its own value and legitimacy. How an individual responds to the existential moment following the death of God is the measure of masculinity for Hemingway and Sartre as well. Does the individual revolt against life's inherent meaninglessness by boldly embracing a world of their own making, or do they take the easy exit, trading in their freedom for comforting illusions or even death?

At the novel's close, Robert Jordan and the other members of his guerilla unit successfully blow up the bridge, a goal that was set out in the novel's opening pages. But Robert's horse crushes his thigh bone after being shot, and this forces Robert's comrades to leave their immobilized friend behind as they flee the scene, for the enemy troops are rapidly approaching and the remaining guerillas, being fewer in number, will not be able to defend Robert or themselves against enemy fire. Overwhelmed by the pain, Hemingway's protagonist contemplates suicide, but, as I mentioned a few pages back, Robert resists the temptation to kill himself and prepares to fight as the fascist enemy appears in the distance. "His leg was hurting very badly now. The pain had started suddenly with the swelling after he had moved and he said, Maybe I'll just do it now," hinting that he might kill himself before the opposition has a chance to or, worse, before they torture him to death. "I guess I'm not awfully good at pain. Listen, if I do that now you wouldn't misunderstand, would you? *Who are you talking to?* Nobody, he said. Grandfather, I guess. No. Nobody."[76] The Catholic Church believes that suicide is a mortal sin, so it would make sense for a Catholic believer in Robert Jordan's situation to plead with God for an exception (he is in excruciating pain and about to be killed anyway), but Robert does not plead with God, despite how it sounds, and nor does he plead with the spirit of his dead grandfather, who looms in his imagination as the ideal of masculinity, for God does not exist and the human soul does not live on after the body dies, according to Robert. Am I talking to God, he wonders? No. Am I talking to grandfather? No. Robert Jordan knows that he has but this one life to live.

It would appear, then, that Hemingway's protagonist is actually addressing himself—would he excuse *himself* for the suicidal act? He thinks of his grandfather at this moment only because the man embodied everything he values—military prowess, a fighting spirit, and heroic bravery—the "good juice," as he calls it, that makes a man a man.[77] Reflecting on their shared qualities, Robert wonders if "he and his grandfather would be acutely embarrassed by the presence of his father," a cowardly man who killed himself.[78] "Anyone has a right to do it, he thought. But it isn't a good thing to do. I understand it, but I do not approve of it. *Lache* was the word."[79] This French word for coward also means *loose*, or a lack of control. Robert utters the word in French because saying it aloud in English is too embarrassing. Again reflecting on his father's suicide, Robert then utters the word in Spanish:

> I wish Grandfather was here, he thought. For about an hour anyway. Maybe he sent me what little I have through that other one that misused the gun. Maybe that is the only communication that we have. But, damn it. Truly damn it, but I wish the time-lag wasn't so long so that I could have learned from him what the other one never had to teach me. . . . maybe the good juice only came through straight

again after passing through that one? I'll never forget how sick it made me the first time I knew he was a *cobarde*. Go on, say it in English. Coward. It's easier when you have it said and there is never any point in referring to a son of a bitch by some foreign term. He wasn't any son of a bitch, though. He was just a coward and that was the worst luck any man could have.[80]

Suicide is a weak, cowardly act, according to Robert Jordan. That his father killed himself is truly humiliating. In fact, Robert only seems to mention his father in order to dismiss him, regarding the man as a kind of genetic anomaly that stands between him and his grandfather.[81] He says that "thinking of his father had thrown him off. He understood his father and he forgave him everything and he pitied him but he was ashamed of him."[82] Robert Jordan models an existential ethic. He disparages the suicidal for their cowardice and admires those who, by contrast, demonstrate a fighting spirit. Built into the modus operandi exhibited by Robert's grandfather and Hemingway's other code heroes is the proper use of weaponry, which should never be turned against oneself—as Robert states above, his father "misused the gun"—but can and even *should* be used against others. Put differently, the use of deadly force against one's opponent is not only condoned under the Hemingway ethic, it is encouraged. In the following passage, Robert glorifies deadly weapons and reveals a scandalous truth about his grandfather's past:

> Remember grandfather's saber, bright and well oiled in its dented scabbard and Grandfather showed you how the blade had been thinned from the many times it had been to the grinder's. Remember Grandfather's Smith and Wesson. It was a single action, officer's model .32 caliber and there was no trigger guard. It had the softest, sweetest trigger pull you had ever felt and it was always well oiled and the

bore was clean although the finish was all worn off and the brown metal of the barrel and the cylinder was worn smooth from the leather of the holster. It was kept in the holster with a U.S. on the flap in a drawer in the cabinet with its cleaning equipment and two hundred rounds of cartridges. Their cardboard boxes were wrapped and tied neatly with waxed twine.

You could take the pistol out of the drawer and hold it. "Handle it freely," was Grandfather's expression. But you could not play with it because it was "a serious weapon."

You asked Grandfather once if he had ever killed any one with it and he said, "Yes."

Then you said, "When, Grandfather?" and he said, "In the War of the Rebellion and afterwards."[83]

The saber and pistol are military weapons used to kill other human beings, not animals, and yet, for Robert Jordan, they have a sensuous and perhaps even sensual allure. As with many gun owners, Grandfather Jordan must have relished listing off the firearm's notable features—single action, officer's model, .32 caliber, no trigger guard—and you can hear his voice echoed in Robert's observation that it had the "softest, sweetest trigger pull." Fetishistically, the gun represents his grandfather's military prowess—"he was a hell of a good soldier, everybody said"[84]—but the gun almost certainly represents his *manhood* as well (i.e., his phallus). The "bright and well oiled" saber is actively cared for, but its "dented scabbard" and "thinned" blade show that the sword is also well used. The Smith and Wesson is likewise "well oiled and the bore was clean" but "the finish was all worn off" and "the cylinder was worn smooth from the leather of the holster." Robert's grandfather takes pride in the weapon. He neatly wraps the cartridges in boxes with waxed twine, and when his grandson asks to handle the deadly firearm, he encourages Robert to do so, but reminds him of its seriousness. Robert then asks his grandfather if he has ever killed anyone, and his grandfather answers in the positive: during the Civil War *and afterwards*, he states. The implication is that Grandfather Jordan killed someone (or even multiple people) outside of military warfare, where killing is legally sanctioned. Put more explicitly, Robert's grandfather may have committed murder, or at least manslaughter. When pressed for more information, his grandfather answers: "I do not care to speak about it."[85]

And yet Grandfather Jordan's silence on the matter is not due to the remorse he feels over taking a human life. Were the old man ashamed of the killings he would not display the murder weapons with pride, regularly attending to their maintenance. After all, killing people is not something you openly talk about, especially to a child. As a matter of fact, Grandfather Jordan is not required to share this information at all; were he truly ashamed of the actions, he could simply dismiss the conversation altogether, explaining to Robert that matters of this nature are not to be discussed with children. Instead, Grandfather Jordan withdraws from the conversation after already confessing to murder. This allows the old man to observe decorum and, at the same time, sneak in a boast that will garner his grandson's admiration. As Hemingway often emphasized, you spoil a thing by talking about it,[86] so there is something of the masculine ideal encoded in Grandfather Jordan's silence. One could say, moreover, that there is something of Hemingway's iceberg theory at work in the pages of this scene, for everything left unsaid by Robert and his grandfather gestures toward a central feature of Hemingway's thought: namely, that killing yourself is cowardly and that killing someone else gives meaning to life. What makes this bizarre equation possible is only ever suggested in the pages of Hemingway's fiction; for this reason, I return to Hemingway's nonfictional *Death in the Afternoon* to explain the matter in detail.

The Faena, *or Becoming Like God*

In the opening pages of *Death in the Afternoon*, Hemingway reports the following:

> I had just come from the Near East, where the Greeks broke the legs of their baggage and transport animals and drove and shoved them off the quay into the shallow water when they abandoned the city of Smyrna, and I remember saying that I did not like the bullfights because of the poor horses. I was trying to write then and I found the greatest difficulty, aside from knowing truly what you really felt, rather than what you were supposed to feel, and had been taught to feel, was to put down what really happened in action; what the actual things were which produced the emotion that you experienced. In writing for a newspaper you told what happened and, with one trick and another, you communicated the emotion aided by the element of timeliness which gives a certain emotion to any account of something that has happened on that day; but the real thing, the sequence of motion and fact which made the emotion and which would be as valid in a year or in ten years or, with luck and if you stated it purely enough, always, was beyond me and I was working very hard to try to get it. The only place where you could see life and death, *i.e.*, violent death now that the wars were over, was in the bull ring and I wanted very much to go to Spain where I could study it.[87]

Hemingway wanted to study violent death, which, according to the writer, was at this time only observable in the bullring, so he traveled to Spain. There, he met up with Alice Toklas and Gertrude Stein, who introduced him to the sport (although, for Hemingway, bullfighting would eventually be seen as less of a sport and more of a ritual practice). A struggling writer at the time, he remembers how the mules were drowned at Smyrna, and this memory compounds the sympathy he feels for the horses, which are regularly killed in the bullring. He comes to recognize, however, that his sympathy for the horses reflects what "he had been taught to feel," rather than what he actually felt, and he knew that, in order to become a great writer, he must learn to rid himself of ideological presuppositions to obtain a pure view of life itself, as it truly exists. Representing this deeper-level truth—which is also discussed in *A Moveable Feast* as "one true sentence"[88]—a writer must capture the emotion produced by a sequence of actions and, therefore, must also "put down what really happened in action." What *really* happened is difficult to define, of course, but, if we take the quay at Smyrna as an example, Hemingway perceived in the side-by-side drowning of mules and Greek refugees his own animal nature—a dissolution of the *imago Dei* through the radical breakdown of the human/nonhuman distinction.

Hemingway discovered a similar truth in the bullring, a deeper-level truth that he would build upon and revise with new insights. Not only would he observe human mortality in the ring, where man and bull meet each other as existential equals; he would catch glimpses of immortality in what might be called the *rehumanization* of mankind, an anthropogenic, signifying act that reasserts the difference between human and nonhuman lifeforms. Mortality and immortality, human and animal nature converge in the bullring during the *faena*, a series of passes conducted by the matador that, when performed properly, put his life at serious risk. The competent matador—a masculine code hero—will lure the bull in very closely as it passes by him, for the "greatest pass" is "the most dangerous to make and the most beautiful to see."[89] Hemingway explains:

> If the spectators know the matador is capable of executing a complete, consecutive series of passes with the muleta in which there will be valor, art, understanding and, above all,

beauty and great emotion, they will put up with mediocre work, cowardly work, disastrous work because they have the hope sooner or later of seeing the complete faena; the faena that takes a man out of himself and makes him feel immortal while it is proceeding, that gives him an ecstasy, that is, while momentary, as profound as any religious ecstasy; moving all the people in the ring together and increasing in emotional intensity as it proceeds, carrying the bullfighter with it, he playing on the crowd through the bull and being moved as it responds in a growing ecstasy of ordered, formal, passionate, increasing disregard for death that leaves you, when it is over, and the death administered to the animal that has made it possible, as empty, as changed and as sad as any major emotion will leave you.[90]

This passage embodies the crux of Hemingway's thought. Without it, the central claims of this book are much harder to corroborate. In particular, the passage reveals the manner in which Hemingway secularizes theism as an expression of both masculinity and Sartrean existentialism. These connections will be fleshed out in due course, but, at the present moment, it is more important that readers comprehend specific details in the passage itself. Directly quoting from these lines, we learn that the *faena* "takes a man out of himself and makes him feel immortal," giving him "an ecstasy, that is, while momentary, as profound as any religious ecstasy." This momentary, profound, pseudo-religious feeling, in turn, fills the matador with an "increasing disregard for death" that leaves him, we are told, the moment the bull passes. Paraphrasing, one could say that, when the bull gallops by the matador, nearly goring him to death with razor-sharp horns, the matador is as close to death as a person can get without actually tasting it. Having this level of control over the situation, which is only achieved through a practiced mastery of the art, the matador experiences the delusion of immortality, for in that moment, he exerts—what feels like—his power over death. When the matador finally kills the bull, driving his sword between the bull's shoulders and into its heart, he symbolically conquers death, putting an end to that which threatened his life. In short, the matador brings death as close as possible, exercises control over it, and, during these flashes of ecstasy, he feels eternal. This is the *religious feeling* discussed by Frederic Henry and embodied by a handful of Hemingway heroes.

The spectator (and especially the aficionado) experiences these feelings of immortality vicariously but, after the bull is killed, the feelings go away, and, as Hemingway writes, the spectator feels "as changed and as sad as any major emotion will leave you." What reappears in place of the spectator's vicarious experience of religious ecstasy is the recognition that every one of us is mortal, the recognition, in other words, that bullfighting is not a sport, but a "tragic spectacle," for certain death comes inevitably for either the bull or his opponent.[91] Just as the existentialist must pass through nihilism to understand the metaphysical purchase of sovereign decision making, so too must the bullfighter first recognize his mortality and, with it, his animality in order to understand the *faena* and exercise a godlike power over death. "The bull is death on four legs," writes Angela Alaimo O'Donnell. "But the matador stands his ground. He taunts death. He prods death, poking him with *banderillas*. And he dances with death, arching and turning his body, . . . doing what we all seek to do—evade our inevitable mortality."[92] Due to the nature of his profession, the bullfighter is constantly reminded of his impending doom, "living every day with death,"[93] and yet the true artist of bullfighting, whom the author describes as a messianic figure,[94] is also a kind of existential hero who everyday revolts against death by creating meaning in the face of meaninglessness, accepting death in order to affirm the momentary value of life, which, being practiced under intense conditions, gives the matador a feeling of immortality.

"Bullfighting is the only art in which the artist is in danger of death and in which the degree of brilliance in the performance is left to the fighter's honor";[95] for the Spaniards especially, "honor is a very real thing. Called pundonor, it means honor, probity, courage, self-respect and pride in one word. Pride is the strongest characteristic of the race and it is a matter of pundonor not to show cowardice."[96] Hemingway felt a natural kinship with the Spaniards and he too regarded courage and cowardice as opposite ends of the masculinity spectrum. The cowardly bullfighter, he says, was shown as little respect as the "suicide,"[97] who accepts the nihilistic reach of death by failing to seize the existential moment, while the courageous bullfighter is deified for doing the opposite. Rather than killing himself, as the coward sometimes does, the masculine, existential hero—i.e., the matador—kills another living being, as Hemingway explains:

> The truly great killer must have a sense of honor and a sense of glory far beyond that of the ordinary bullfighter. In other words he must be a simpler man. Also he must take pleasure in it, not simply as a trick of wrist, eye, and managing of his left hand that he does better than other men, which is the simplest form of that pride and which he will naturally have as a simple man, but he must have a spiritual enjoyment of the moment of killing. Killing cleanly and in a way which gives you aesthetic pleasure and pride has always been one of the greatest enjoyments of a part of the human race. Because the other part, which does not enjoy killing, has always been the more articulate and has furnished most of the good writers we have had a very few statements of the true enjoyment of killing. One of its greatest pleasures . . . is the feeling of rebellion against death which comes from its administering. Once you accept the rule of death thou shalt not kill is an easily and naturally obeyed commandment. But when a man is still in rebellion against death he has pleasure in taking to himself

one of the Godlike attributes; that of giving it. This is one of the most profound feelings in those men who enjoy killing. These things are done in pride and pride, of course, is a Christian sin, and a pagan virtue. But it is pride which makes the bullfight and true enjoyment of killing which makes the great matador.[98]

The existentialist accepts death only to rebel against it, positively affirming the present moment through creative acts of volition. As I demonstrated in Chapter 2, sovereign, existential choices often have violent consequences because, as Agamben does well to demonstrate, they are at once divisive and self-authorizing. As Agamben explains, the sovereign decision is a "zone of indistinction" where "pure potentiality and pure actuality" become "indistinguishable,"[99] where the absolute freedom of being-for-itself and the absolute ontology of being-in-itself are combined as being-in-itself-for-itself, to use Sartre's terminology, and thus empower the sovereign subject to dictate, at will, the ontic nature of human identity. Put simply, existential choices are divisive significations of humanity that pass themselves off, not as the arbitrary significations that they in fact are, but as ontological absolutes. It is not surprising that Hemingway describes morality earlier in the document as a relative construct,[100] for "the great matador"—our masculine, existential hero—assumes divine authority when administering death. Hemingway even contrasts the matador's godlike decision to take someone's life with the biblical injunction against murder, so readers can safely assume that morality, in Hemingway's worldview, originates with the sovereign subject, not with the Decalogue, and that the love of killing, deep within each of us, applies as much to humans as it does to animals. A person rebels against their mortality by acting like God, taking the life of another creature—be they human or animal—to make themselves feel immortal.[101]

Historically, the "whole end of the bullfight was the final sword thrust, the actual encounter between the man and the animal, what the Spanish call the moment of truth, and every move in the fight was to prepare the bull for that killing,"[102] so the matador "must love to kill," Hemingway explains, for this has always been an essential part of the performance.[103] Commenting on this crucial element, John Killinger argues that "the 'moment of truth' is the existential moment of anguish or dread crystallized into ritual . . . In this sense, the moment of truth is symbolic, and applies to the facing-death situations of all of Hemingway's heroes."[104] Hemingway admires matadors and takes vicarious pleasure in their performances because the ritualistic killing of bulls, much like religious ritual, enacts and re-enacts his core belief that real men confront death courageously through sovereign acts of volition, constructing meaning out of the meaningless and asserting individual value where no inherent value can be found. What Hemingway fails to notice—or what he does not explicitly write about—is how the act of killing animalizes the victim at the same time that it humanizes the killer, but, as Chapter 2 of this book demonstrated, this is one of the natural consequences of Sartrean thought. Because the sovereign individual is a lawmaker who "choos[es] for all men," their choices are *man-making*, according to Sartre, for "in creating the man each of us wills ourselves to be, there is not a single one of our actions that does not at the same time create an image of man as we think he ought to be."[105] The act of killing, more than any other sovereign act, divides the human from the nonhuman, the legally protected citizen from *bare life*, as Agamben puts it, so it is death that fuels the anthropological machine. Hemingway, like Sartre, reclaims the *imago Dei* after first denying its existence, humanizing the masculine code hero through the sovereign animalization of his opponents.

Given Hemingway's interpretation of bullfighting, it would be misleading to describe the practice as properly

Catholic, but one should nevertheless acknowledge that bullfighting, as a ritual performance, at the very least resembles Catholic Mass. For just as believers gather in ceremony to partake of the Holy Sacrament, ingesting the body and blood of a savior who rose from the dead, so too do aficionados gather in the arena to witness the matador conquer death. O'Donnell makes the following observations after her visit to the bullring:

> Without blood there is no faith, no resurrection, no salvation. The death of the bull is somehow part of this tradition. The animal is sacrificed. Its meat is eaten. Its death gives life. The killing is lamentable and necessary. It is a telling fact that the word *blessing* in English comes from the Old English word, *blud*. There is no blessing without blood. What I did not expect to discover during my two hours at the bullring is the deeply Catholic nature of bullfighting, the way the ritual echoes the sacrifice of the Mass. For, weirdly, the bull is Jesus, too—the beautiful god who must die, whose flesh is eaten and whose blood is drunk. This is not such a stretch as it might seem. In ancient times, among some cultures, the bull was regarded as a sacred creature and was thought to be divine. Bullfighting (as in Pamplona) took place in the context of a larger religious celebration. This might help to account for its irresistible appeal to the Catholic convert, Hemingway, as well as its appeal to the people of Spain, a country where Catholicism has taken bloody forms for centuries.[106]

Hemingway's interpretations of the *faena* and *moment of truth* do not align with Catholic theology, but Hemingway clearly values the Church's devotion to ritual performance, in which he discovers an analogue for bullfighting. Much like Jake Barnes, the protagonist of Hemingway's 1926 debut novel *The Sun Also Rises*, Hemingway regularly attended the Festival of San Fermin, participating in a religious pilgrimage organized around the bullfight. Serious observers like himself will recognize through ritual practice, first, that they are mortal, and second, that killing affords them an experience of immortality. As high priest, the matador models this lesson, which Hemingway then models in fictional portrayals of the masculine code hero.

The Masculine, Existential Hero

Foremost among Hemingway's code heroes is Francis Macomber, whose short, happy life captures the same feelings of masculinity, sovereignty, and immortality as the *faena*. Published in the *Winner Take Nothing* collection six years after Hemingway's Catholic marriage to Pauline Pfeiffer and seven years before their divorce in 1940, "The Short Happy Life of Francis Macomber" is about an "existential hero" who "fills meaninglessness with a new essence," in the words of Ben Stoltzfus, by courageously hunting dangerous animals.[107] Francis Macomber, he states, "forges a new identity and, although he dies (his wife, Margot, shoots him in the head—a Freudian slip of the finger)[, h]e dies happy, knowing that he is a winner."[108] Turning his attention to Robert Wilson, the Macombers' hunting guide, Warren Beck observes the following:

> The opening pages, with some centering on Wilson's consciousness, emphasize his ambivalent, at times uncertain, and even baffled attitude toward a pair whom he then repeatedly categorizes as familiar types, the wealthy, soft American sportsman and his glitteringly hard wife.... He had a word for Margot Macomber, of five letters, and apparently he made no substitution for it. He had a four-letter word for Francis, but he dropped that, because Francis had done something that Wilson could understand, had lived up to the code of physical courage, thereby coming of age, as Hemingway has Wilson put it.[109]

Not only is the story at times imbued by Wilson's consciousness, but Wilson is the moral center of the story. And though Wilson, by conventional standards, is a rather cruel person (as is Margot Macomber, who cuckolds, verbally abuses, and shames her husband for running from an attacking lion), Wilson is the masculine, existential standard against which Francis is at first judged as inadequate and eventually declared a code hero. Following Wilson's example, Francis puts himself in mortal danger, staring down a charging buffalo in order to exert his power over death. During these final moments of ecstasy, Francis becomes a *real man* and thus fulfills the masculine ideal modelled by his opposite, the testosterone-charged Wilson, undergoing a kind of "religious conversion" that leaves Francis completely transformed.

Yet again Hemingway presents his readers with contrasting male figures, the coward and the masculine hero, the latter of whom is a secularized theist. To understand this conclusion, let us first unpack the differences between Wilson and Francis Macomber. Francis "was very tall, very well built if you did not mind that length of bone, dark, his hair cropped like an oarsman, rather thin-lipped, and was considered handsome."[110] As far as physical appearances go, Francis seems to be Wilson's equal, for he "was dressed in the same sort of safari clothes that Wilson wore except that his were new, he was thirty-five years old, kept himself very fit, was good at court games, [and] had a number of big-game fishing records."[111] The difference between the two men was internal, a matter of personal character, and, as we learn from the opening pages, Francis "had just shown himself, very publicly, to be a coward."[112]

After injuring a big-game animal, who then retreats into the bush for protection, it is customary to move in close for a viable shot. Once the hunter is close enough to make a kill, the animal will charge, and, in this moment of extreme danger, the hunter must quickly shoot it to death before the animal mauls them, tramples them, or stabs them through with its horns. This is the big-game hunter's version of the *faena*, while the final, deadly shot is comparable to the moment of truth. But when the lion rushes forward, Francis retreats, "running wildly, in panic," and it is Wilson who, in the style of a great matador, stands his ground to kill the beast.[113] After this humiliating event, fear follows Francis "like a cold slimy hollow."[114] He is not like the great matador who exerts his power over death through fleeting gestures of defiance, and Macomber's poorly executed *faena* does not culminate in the moment of truth but in a shameful retreat over the arena wall.

Wilson reflects on Macomber's cowardice: "It's that some of them stay little boys so long, Wilson thought. Sometimes all their lives. Their figures stay boyish when they're fifty. The great American boy-men. Damned strange people."[115] According to Wilson, cowardice in the face of death is childlike behavior, the mark of someone who has not yet matured into adulthood. The fully formed man accepts mortality in order to rebel against it, positively affirming their present existence through sovereign acts of volition, the most potent of which is the act of killing. Being himself a "professional hunter,"[116] Wilson is the epitome of masculine development. Remarking on the fundamental difference between Robert Wilson and her husband, Margot asks: "What importance is there to whether Francis is any good at killing lions? That's not his trade. Mr. Wilson is really very impressive killing anything. You do kill anything, don't you?" to which Wilson replies: "Oh, anything, . . . Simply anything."[117] That Wilson would kill another human being is implied here, I think, and the story's bloody ending demonstrates that Margot might even have murder in mind when she asks Wilson the question. By taking the life of another living being, Wilson makes himself like God, a sovereign, existential subject whose ostensible courage is, for Hemingway and his fictional characters, tied to masculinity. "[H]e had seen men come of age before and it . . . was not a matter of their twenty-first birthday," the narrator observes. "He'd seen it in the war work the same way. More of a change than any loss of virginity. Fear gone like an operation. Something else grew in its place. Main thing a man had. Made him into a man. Women knew it too. No bloody fear."[118] Before his radical transformation, Francis is crippled by the fear of death, emasculated by his wife, and incompetent at killing. Wilson, by contrast, is an expert assassin who, in the act of killing, asserts his manliness (his superiority over women and emasculated men), his humanity (his superiority over animals), and, with it, his divinity (the religious feeling of immortality, under discussion here as the *imago Dei*).

Sifting through the author's works, one notices that Hemingway rejects human exceptionalism through an ostensible deconstruction of the human/animal divide. Along with human exceptionalism Hemingway rejects its ideological substructure, the *imago Dei*, for he spurns the natural theological proposition that human nature bears evidence of God's design, as I showed through an analysis of "A Natural History of the Dead." It is my belief, however, that after first rejecting the *imago Dei*, Hemingway tacitly reinstates it, and that after collapsing the human/animal divide, Hemingway promotes masculine heroes who assert their superiority over the nonhuman world through the ritualistic killing of dangerous animals. For it is during the so-called moment of truth—when an individual puts their life at risk to kill another living being—that humanity experiences the feeling of immortality, the closest we will ever get to divinity or a spiritual afterlife. "It's trying to kill to keep yourself alive," the protagonist Harry states in "The Snows of Kilimanjaro," Hemingway's much-celebrated short story of 1936.

In Chapter 2 of this book, I examined the philosophical work of Giorgio Agamben to show that killing—and, to a lesser degree, every other sovereign act—divides humanity from the nonhuman. I then applied Agamben's theoretical framework to a study of Sartrean decisionism to demonstrate, in turn, how this study might lend itself to a reading of Hemingway. My discovery, explicated over the course of many pages now, is that Hemingway replaces a theological account of human exceptionalism with a pseudo-secular account, supplanting his belief in the *imago Dei* with the feeling of immortality. To be clear, I do not claim that Hemingway transitions from one set of beliefs to another at any particular moment in his writing career, but that both elements—secular and religious—are ever-present, for just as the existentialist must pass through nihilism to understand the metaphysical purchase of sovereign choice, Hemingway too must first reject the *imago Dei* in order to then resurrect a secularized form of it. Identifying mankind with other members of the animal kingdom is the first step toward asserting humanity's superiority over nonhuman life. The difference, of course, is that human superiority is no longer the result of an essential, God-given nature, as Christianity teaches, but the power that each of us has to demonstrate our superiority over other lifeforms through a sheer force of will.

We have already discussed the decentering effect of the lion's first-person perspective as a formalistic critique of anthropocentrism. Critical consensus, I demonstrated, is that the lion's objectification of the hunters introduces a shift in power which then permits readers to second-guess the heroic representation of Wilson and Francis Macomber. But a closer reading of the passage shows something else afoot: the interlaying of human and animal perspective:

> The lion still stood looking majestically and coolly toward this object that his eyes only showed in silhouette, bulking like some super-rhino. There was no man smell carried toward him and he watched the object, moving his great head

a little from side to side. Then watching the object, not afraid, but hesitating before going down the bank to drink with such a thing opposite him, he saw a man figure detach itself from it and he turned his heavy head and swung away toward the cover of the trees as he heard a cracking crash and felt the slam of a .30-06 220-grain solid bullet that bit his flank and ripped in sudden hot scalding nausea through his stomach. He trotted, heavy, big-footed, swinging wounded full-bellied, through the trees toward the tall grass and cover, and the crash came again.[119]

The passage is told almost entirely from the lion's perspective, but after the bullet penetrates the animal's flesh, suddenly the human perspective reappears. The small piece of metal is described to readers as a .30-06 220-grain solid, clearly reflecting the perspective of a human hunter, who recognizes the description as a kind of bullet. Later we read:

> That was the story of the lion. Macomber did not know how the lion had felt before he started his rush, nor during it when the unbelievable smash of the .505 with a muzzle velocity of two tons had hit him in the mouth, nor what kept him coming after that, when the second ripping crash had smashed his hind quarters and he had come crawling on toward the crashing, blasting thing that had destroyed him. Wilson knew something about it and only expressed it by saying "Damned fine lion," but Macomber did not know how Wilson felt about things either.[120]

Here, the human perspective, which in the previous passage flashed before the reader's eyes with a single bullet strike, now competes against the animal's point of view for the reader's attention. Words like "smash" and "crash" represent how the lion perceives gunfire, and "blasting thing" represents how the lion perceives the hunter's firearm. These phrases are read alongside of the phrases ".505 with a muzzle velocity of two tons," "Macomber did not know how the lion had felt," and he "did not know how Wilson felt about things either," all of which reflect Macomber's perspective. As the struggle between man and beast intensifies, readers are shuffled between human and animal perspectives, Francis giving one account of the events and the lion giving another. Because the victor lives another day to tell their story, whoever wins the battle also gains story-telling privileges, as it is ultimately their narrative point of view with which readers are left. The act of killing all but eliminates the victim's capacity to tell their story and thus insists upon the killer's narrative point of view. It would appear, in light of this observation, that Hemingway's formal techniques complement the story's themes: sovereign decision making is sovereign story-telling—or, as Sartre will put it, our every decision is a man-making act of creation.

But it is not only Francis and the lion who vie for discursive power; it is the lion, the buffalo, Wilson, and Margot Macomber as well. In fact, the human characters of the story actively seek to dominate each other. Margot sleeps with Wilson to humiliate Francis, for example, and she repeatedly underscores his cowardice to gain power over him. Francis, likewise, refers to Margot as a *bitch* multiple times, just as Wilson refers to her, and Wilson, whom I identified earlier as the moral center of the story, treats both Francis and Margot as predictable American stereotypes. The characters *name* each other in order to dominate each other, obstructing their rival's ability to self-identify through sovereign, self-originating acts of their own. Sartre described this experience of being dominated by your peers as *being-for-others*, the sense that our identity has been decided by people who objectify us as fundamentally one way or another, imposing a stable identity in order to limit our freedom. Breaking loose from these oppressive chains, Francis discovers his freedom in the buffalo chase and undergoes a radical transformation:

> "By God, that was a chase," he said. "I've never felt any such feeling. Wasn't it marvellous, Margot?"
> "I hated it."
> "Why?"
> "I hated it," she said bitterly. "I loathed it."
> "You know, I don't think I'd ever be afraid of anything again," Macomber said to Wilson. "Something happened in me after we first saw the buff and started after him. Like a dam bursting. It was pure excitement. . . . You know, something did happen to me," he said. "I feel absolutely different."
> His wife said nothing and eyed him strangely. She was sitting far back in the seat and Macomber was sitting forward talking to Wilson who turned sideways talking over the back of the front seat.
> "You know, I'd like to try another lion," Macomber said. "I'm not really afraid of them now. After all, what can they do to you?"
> "That's it," said Wilson. "Worst one can do is kill you."[121]

When the charging lion comes after Francis, the coward runs to save his life. But after accepting death as the inevitable outcome of life—moving, as he does, from cowardice to nihilism and finally to existentialism—Francis takes ownership over his story-telling powers and embraces the present, existential moment as the site of absolute freedom. "[C]onsciousness of death affirms our awareness of life and enhances its intensity," Stoltzfus writes. "Macomber's exhilaration derives from . . . the knowledge that Margot can no longer influence his choices. He has passed through the valley of the shadow of death and come out on the other side, transformed."[122] Moreover, Francis "takes pleasure in shooting animals," Stoltzfus continues, "because killing usurps one of God's prerogatives: the killer experiences a sense of exaltation"[123] — a sense that he decides his own identity, originates his own moral values, and is greater than the animal he just killed. Hemingway's short story is "a quintessential example of Sartre's philosophy in action."[124]

In short, Francis becomes a masculine, existential hero who, like the great matador, accepts his mortality in order to defy it, inching his way ever closer to death in order to demonstrate his control over it. After injuring the buffalo, who then retreats into the bush, the men move in closer for a deadly shot. An attendant investigates the scene and informs Wilson that the buffalo is dead, but just as Wilson goes to congratulate Francis, the buffalo rushes "out of the bush sideways, fast as a crab, and the bull coming, nose out, mouth tight closed, blood dripping, massive head straight out."[125] Francis has the opportunity to redeem himself during this big-game hunting version of the *faena*, but this time, instead of running, Francis "st[ands] solid and sho[ots] for the nose" as the bull gets closer and closer.[126] As the buffalo is about to gore Francis, Wilson kills the bull, and Margot shoots Francis in the back of the skull; afterwards, their bodies lay no more than "two yards" apart, thus illustrating Macomber's willingness to stand his ground no matter the outcome.[127] When writing this scene, Hemingway seems to have had the comparison to Spanish bullfighting in mind, for he refers to the buffalo eighteen times as a *bull*. Indeed, the African Cape buffalo shares striking similarities with the Spanish fighting bull; both are massive bovines with a dark hide and long, dangerous horns. Of course, Francis and the bull are not able to meet each other in the so-called moment of truth, but Francis nevertheless captures the feeling of immortality in his version of the *faena*, and this experience accounts for the nature of his short, happy life.

The love of killing reflects a desire to feel eternal, if only for a moment, while the act of killing, like all sovereign choices, separates subject from object, superior from inferior, human from animal. The combination amounts to a form of human exceptionalism that, at once, secularizes the *imago Dei* and instills humanity with the godlike ability to create objective moral values. This secularized theism, as Agamben calls it, embodies the logic of Sartrean existentialism, which presents human freedom as the metaphysical source of moral law. These moral choices, in turn, reflect valuations of human identity, which, Agamben demonstrates, must define itself against various constructions of the nonhuman other. For this reason, all human choices are morality-making, man-making, and world-making by proxy. When these choices are conceptualized as self-originating, moreover, the individual lawmaker becomes like God, creating the moral universe *ex nihilo*. Ironically, then, annihilation is also the supreme act of creation, for the pinnacle of Hemingway's secularized religion is the act of killing.

Not surprisingly, this is also the case with Sartre. His 1943 stage adaptation of the Electra myth, "The Flies," is organized around a revenge plot. The play's protagonist, Orestes, returns to the city of Argos to avenge his father Agamemnon, the former king of Argos, who was killed by his wife, Queen Clytemnestra, and her adulterous lover, Aegistheus, who subsequently takes the throne. Afraid for his life, Aegistheus implores Zeus to kill Orestes with a thunderbolt, but the gods are powerless against individuals who, like Orestes, know that they are free. Afraid that Orestes will awaken the people of Argos to their own freedom, Zeus commands Aegistheus to kill Orestes, but Aegistheus regrets his crime against Agamemnon and does not defend himself against Orestes, who murders both Aegistheus and Clytemnestra in cold blood. Orestes' sister, Electra, urges him to kill both Aegistheus and their mother, but when the act is finally completed, Electra is filled with crippling guilt and swarmed by the flies, the goddesses of remorse. Orestes, by contrast, does not experience any guilt for, like so many of Hemingway's protagonists, he is a masculine, existential hero, who, in the act of killing, becomes the godlike origin of moral value.

The tension between human freedom and objective moral value is set out early in the play during a conversation between Zeus and Aegistheus.

> ZEUS: Aegistheus, you are a king, and it's to your sense of kingship I appeal, for you enjoy wielding the scepter.
> AEGISTHEUS: Continue.
> ZEUS: You may hate me, but we are akin; I made you in my image. A king is a god on earth, glorious and terrifying as a god.
> AEGISTHEUS: You, terrifying?
> ZEUS: Look at me. [*A long silence.*] I told you you were made in my image. Each keeps order; you in Argos, I in heaven and on earth—and you and I harbor the same dark secret in our hearts.
> AEGISTHEUS: I have no secret.
> ZEUS: You have. The same as mine. The bane of gods and kings. The bitterness of knowing men are free. Yes, Aegistheus, they are free. But your subjects do not know it, and you do.
> AEGISTHEUS: Why, yes. If they knew it, they'd send my palace up in flames. For fifteen years I've been playing a part to mask their power from them.
> ZEUS: So you see we are alike.[128]

Moral authority as with legal authority is illusory—both lack an objective, metaphysical basis, and yet both god and king, as administrators of the law, exercise power over their subjects. According to Zeus, this is because people erroneously believe that the law is objective, or built into the nature of being. They think, for example, that morality has eternal, unchanging value as something created by the gods. Therefore, any contradiction of moral law is not only a sin but a violation of nature itself. People subject themselves to gods and kings because they believe there is no other choice. Were they to become aware of their freedom, as Zeus fears will someday happen, the people of Argos would no longer believe in objective morality and, as a direct result of this, Zeus would lose his power over them. "If they knew" they were free, Aegistheus echoes, "they'd send my palace up in flames." But there is another secret that Zeus has yet to reveal:

> ZEUS: Aegistheus, my creature and my mortal brother, in the name of this good order that we serve, both you and I, I ask you—nay, I command you—to lay hands on Orestes and his sister.
> AEGISTHEUS: Are they so dangerous?
> ZEUS: Orestes knows that he is free.
> AEGISTHEUS [*eagerly*]: He knows he's free? Then, to lay hands on him, to put him in irons, is not enough. A free man in a city acts like a plague-spot. He will infect my whole kingdom and bring my work to nothing. Almighty Zeus, why stay your hand? Why not fell him with a thunderbolt?
> ZEUS [*slowly*]: Fell him with a thunderbolt? [*A pause. Then, in a muffled voice*] Aegistheus, the gods have another secret.
> AEGISTHEUS: Yes?
> ZEUS: Once freedom lights its beacon in a man's heart, the gods are powerless against him. It's a matter between man and man, and it is for other men, and for them only, to let him go his gait, or to throttle him.[129]

As before, those who believe in objective moral values do not feel at liberty to violate these ostensible laws. When they do violate them—performing an action that they believe to be objectively wrong and therefore "sinful"—they experience feelings of remorse and even guilt, which is thereafter internalized as self-punishment. Those who, like Orestes, have awakened to their freedom, however, no longer believe in objective moral values, so their freedom is not obstructed by the gods, as it is with the citizens of Argos, but by other individuals—those who struggle against them for story-telling privileges, or the rights to sovereignty. Sartre describes this in his discussion of being-for-others, the process whereby an individual is objectified by another person. Here, as in Hemingway's works, the most extreme example of this is killing, a signifying act that separates the beast from the sovereign, the humanized from the animalized, and subject from object by locating moral authority with free will, the home of self-origination. This is why Zeus describes the battle for freedom as "a matter between man and man"; you must either submit to your opponent or "throttle him" in this zero-sum fight for sovereign power.

"On the individual level, my freedom is such that, through negation, I can choose what I want to be. But on the social level, my freedom is only one of many freedoms, and my being is subject to other powers of negation," writes Kate Kirkpatrick in her examination of being-for-others.[130] "But I can only found my freedom if I assimilate the freedom of the Other. . . . For Sartre, there is no room for two selves; intersubjective relationality is a ruse. We always inevitably turn to the human Other to justify our existence, reducing the Other to a means to my ends."[131] This notion is illustrated from multiple angles in Sartre's 1944 play *No Exit*. Three characters—Garcin, Estelle, and Inez—find themselves trapped in hell, a luxurious, moderately comfortable drawing room fashioned in the style of the Second Empire. Garcin is surprised that hell lacks the fire and brimstone depicted in Christian art, but after a short time with his roommates, Garcin yells out in misery that "Hell is—other people!"[132] On the one hand, Garcin knows that a "man is what he wills himself to be,"[133] but, as Inez points out, a person's identity is also determined by what other people think of them, as she rebuts: "You're a coward, Garcin, because I wish it.

I wish it—do you hear?—I wish it. And yet, just look at me, see how weak I am, a mere breath on the air, a gaze observing you, a formless thought that thinks you."[134] By simply thinking about another person you assimilate them into your story of the world, becoming, in effect, the author of their identity. This person can regain their subjectivity, or the power to self-determine, either by killing you, which brings an end to your story-telling capacity, or by persuading you of their viewpoint, but this, in turn, leaves you objectified by them. The characters of Sartre's play are already dead, of course, so Garcin must persuade Inez of his viewpoint to regain his subjectivity; murder is not an option. As Inez points out to Garcin: "You can't throttle thoughts with hands. So you've no choice, you must convince me, and you're at my mercy."[135]

If hell is other people, or, more specifically, the power that other people have to objectify an individual as their inferior, then salvation comes in the form of self-insistence, the exercise of sovereign control over those who wish to objectify the individual in question. Orestes and Electra model opposite ends of this religious spectrum: Orestes discovers salvation in his ability to self-determine and comes to regard himself as the man-making origin of moral law; Electra, by contrast, becomes trapped in her own personal hell and accepts as divinely authorized the moral laws that she already violated. Zeus threatens to punish Orestes for the bloody murders that he and Electra orchestrated, but Orestes retorts that "I am no criminal, and you have no power to make me atone for an act I don't regard as a crime. . . . [Electra] is dearer to me than life. But her suffering comes from within, and only she can rid herself of it. For she is free."[136] Failing to realize her freedom, Electra is swarmed by the Furies, who crawl over her body with "thousands of tiny clammy feet,"[137] until she finally repents of her crimes and vows to worship Zeus.

Orestes, however, rebels against the gods, discovering a kind of religious salvation in the act of killing. "Your whole universe is not enough to prove me wrong," he says to Zeus. "You are the king of gods, king of stones and stars, king of the waves of the sea. But you are not the king of man."[138] Orestes appears to deify himself, taking on the moral authority of the gods at the same time that he profanes divine authority. But this is no different than Sartre, who declares the end of moral absolutes and at the same time defends the lawmaking procedures of sovereign, self-originating choice. "I am doomed to have no other law but mine," Orestes declares. "For I, Zeus, am a man, and every man must find out his own way."[139] The tension here between *anomie* and *nomos*, lawlessness and lawmaking choices, again marks the difference between nihilism and existentialism, for nihilists reject divine law through an acceptance of their mortality while existentialists rebel against mortality through a kind of delusional self-insistence, assuming the right, in this ostensible moment of religious ecstasy—the moment of truth—to take another creature's life. This *love of killing*, as Hemingway called it, is the highest expression of masculine self-determination, the foundation of Hemingway's and Sartre's secularized theism.

Finding Religion Without God

In Hemingway's 1926 novel *The Sun Also Rises*, the protagonist, Jake Barnes, is asked by another character about his religious orientation. Jake and Bill Gorton, a friend from the war, are fishing in Burguete, Spain, before they attend the Festival of San Fermin in Pamplona. The two exchange quips, and Jake reveals that, prior to the war, he "went to Loyola with Bishop Manning."[140] The conversation develops in multiple directions and, after a few drinks, Bill decides to take a nap. He places a newspaper over his face and mutters the following:

> "Listen, Jake ... are you really a Catholic?"
> "Technically."
> "What does that mean?"
> "I don't know."
> "All right, I'll go to sleep now."[141]

Bill's question—is Jake *really* a Catholic?—seems to grow out of skepticism, as though Bill were surprised to learn this new information about his longtime friend. Moreover, Jake's response comes across as somewhat defensive, or at least evasive. Is Jake embarrassed to identify as a Catholic? If not, why not simply admit to the fact? To call oneself *technically* a Catholic is like saying that a fighter *technically* won a boxing match. In the popular parlance, this means that he did not *actually* win, having fought better than his opponent, but was nevertheless announced the winner by officials on the grounds of a technicality. A surface reading of the passage suggests that Jake was baptized Catholic, raised in the Church, and still attends Mass despite the fact that he no longer believes, or some variation of this. We also discover, after closer analysis, that Jake values Catholic ritual as something that aids his atheistic pursuit of the "religious feeling," what I call secularized theism. It is in this sense that Jake is *technically* a Catholic. When Bill presses him for more of an explanation, Jake evades the question, saying "I don't know." Jake, of course, does know what he means by the comment, but it is too difficult to explain to Bill in this setting. Important to note, however, is that Jake does not answer a simple question with a simple response. To identify himself as an outright Catholic would be inaccurate; Jake is *technically* a Catholic.

H. R. Stoneback disagrees with this reading. In his view, Jake's response is not evasive, but meticulously accurate—a highly technical response to a casual question asked in passing. To answer with this degree of technical accuracy would be somewhat annoying in this context; it is not in keeping with Jake's personality or the tone of the conversation, but Stoneback doubles down. Because "the passage is sometimes read as an indication that Jake is not really a Catholic, that he doesn't believe in or truly practice his faith," Stoneback warns that

> Jake's response must be considered carefully. The word "technically" may have many meanings, but all of them have to do with *technique*, with the careful practice of an art or craft, the execution or performance of something in relation to formal or practical details; and the older sense of "technical," with regard to a thing skillfully done, or a person "skilled in or practically conversant with some particular art of subject" (*OED*), should not be overlooked either, especially in a novel so concerned with, say, the technique of bullfighters, the style or technique of all things, including the chilling and opening of bottles of champagne. To take Jake's response—technically—as an indication that he is some kind of skeptic about his Catholicism is to miss the point entirely. The Catholic Church places great emphasis on not just the right matter and the right intention but also the "right form" when it comes to "the technicalities of Sacramental theology" (Cross 1198). In going to confession and Mass, Jake practices the technique, the form of two of the major sacraments of his church—penance and Eucharist. As the "laying on of hands" scene with Montoya (131–32) and the swimming scenes in San Sebastian (235–38) demonstrate, he is also alert to the sacramental overtones of secular activities that serve as analogues to the sacraments of confirmation and baptism.[142]

Stoneback's interpretation fails to account for the context of this passage. It would be unlike Jake to answer Bill's question with such a loaded but also tacit response, which is not in keeping with the tone of the conversation. But I like Stoneback's interpretation all the same because it draws readers' attention to the true character of Jake's Catholicism, highlighting an element that supports Stoneback's view but that ultimately, after further analysis, undermines Stoneback's position by exposing Jake as a secularized theist.

A central difference between Protestantism and Roman Catholicism is that the former prioritizes the salvific efficacy of personal faith while the latter prioritizes the ritualistic exercise of divine sacraments. With the same fervor that Protestants emphasize *sola fide* over against the sacramental theology of the Roman Catholic Church do those of the Catholic faith emphasize the salvific quality of the sacraments. It is in the ritual practice of Catholicism, after all, that one is saved, according to Catholic theology. As Stoneback puts it, "Protestantism, in many of its manifestations, is most notable for the manner in which it discards technique, form, and discipline, for its celebration of the individualized gesture over the technique, the form, rooted in [the Catholic] tradition."[143] But Jake weighs these contrasting approaches equally, placing as much importance on the individual's personal beliefs as he does on the technical performance of religious ritual. Both elements are emphasized in the following passage:

> At the end of the street I saw the cathedral and walked up toward it. The first time I ever saw it I thought the façade was ugly but I liked it now. I went inside. It was dim and dark and the pillars went high up, and there were people praying, and it smelt of incense, and there were some wonderful big windows. I knelt and started to pray and prayed for everybody I thought of, Brett and Mike and Bill and

Robert Cohn and myself, and all the bullfighters, separately for the ones I liked, and lumping all the rest, then I prayed for myself again, and while I was praying for myself I found I was getting sleepy, so I prayed that the bullfights would be good, and that it would be a fine fiesta, and that we would get some fishing. I wondered if there was anything else I might pray for, and I thought I would like to have some money, so I prayed that I would make a lot of money, and then I started to think how I would make it, . . . and as all the time I was kneeling with my forehead on the wood in front of me, and was thinking of myself as praying, I was a little ashamed, and regretted that I was such a rotten Catholic, but realized there was nothing I could do about it, at least for a while, and maybe never, but that anyway it was a grand religion, and I only wished I felt religious."[144]

Why does Jake feel like a rotten Catholic? He dutifully goes to church, he prays, he kneels with his forehead pressed against the wooden pew. It would seem that Jake performs the technical procedures as they were meant to be practiced. What makes Jake a rotten Catholic, then, is not his lack of participation in religious ritual but his personal thoughts and feelings, which, according to Jake himself, do not align with sincere belief. Jake bemoans the fact that, after praying for his friends, his thoughts become shallow and self-oriented. He dreams of striking gold, becomes distracted by bullfighting, and nearly falls asleep. The external performance is up to par, but the internal, subjective experience is lacking; as Jake states, "I only wished I felt religious."

In this regard, he is like Santiago, protagonist of *The Old Man and the Sea*. We learn in the opening pages of the novel that hanging on the walls of Santiago's shack are "a picture in colour of the Sacred Heart of Jesus and another of the Virgin of Cobre."[145] The presence of these Catholic emblems on the wall of Santiago's home suggests that the novel's protagonist is a believing Catholic, but, later in the novel, Santiago states very plainly that "I am not religious, . . . [b]ut I will say ten Our Fathers and ten Hail Marys that I should catch this fish."[146] The prayers are recited in a mechanical way that seems to lack heartfelt sincerity. "He commenced to say his prayers mechanically. Sometimes he would be so tired that he could not remember the prayer and then he would say them fast so that they would come out automatically. Hail Marys are easier to say than Our Fathers, he thought."[147] Like Jake, Santiago lacks genuine belief in the gospel message—he even identifies as a non-religious person—but he nevertheless performs Catholic ritual to help him catch the marlin, praying to a God he does not believe in. In this manner, Santiago resembles the protagonist of Hemingway's short story "A Clean, Well-Lighted Place," who recites his own renditions of the Lord's Prayer: "Our *nada* who art in *nada*, *nada* be thy name," and the Hail Mary: "Hail nothing full of nothing, nothing is with thee."[148]

Here, the protagonist replaces key words with *nada* or *nothing*—reflecting the existential belief that God's death gives way to absolute freedom, a negative ontology that, in the Roman Catholic tradition, derives from the absence of God, the one true source of being. This is Catholicism emptied of its religious content—a theological system without God—and, as numerous scholars have argued, it forms the basis of Sartrean existentialism. Comparing Santiago with the protagonist of "A Clean, Well-Lighted Place" draws attention to the philosophical value of Catholic ritual, for just as the "older waiter"[149] recites Catholic prayer to confront nothingness, or God's nonexistence, so too might Santiago, a self-identified unbeliever, find value in a ritual practice that reveals *nada* at the heart of Catholicism, reminding Santiago of his power to self-determine. Stoneback seems to agree that unbelievers can benefit from ritual, as well: "On this subject, one might consult many Christian saints and mystics or, for that matter, Confucius, who understood very well . . .

the feeling of magical power that emanates from the authentic ritual gesture."[150] Even a non-Christian like Confucius understood the value of ritual, which Stoneback sees performed in "the church, the bullfight, and fishing, or even travel and work, as well as the smaller but no less important ceremonies of dailiness such as wine drinking,"[151] so it is clear that Hemingway's use of ritual should not be proof, for Stoneback, that Hemingway also *believed* in Catholicism.

There is no question that Hemingway makes use of Catholic ritual and may, for this reason, identify as a member of the Catholic Church, just as Jake Barnes identifies as *technically* Catholic, but Chapters 3 and 4 of this book demonstrate that Hemingway did not believe in God or the Christian afterlife. Like Sartre, Hemingway discovered absence at the heart of Catholicism, so the ritual performance of Catholic sacraments was a reminder of his own nothingness, which is to say, his capacity for sovereign, self-originating choice—the foundation of Hemingway's secularized theism. But he would also discover this capacity and, with it, the "religious feeling" in secular rituals like bullfighting, big-game hunting, and deep-sea fishing.

Hemingway's first novel, *The Sun Also Rises*, and the last novel published in his lifetime, *The Old Man and the Sea*, mark the span of a quarter-century, and yet both titles present their protagonists as religious pilgrims who march toward death in search of immortality. Jake Barnes visits cathedrals and other religious sites during his pilgrimage, but the Plaza de Toros is his ultimate destination. This is because Jake is an "aficionado . . . one who is passionate about the bullfight" and understands its "spiritual" value.[152] As we have already discussed at length, Hemingway took refuge in the two-part nature of the fight: the *faena*, which confronts the spectator with their mortality and animal nature; and *the moment of truth*, in which spectators vicariously reclaim the *imago Dei*—a symbol of human exceptionalism. "Outside the ring, after the bullfight was over, you could not move in the crowd," Jake recalls. "We could not make our way through but had to be moved with the whole thing, slowly, as a glacier, back to town. We had that disturbed emotional feeling that always comes after the bullfight," the feeling of mortality, or certain death, "and the feeling of elation that comes after a good bullfight," the feeling of immortality, that is, which follows the *moment of truth*.[153] Twenty-six years later, Hemingway would write about Santiago's religious pilgrimage, and yet, in spite of the considerable time lapse between his first novel and his last, Hemingway's depiction of the *faena* and *moment of truth* appear nearly identical. Santiago wonders if killing the marlin is a "sin," questioning the boundary between human and animal nature, but the old fisherman ultimately recognizes that killing the fish is a spiritual duty that, in turn, will finally prove his own greatness and masculine heroism.[154]

> The old man dropped the line and put his foot on it and lifted the harpoon as high as he could and drove it down with all his strength, and more strength he had just summoned, into the fish's side just behind the great chest fin that rose high in the air to the altitude of the man's chest. He felt the iron go in and he leaned on it and drove it further and then pushed all his weight after it. Then the fish came alive, with his death in him, and rose high out of the water showing all his great length and width and all his power and his beauty. He seemed to hang in the air above the old man in the skiff. Then he fell into the water with a crash that sent spray over the old man and over all of the skiff. The old man felt faint and sick and he could not see well. But he cleared the harpoon line and let it run slowly through his raw hands and, when he could see, he saw the fish was on his back with his silver belly up. The shaft of the harpoon was projecting at an angle from the fish's shoulder and the sea was discolouring with the red of the blood from his heart.[155]

The marlin comes alive with "death in him," passing by Santiago in this aquatic version of the *faena*, and like the great matador, Santiago sends his blade through the creature's heart. In this existential *moment of truth*, Santiago joins a long line of Hemingway heroes who discover a "religious feeling" in the sovereign exercise of free will. But this theological expression of masculine volition is epitomized in the ritualistic killing of animals, a signifying act that separates man from beast, superior being from inferior being. As the ritual basis of his secularized theism, this so-called *love of killing* unites the Oak Park Congregationalism of Hemingway's youth, his existential disillusionment after the war, and his conversion to Roman Catholicism years later by unveiling a *nothingness* at the heart of existence that must—for the sake of humanity—be overcome. Were Hemingway to embrace this *nothingness* rather than fight against it, accepting God's death and its logical consequences without reservation, he would accomplish the stated goal of materialistic atheism and dissolve the humanist fantasy, transforming himself from a sacred man back into a mortal beast. But this is an outcome that Hemingway could not bring himself to accept, ultimately, as the writer converted from theist to atheist and, finally, to secularized theist.

Cause for Question in Hemingway's Posthumous Works

There are two late works in the Hemingway canon that seem to complicate or at least bring into question my argument in this book—*The Garden of Eden* and *Under Kilimanjaro*,[156] both of which remained unfinished in Hemingway's lifetime. What can be interpreted as Hemingway's growing sympathy for animals, keenly illustrated by the elephant hunt in *The Garden of Eden*, may indicate a final shift in Hemingway's thought, according to critics. After all, the novel's protagonist, David Bourne, mourns the death of an elephant after revealing its whereabouts to his father and their African hunting guide (who track down and kill the beast) to the same degree that one might mourn the loss of a fellow human being. Under this reading, David is thought to believe in the moral value of animal life, and one is tempted to imagine him, in response to this traumatic event, turning to vegetarianism as an advocate of animal rights. But readers of the novel will note that David kills two spurfowl after expressing his deep regret for revealing the elephant's location. It may be that David values elephants over spurfowl due to the elephant's superior intelligence, capacity for love, or some other human-like quality that allows the young man to see himself in the elephant; indeed, it may be that David, like many human beings, values animals to the degree that he is able to identify with them. Under this matrix—which I described earlier as positive egalitarianism—nonhuman lifeforms are elevated from their inferior station so as to be included within the fold of humanity as equal members with the sacred right to life. Were this the case, it would explain why David is willing to kill a spurfowl but not the elephant, which too closely resembles humanity in his eyes. It does not, however, indicate that Hemingway, represented here by David, loses the love of killing and, as such, abandons the human/nonhuman, superior/inferior hierarchy that characterizes the author's secularized theism, despite what some critics have argued.

Cary Wolfe, for one, argues that David crosses the gender line with his wife Catherine precisely in order to cross the species line in their shared exploration of alterity. He writes that

> the childhood trauma of the elephant's murder—in which the cross-species identification common among children is violently foreclosed by the father—may be seen not only as retroactively expressive of but also as the traumatic "origin" of David's compensatory cross-gender identification with

Catherine and her explorations of otherness in an attempt to break with the sacrificial regime of the father who mandated the killing of the elephant in the first place.[157]

In Wolfe's reading, David's father represents heteronormativity on a local scale and, on a global scale, the sovereign subject of Enlightenment humanism who mandates the divisions between male and female, human and nonhuman, superior and inferior species in their conquest of the natural world. Highlighting Catherine's darkened skin, which David, paradoxically, likens to ivory, Wolfe argues that the couple's cross-gender exploration, which violates the heteronormative demands of patriarchy, is entangled with their cross-racial and cross-species explorations, the darkened skin tying Catherine to Africa, the ivory skin tying Catherine to the elephant. Catherine's "fantasies of racial and species miscegenation don't reproduce the father's [imperialist] Africanism because they in fact question its constitutive terms—that is, they question the sacrificial economy (of child, of woman, of animal) on which that discourse is based."[158] In other words, the Bournes' gender play leads to the deconstruction of racial and species boundaries as well. The fact that David identifies with the elephant over against his father should therefore be understood as a rejection of the human/animal hierarchy that bolsters his father's patriarchal, imperialist humanism. Racism sustains itself only if the "distinction between human and nonhuman is assumed to be unproblematically coterminous with the distinction between subject and object," Wolfe writes. "Hemingway's novel, then, attacks racism, but not on the terrain of racial discourse itself, using instead the 'off-site' of species discourse to undermine racism's conditions of possibility."[159]

Ryan Hediger similarly argues that "David finds himself identifying with an elephant, across the boundaries of species and against his ivory-hunting father whom he criticizes sharply."[160] He writes that "David identifies with the elephant, against his father and Juma,"[161] the hunting guide, in order to "surrender[] his place among the humans" and identify "as a vulnerable third member of the elephant group."[162] According to Hediger, David forsakes human exceptionalism in favor of what I call negative egalitarianism, a recognition of humanity's animal nature that collapses the metaphysical hierarchies upon which humanity establishes their moral absolutes. Now, it is certainly true that David identifies with the elephant, calling it his "hero," "brother," and "friend,"[163] but it is not true that David surrenders his *humanity*, which is to say, his exceptional status as a superior lifeform. David "had come to the knowledge that he hated elephant hunting,"[164] we learn in the novel, but he nevertheless remains a killer, killing two spurfowl and wishing that the elephant—his hero, brother, and friend—had killed Juma. In short, David objects to killing the elephant, an act that he finds morally reprehensible, but he does not object to killing spurfowl and, it is crucial to note, he does not object to killing human beings. After Juma and David's father kill the elephant, David and his father exchange the following words:

> "He was a murderer you know, Davey," h[is father] had said. "Juma says nobody knows how many people he has killed."
> "They were all trying to kill him weren't they?"
> "Naturally," his father said, "with that pair of tusks."
> "How could he be a murderer then?"
> "Just as you like," his father had said. "I'm sorry you got so mixed up about him."
> "I wish he'd killed Juma," David had said.
> "I think that's carrying it a little far," his father said. "Juma's your friend you know."
> "Not anymore."[165]

For David, as for the artillery officer in "A Natural History of the Dead," humane, morally upright behavior is performed by human beings while inhumane behavior is performed by the inhuman, those individuals whose actions are so morally egregious that they fall beyond the pale of comprehension. For David, who appears to be a sovereign, self-authorizing moralist, such behavior empties these individuals of their humanity. It would appear, then, that the line separating human from nonhuman, superior from inferior lifeform is synonymous, in David's mind, with the line that separates friend from enemy, which moves along a sliding scale. As David says to his father, he wishes the elephant had "killed Juma" because Juma is no longer his "friend." By contrast, his new friend, the elephant, is described as "the most alive thing that David had ever seen," which is to say, the most deserving of life.[166] The elephant, for David, is more human than Juma or even his own father. David authorizes these categorizations in his own mind through an appeal to moral absolutes. The elephant is in; Juma is out.

As Hediger himself observes, "the capacity for ethical behavior is often used to mark the difference between humans and non-human animals . . . in *The Garden of Eden* the elephant shows signs of complex feelings that move David, even though he is still a child, to criticize his father's inhumanity, his *brutality*."[167] David's humanization of the elephant results in the dehumanization of his father; thus, David does not *surrender* his humanity in order to identify with the elephant, as Hediger argues. On the contrary, David assumes the role of sovereign decision maker, animalizing some lifeforms and humanizing others. As we see in the passage quoted above, he and the elephant are attributed the right to life, but Juma and the spurfowl are not. Attempting to account for this inconsistency—i.e., David rejects the human/animal hierarchy in defense of the elephant but retains the paradoxical right to kill spurfowl—Hediger writes off the killing of spurfowl as an ethical compromise, stating that David "was too weak not to kill the birds. The party was low on food, and having enough energy simply to cover the miles was very much at issue for David, whereas his father and Juma patently did not need the wealth from more ivory."[168] Were David's sympathy for the elephant a rejection of the human/animal hierarchy, as both Wolfe and Hediger contend, either no being would have the right to life, or every being would have the right to life, including the spurfowl. A person's hunger or even their desire for material wealth would be of no consequence. Wolfe, too, recognizes the inconsistency here, writing that David's "systematic parsing of the animal other into quite different and discrete ontological categories" reflects his "inability to establish any ethical linkage between the multiplicity of animal others he encounters in the novel, such as the 'two spur fowl' David kills with his slingshot while his father and Juma track the elephant."[169] At first glance, *The Garden of Eden* presents an unlikely figure in the character of David, who protests the killing of an elephant on moral grounds, but a closer examination reveals that David is yet another secularized theist who, in defense of metaphysical hierarchy, wields moral authority in his creation of humans and nonhuman others.

Editors Robert W. Lewis and Robert E. Fleming write in their introduction to *Under Kilimanjaro*, Hemingway's nonfictional account of his African safari in 1953, that the writer's attitude toward hunting had clearly changed since his first safari in 1933:

> Hemingway as hunter has no desire to kill trophy game ... Instead, he shoots meat for the camp and takes greater pleasure in merely watching the wildlife. His greatest moment of pleasure during the hunt for Mary's lion is not the spectacular long-range shot that drops the lion Mary

has wounded but an earlier view of that same great cat lying on a mound one evening, surveying his kingdom. On another occasion he carefully stalks a massive old buffalo bull but merely dry-fires on it. The stalk was enough; killing the bull would have poisoned the pleasure of the hunt. Whenever possible his party avoids contact with rhinos, and Hemingway is relieved when a herd of elephants bypasses a nearby Kamba village without damaging it, for if it had, as an Honorary Game Ranger, he would have been forced to take action against the herd.[170]

Hemingway's bloodlust seems to have cooled in this late stage of his career. There are times when he does not wish to kill in *Under Kilimanjaro* and times when he has the opportunity to kill but chooses not to. This is in stark contrast with the younger Hemingway of *Green Hills of Africa* who fiercely—one might say desperately—competes with his fellow hunter, Karl, for bragging rights and masculine superiority. It is my belief, however, that we are presented in *Under Kilimanjaro* with a more confident Hemingway, a Hemingway secure in his masculinity and sure of his exceptional status, a Hemingway, that is, whose love of killing, though tempered, remains intact. There are times when Hemingway does not want to kill, certainly, but he still recognizes that killing, as a ritual practice, is the means through which an individual becomes truly human.

As Lewis and Fleming note, Hemingway hoped not to kill any elephants on the safari, but we learn in the opening pages of *Under Kilimanjaro* that this is not the result of his sympathy for the animals. On the contrary, Hemingway asks Philip Percival how to kill elephants effectively, and Percival answers: "the seventh wrinkle on the nose counting from the first wrinkle on the high forehead."[171] It would appear that Hemingway is perfectly willing to kill elephants; his only reluctance is due to the fact that elephant-killing is an inconvenience and not really an instance of big-game hunting at all.

"Never give them a thought," Percival remarks. "Enormous silly beasts. Harmless everyone says."[172] Elephants are certainly dangerous at times, but Hemingway does not view them as big game, nor does he view them as a food source. Thus, Hemingway would only kill the elephants if he was forced to as an Honorary Game Ranger. Even when it comes to big game, we learn, there is "as much difference between a wild lion and a marauding lion ... as there is between the old grizzly that will follow your trap line and ruin it and tear the roofs off your cabins ... and the bears that come up alongside the road to be photographed in Yellowstone Park."[173] Hemingway says that big game should be "intelligent, destructive, and much hunted in a way that had been defined, if not by our religion, by certain ethical standards."[174] In short, the quality of the animal matters. Hemingway kills ritualistically in accordance with his "religion," but he also kills *selectively* in accordance with certain ethical standards.

Describing these ethics, Hemingway writes that he "still loved to shoot and to kill cleanly" but that the "time of shooting beasts for trophies was long past with me."[175] Again, it appears that we encounter a matured Hemingway in 1953; he does not feel the need to prove himself by collecting trophies but, as the author clearly states, he still loves to kill and to do so cleanly, demonstrating his skilled mastery over death. Commenting on Mary's lion hunt, which he likens to a bullfight, Hemingway observes:

> Probably no one is as happy as hunters with the always new, fresh, unknowing day ahead and Mary was a hunter too. But she had set herself this task and being guided and trained and indoctrinated into absolute purity and virtue of killing a lion by Pop [Philip Percival], who had made her his last pupil and given her ethics he had never been able to impose on other women so that her killing of her lion must not be the way such things are done but the way such

things should ideally be done; Pop finding finally in Mary the spirit of a fighting cock embodied in a woman; a loving and belated killer.[176]

Make no mistake; the elder Hemingway fails to demonstrate his youthful bloodlust in the pages of *Under Kilimanjaro*, but he identifies himself, Mary, and all other hunters in the tradition of Philip Percival as "matador[s],"[177] killers who, through well-practiced technique, demonstrate their mastery over death to achieve the feeling of immortality. Such killers are "indoctrinated into absolute purity," where the "virtue of killing a lion"—not a marauding lion but a fierce and practiced killer itself—is motivated by the love of killing. As Hemingway observes, Percival found in Mary "the spirit of a fighting cock embodied in a woman." Thus, critics are right to notice a change in Hemingway's late career, but these changes must not be overstated. The author still loved to kill; he had simply grown selective about his prey. What we find in *The Garden of Eden* and *Under Kilimanjaro*, then, are not reasons to question my thesis but further evidence of its accuracy.

Conclusion: The Death of God, the Death of Man

In my quest to resolve the critical disagreement over Hemingway's religious orientation, I have described secularization as a failure. Rather than bar the use of theological dogma to justify society's moral, political, and legal procedures, secular society replaces theological transcendence with a God-surrogate to carry out the same operations. Human exceptionalism—or the belief that human beings have self-evident, metaphysical value guarded by their legal rights—has taken the place of God, a sacred standard beyond reproach or re-evaluation that is questioned only, human rights advocates will contend, by the fascist, the bigot, or some other such anathema. To be anti-humanist in the current political climate is, ironically, to be inhumane—that is, *inhuman*, as the artillery officer says of the Captain Doctor in "A Natural History of the Dead"; it is to act in a way, according to mainstream human rights discourse, that disfigures our higher nature. But as historian Stefanos Geroulanos points out, anti-humanism[178] emerged in the interwar and postwar era as a philosophical response to the humanist ideologies—be they democratic, communist, or national socialist—that led to global warfare. This anti-humanism "did not simply 'overcome' religion and institute a divine humanity that dominates this otherwise godless universe, but instead remained lost in a world [both] without God" or his secular counterpart.[179] Among these anti-humanists was Sartre, whose reconstruction of human identity as ontological nothingness—a veritable non-identity—allowed people, Geroulanos explains, "to be suspicious of the failures, religious implications, and violence of any humanism," whether Christian, secular, or otherwise.[180]

This, of course, was among the stated goals of Sartrean existentialism, but I have shown that Sartre too would divinize human beings by assigning them objective moral value, falling back—unwittingly, it seems—into the essentialist paradigms that he sought to overturn. Where justice refers to an equal administration of the law, and equality to the identical treatment of individual persons, there emerges a notion of human identity that universalizes our shared values and corresponding morality as objectively true. Lacking metaphysical objectivity, the system will acquire universal authority only if powerful leadership or some other hegemonic force imposes their valuation of human identity upon those who dissent. For this reason, every attempt at social justice objectifies morality and essentializes human nature at the expense of those who conceptualize these notions differently. To conceive of humanity, moreover, always pushes the nonhuman beyond the reach of equal moral treatment because the "human being," no matter how we choose to define it, is meaningful only in relationship to its conceptual opposites. It is no surprise that Sartre's moral commitments justified his support of Soviet concentration camps, which stood at the heart of his conflict with Albert Camus; likewise, it is no surprise that Hemingway's moral valuations were grounded in the love of killing. Absolute morality authorizes differential representations of humanity that, in turn, produce dehumanizing violence. The human gives birth to the nonhuman; moral authoritarianism breeds violent behavior.

In my critique of both Hemingway and Sartre, I leveraged the philosophical insights of Agamben to deauthorize sovereign decisionism, unpacking the contents of Hemingway's and Sartre's failed atheism to uncover its latent theological foundation. Agamben provides the antidote to sovereign decision making, to which Hemingway and Sartre would eventually find themselves bound through a series of logical missteps, as both writers failed to recognize the implications of their moral commitments. But I am not certain that Agamben's philosophical alternative fits the bill. In *The Open: Man and Animal*, Agamben calls for a deactivation of the anthropological machine, what he describes in *The Time That Remains* (2005) as "the revocation of each and every concrete factical vocation," the revocation, in other words, of any concrete identity.[181] Hoping to deauthorize sovereign representations of the human being, Agamben describes its nature as an impotent potentiality—which is to say, the potential to become an ontological essence that never succeeds in actualizing. In this sense, human beings are *pure* potentiality—what Sartre refers to as nothingness—and, as such, they have no identity; they are, in effect, non-identities. By conceptualizing the human being as an impotent potentiality that refuses to self-identify—suspended, as it were, in a permanent state of undecidability—Agamben renders the sovereign decision inoperative and as therefore incapable of producing representational violence against the nonhuman. If Sartre believed that existence precedes essence, then Agamben believes that existence *prevents* essence, for each of us is a pure potentiality that can never actualize as an ontic being, a nothingness, that is, who renders being-in-itself-for-itself impossible.

And yet Agamben himself appears committed to human rights, devoting his career to philosophical arguments against sovereign violence. He mourns the dehumanizing treatment of concentration camp prisoners in *Remnants of Auschwitz* (1999), and, in fact, the entire *Homo Sacer* series, which consists of nine volumes written over the span of two decades, is geared toward the redemption of *bare life*, those individuals separated from humanity and deprived of their rights by the sovereign powers that be. I wrote earlier that Agamben's philosophical project exceeds the scope of this book, but readers may wonder, in light of his ethical concerns, whether Agamben's defense of marginalized figures translates into a moral imperative. Can Agamben prescribe the fair treatment of society's victims on moral grounds without inciting representational violence of his own? And if this prescription lacks moral authority, should we not call it a *suggestion* rather than a *prescription*, as something that one *can* do but not as something that one *ought* to do? Put differently, were it not for humanity's inherent moral value, the ethical imperative *thou shalt not kill* would make little sense to the individual who wants nothing more than to see their enemy laid to waste. Without the *imago Dei* or some other such metaphysical foundation, moral suggestions of any kind would lack their universal force. Whether Agamben can adopt a moral stance without reinscribing the sovereign violence he seeks to overcome therefore appears doubtful, but I will leave this query to the seasoned scholars of Agamben's work.

The more pressing question for readers of this book is whether Hemingway's secularized theological views should be condemned as morally wrong. As I fail to distance myself from the author's conclusions, readers might assume, moreover, that I condone Hemingway's defense of sovereign violence. I can say, however, without any reservation, that sovereign decisionism is a fiction—the slaughter of dangerous animals does not instill their killer with metaphysical superiority, and, likewise, the sovereign act does not create a zone of indistinction between potentiality and actuality that results in being-in-itself-for-itself. Hemingway's belief in theological transcendence is delusional. That being said, I will not, in turn, condemn Hemingway's defense of violence as morally wrong. Killing might be distasteful, destructive, traumatizing, and unwanted, but it is not morally wrong. For morality too is a fiction, based on the exceptional value of human life, and its application is dehumanizing, itself a justification or defense of sovereign violence against the non-human others of this world. Readers of this book can opt out of the morality game altogether, refusing to enact the violent consequences of moral authoritarianism, but they can also respond to sovereign violence with a counter-violence of their own. This is ultimately their prerogative. I, for one, have chosen to opt out, leaving behind morality, human exceptionalism, and its violence.

Notes

1. Ernest Hemingway, *Death in the Afternoon* (London: Arrow Books, 2004), 104.
2. Michael Pollan, "An Animal's Place," in *The Norton Reader: An Anthology of Nonfiction*, 14th edn, ed. Melissa A. Goldthwaite et al. (New York/London: W. W. Norton & Company, 2017), 694.

3. Ernest Hemingway, *A Farewell to Arms* (New York: Charles Scribner's Sons, 1929), 116.
4. Ibid., 13.
5. Ibid., 325.
6. Ibid., 327.
7. Ibid.
8. Ibid., 263.
9. Ibid., 330.
10. Ibid., 327–8.
11. Jean-Paul Sartre, *The Wall and Other Stories*, trans. Lloyd Alexander (New York: New Directions Publishing Corporation, 1948), 11.
12. Ibid., 12.
13. Ernest Hemingway, *In Our Time* (New York: Scribner, 2003), 51.
14. Hemingway uses this motif again in "The Killers," where the boxer Ole Andreson, while avoiding a confrontation with two hitmen, stares at the wall in his bedroom for hours at a time. Hemingway also uses the motif in "In Another Country," as I describe in the next paragraph. In each of these instances, "the wall" symbolizes an individual's confrontation with death.
15. Sartre, *The Wall*, 13.
16. Ibid., 14.
17. Ernest Hemingway, *Men Without Women* (New York: Scribner Paperback Fiction, 1997), 44.
18. Ibid., 49.
19. Ibid., 45.
20. Hemingway, *In Our Time*, 76.
21. Sartre, *The Wall*, 5.
22. Ibid., 6.
23. Hemingway, *Men Without Women*, 47.
24. Ibid., 48.
25. Ibid., 46.
26. Ibid., 145.
27. Ibid., 149.
28. Hemingway, *A Farewell to Arms*, 54.

29. Sandra Spanier and Robert W. Trogdon, eds., *The Letters of Ernest Hemingway Volume 1, 1907–1922* (Cambridge, UK: Cambridge University Press, 2011), 147.
30. More on this work, including its publication history, will be discussed later.
31. Ernest Hemingway, *Under Kilimanjaro*, ed. Robert W. Lewis and Robert E. Fleming (Kent, OH: Kent State University Press, 2005), 220.
32. Matthew Nickel, *Hemingway's Dark Night: Catholic Influences and Intertextualities in the Work of Ernest Hemingway* (Wickford, RI: New Street Communications, 2013), 93.
33. Ibid., 97.
34. Ibid.
35. Hemingway, *Men Without Women*, 145.
36. Nickel, *Hemingway's Dark Night*, 96.
37. Hemingway, *Men Without Women*, 145.
38. Ibid.
39. Ibid., 147.
40. Ibid.
41. See, for example, James L. Green, "Symbolic Sentences in 'Big Two-Hearted River,'" *Modern Fiction Studies* 14.3 (1986): 307–12.
42. Hemingway, *Men Without Women*, 149.
43. Ibid., 47.
44. Hemingway, *Death in the Afternoon*, 104.
45. Hemingway, *Men Without Women*, 152.
46. Ibid., 153.
47. Ibid.
48. Lesley M. M. Blume, *Everybody Behaves Badly: The True Story behind Hemingway's Masterpiece 'The Sun Also Rises'* (Boston, MA: Houghton Mifflin Harcourt, 2016).
49. Hemingway, *Men Without Women*, 146.
50. Ibid.
51. Hemingway, *A Farewell to Arms*, 330.
52. Scott Donaldson, "Hemingway and Suicide," *The Sewanee Review* 103.2 (1995): 287.

53. Albert Camus, *The Myth of Sisyphus and Other Essays*, trans. Justin O'Brien (New York: Vintage Books, 1959), v.
54. Which is to say, lawmaking decisions that originate their own metaphysical value. This understanding of existential choice was established in Chapter 2 of this book through a close reading of Sartre.
55. Donaldson, "Hemingway and Suicide," 292.
56. Dylan Thomas, "Do not go gentle into that good night," Poets.org, accessed May 28, 2021, https://poets.org/poem/do-not-go-gentle-good-night.
57. Harvey Mansfield, "Manly Assertion," in *Hemingway on Politics and Rebellion*, ed. Lauretta Conklin Frederking (New York: Routledge, 2010), 94.
58. Richard K. Sanderson and Rena Sanderson, "Suicide and Literary Biography: The Case of Hemingway," *Biography* 20.4 (1997): 406.
59. "Hemingway's Sister Calls Death Accident," *Idaho Daily Statesman* (Boise), July 4, 1961, 2, quoted in Sanderson and Sanderson, "Suicide and Literary Biography," 407.
60. Sanderson and Sanderson, "Suicide and Literary Biography," 409.
61. Hemingway, *In Our Time*, 17.
62. Ibid., 18.
63. Ibid., 19.
64. Ibid.
65. Indeed, the Indian's suicide has perplexed critics, leading some to postulate alternate explanations. Larry Grimes, Kenneth Bernard, Peter Hays, and Gerry Brenner all speculate, for example, that Uncle George impregnated the Indian woman. Therefore, the cuckolded father does not kill himself because the Cesarean section is difficult to witness, but because he is humiliated by Uncle George and tortured by his broken romance. For a discussion of their findings, see Jeffrey Meyers, "Hemingway's Primitivism and 'Indian Camp,'" *Twentieth-Century Literature* 34.2 (1988): 211–22. My point here is not that the Indian's suicide demands an alternate explanation, but that, without an alternate explanation, the Indian's

suicide appears unwarranted. This is why Nick's father, Doctor Adams, must himself venture an explanation, stating, "I don't know, Nick. He couldn't stand things, I guess." A real man would have endured the situation. The Indian's suicide is an unexplainable failure in masculinity.
66. Hemingway, *In Our Time*, 15.
67. Ibid.
68. Charles E. May, "Introduction," in *The New Short Story Theories*, ed. Charles E. May (Athens, OH: Ohio University Press, 1994), xvii.
69. Hemingway, *In Our Time*, 16.
70. Ibid., 18–19.
71. This same kind of survival mode is portrayed in "Chapter VII" of *In Our Time*, a subsequent story in the collection: "While the bombardment was knocking the trench to pieces at Fossalta, he lay very flat and sweated and prayed oh jesus christ get me out of here. Dear jesus please get me out. Christ please please please christ. If you'll only keep me from getting killed I'll do anything you say. I believe in you and I'll tell every one in the world that you are the only one that matters. Please please dear jesus. The shelling moved further up the line. We went to work on the trench and in the morning the sun came up and the day was hot and muggy and cheerful and quiet. The next night back at Mestre he did not tell the girl he went upstairs with at the Villa Rossa about Jesus. And he never told anybody" (67). Obviously, Nick does not beg the Christian God to save his life, but, like this soldier, he does resort to an alternate account of death in a moment of panic. Just as the unfaithful soldier becomes faithful in the face of imminent destruction, so too does Nick resort to a belief in immortality when confronted with his mortality.
72. Hemingway, *In Our Time*, 21.
73. Ernest Hemingway, *For Whom the Bell Tolls* (New York: Scribner, 1940), 166.
74. Ibid., 169.
75. Sartre, *The Wall*, 12.
76. Hemingway, *For Whom the Bell Tolls*, 469.

77. Ibid., 339.
78. Ibid., 338.
79. Ibid.
80. Ibid.
81. Perhaps worth noting is that Sartre too idolized his grandfather, Charles Schweitzer, whom he often mistook for "God the Father" (Jean-Paul Sartre, *The Words: The Autobiography of Jean-Paul Sartre*, trans. Bernard Frechtman [New York: Vintage Books, 1964], 22). By contrast, Sartre's father, Jean-Baptiste, died when the philosopher was only two years of age.
82. Hemingway, *For Whom the Bell Tolls*, 340.
83. Ibid., 336–7.
84. Ibid., 337.
85. Ibid.
86. As Robert Wilson states in "The Short Happy Life of Francis Macomber," "Doesn't do to talk too much about all this. Talk the whole thing away. No pleasure in anything if you mouth it up too much" (Ernest Hemingway, *Winner Take Nothing* [London: Arrow Books, 1994], 29).
87. Hemingway, *Death in the Afternoon*, 1–2.
88. Ernest Hemingway, *A Moveable Feast* (New York: Charles Scribner's Sons, 1964), 12. When facing writer's block, Hemingway would say to himself, "'Do not worry. You have always written before and you will write now. All you have to do is write one true sentence, and then go on from there. . . .' Up in that room I decided that I would write one story about each thing that I knew about. I was trying to do this all the time I was writing, and it was a good and severe discipline." The meaning of "one true sentence" is vague, but it corresponds with the topics Hemingway knew well enough to write a story about. In general, short story writers and novelists seek to convey deep insights about the human experience, and Hemingway was no exception. Given the context of this passage, "one true sentence" most likely refers to a deep insight, around which Hemingway would then develop a story.

89. Hemingway, *Death in the Afternoon*, 179.
90. Ibid., 177–8.
91. Ibid., 19.
92. Angela Alaimo O'Donnell, "Death & Life in the Afternoon: A Meditation on Bullfighting," Americamagazine.org, October 2, 2017, 42; available at https://www.academia.edu/34647926/Death_and_Life_in_the_Afternoon_A_Meditation_on_Bullfighting.
93. Hemingway, *Death in the Afternoon*, 49.
94. Hemingway describes this person as both a "messiah" and "a god to drive the half-gods out," ibid., 74.
95. Nathan Guss argues in "Danger and Literature: Michel Leiris and the Corrida," *MLN* 124.4 (2009): 951–69 that the art of bullfighting is comparable to the art of writing. Relying upon Nietzsche's distinction between the Apollonian and the Dionysian, Guss attempts to demonstrate how the formal elements of bullfighting achieve the same aesthetic goals that Hemingway achieved in his fiction. In short, Guss concludes that Hemingway mimicked bullfighting with his writing style, claiming that bullfighting and Hemingway's fiction are similar in form. But this conclusion flies directly in the face of Hemingway's assertion that bullfighting is the only art in which the artist is threatened by the possibility of death, and I would add, moreover, that bullfighting is drastically different from writing insofar as the matador must kill another living creature. Indeed, killing the bull that threatens his life is essential to the matador's artistic performance, and while bullfighting can be represented on the page, as Hemingway demonstrates, fiction writing is not the same as bullfighting. On this point, I stand in agreement with Hemingway, especially because the formal similarities identified by Guss are tenuous at best.
96. Hemingway, *Death in the Afternoon*, 78.
97. Ibid., 17.
98. Ibid., 199–200.
99. Giorgio Agamben, *The Omnibus Homo Sacer* (Stanford, CA: Stanford University Press, 2017), 42.

100. Hemingway, *Death in the Afternoon*, 3.
101. It is worth noting that the bullfight also resembles Catholic Mass.
102. Hemingway, *Death in the Afternoon*, 59.
103. Ibid., 152.
104. John Killinger, *Hemingway and the Dead Gods: A Study in Existentialism* (New York: Citadel Press, 1965), 30–1.
105. Jean-Paul Sartre, *Existentialism Is a Humanism*, ed. John Kulka, trans. Carol Macomber (New Haven, CT: Yale University Press, 2007), 24.
106. O'Donnell, "Death & Life in the Afternoon," 44.
107. Ben Stoltzfus, "Sartre, *Nada*, and Hemingway's African Stories," *Comparative Literature Studies* 42.3 (2005): 207, 206.
108. Ibid., 207.
109. Warren Beck, "The Shorter Happy Life of Mrs. Macomber," *Modern Fiction* 1.4 (1955): 28.
110. Hemingway, *Winner Take Nothing*, 2.
111. Ibid.
112. Ibid.
113. Ibid., 16.
114. Ibid., 8.
115. Ibid., 28.
116. Ibid., 21.
117. Ibid., 6.
118. Ibid., 28.
119. Ibid., 11.
120. Ibid., 17.
121. Ibid., 27.
122. Stoltzfus, "Sartre, *Nada*, and Hemingway's African Stories," 213.
123. Ibid., 215.
124. Ibid., 216–17.
125. Hemingway, *Winner Take Nothing*, 30.
126. Ibid., 31.
127. Ibid.

128. Jean-Paul Sartre, *No Exit and Three Other Plays* (New York: Vintage International, 1989), 100.
129. Ibid., 101–2.
130. Kate Kirkpatrick, *Sartre and Theology* (New York/London: Bloomsbury T&T Clark, 2017), 107.
131. Ibid., 109.
132. Sartre, *No Exit*, 45.
133. Ibid., 43.
134. Ibid., 44.
135. Ibid.
136. Ibid., 113.
137. Ibid., 106.
138. Ibid., 117.
139. Ibid., 119.
140. Ernest Hemingway, *Fiesta: The Sun Also Rises* (London: Vintage Books, 2000), 107.
141. Ibid., 108.
142. H. R. Stoneback, *Reading Hemingway's 'The Sun Also Rises': Glossary and Commentary* (Kent, OH: Kent State University Press, 2007), 223–4.
143. Ibid., 224.
144. Hemingway, *Fiesta: The Sun Also Rises*, 84–5.
145. Ernest Hemingway, *The Old Man and the Sea* (London: Vintage Books, 2000), 8.
146. Ibid., 48.
147. Ibid.
148. Hemingway, *Winner Take Nothing*, 58–9.
149. Ibid., 58.
150. Stoneback, *Reading*, 179.
151. Ibid.
152. Hemingway, *Fiesta: The Sun Also Rises*, 115.
153. Ibid., 142.
154. Hemingway, *The Old Man and the Sea*, 81.
155. Ibid., 72.
156. Published in 2005 by editors Robert W. Lewis and Robert E. Fleming, *Under Kilimanjaro* was preceded by a considerably

shorter 1999 version of the book entitled *True at First Light*, edited by Patrick Hemingway.

157. Cary Wolfe, "Fathers, Lovers, and Friend Killers: Rearticulating Gender and Race via Species in Hemingway," *boundary 2* 29.1 (2002): 237.
158. Ibid., 255.
159. Ibid., 256.
160. Ryan Hediger, "The Elephant in the Writing Room: Sympathy and Weakness in Hemingway's 'Masculine Text,' *The Garden of Eden*," *The Hemingway Review* 31.1 (2011): 79.
161. Ibid., 88.
162. Ibid., 87.
163. Ernest Hemingway, *The Garden of Eden* (New York: Scribner Paperback Fiction, 1995), 201, 197, 198.
164. Ibid., 200.
165. Ibid., 201–2.
166. Ibid., 199.
167. Hediger, "The Elephant," 85.
168. Ibid., 90.
169. Wolfe, "Fathers, Lovers, and Friend Killers," 251.
170. Hemingway, *Under Kilimanjaro*, xiv.
171. Ibid., 6.
172. Ibid., 5.
173. Ibid., 46.
174. Ibid.
175. Ibid., 116.
176. Ibid., 195.
177. Ibid.
178. Heretofore, I have used the term *posthumanist* to describe my approach, so readers may wonder, after the introduction of this new term, what the difference is between posthumanism and *anti-humanism*. As Geroulanos explains, anti-humanism was a mid-twentieth-century critique of anthropocentrism. It was part of a new atheism which no longer believed that humanism was a viable substitute for religion. Posthumanism, by contrast, emerged in the 1990s and was similarly based on the critique of anthropocentrism.

"However, a major distinction between the two movements," Francesca Ferrando writes, "is already embedded in their morphologies, specifically in their denotation of 'post' and 'anti-,'" for posthumanism, Ferrando explains, moved beyond a merely negative critique of anthropocentrism to positive considerations of ecology and animal rights, as reflected in Agamben's concern with the human/nonhuman dialectic. In short, anti-humanism and posthumanism share a critique of anthropocentrism. The latter merely expands its scope of interest to include nonhuman organisms. See Francesca Ferrando, "Posthumanism, Transhumanism, Antihumanism, Metahumanism, and New Materialisms," *Existenz: An International Journal in Philosophy, Religion, Politics, and the Arts* 8.2 (2013): 31.

179. Stefanos Geroulanos, *An Atheism That Is Not Humanist Emerges in French Thought* (Stanford, CA: Stanford University Press, 2010), 8.
180. Ibid., 9.
181. Giorgio Agamben, *The Time That Remains: A Commentary on the Letter to the Romans*, trans. Patricia Dailey (Stanford, CA: Stanford University Press, 2005), 23.

BIBLIOGRAPHY

Agamben, Giorgio. *The Omnibus Homo Sacer*. Stanford, CA: Stanford University Press, 2017.
—. *The Open: Man and Animal*. Translated by Kevin Attell. Stanford, CA: Stanford University Press, 2004.
—. *Profanations*. Translated by Jeff Fort. New York: Zone Books, 2007.
—. *The Time That Remains: A Commentary on the Letter to the Romans*. Translated by Patricia Dailey. Stanford, CA: Stanford University Press, 2005.
Aronson, Ronald. "Camus versus Sartre: The Unresolved Conflict." *Sartre Studies International* 11.1/2 (2005): 302–10.
Assman, Jan. *The Price of Monotheism*. Translated by Robert Savage. Stanford, CA: Stanford University Press, 2009.
Astruc, Alexandre, Michel Contat, and Guy Séligmann. *Sartre by Himself* (1976; New York: Interama Video Classics, 1982), VHS.
Bache, William B. "Craftsmanship in 'A Clean, Well-Lighted Place.'" *Personalist* 37 (Winter 1956): 60–4.
Baker, Carlos. *Ernest Hemingway: A Life Story*. New York: Avon Books, 1968.
Barnes, Hazel E. "Sartre and Sexism." *Literature and Philosophy* 14.2 (1990): 340–7.
Barrett, William. *Irrational Man: A Study in Existential Philosophy*, 2nd edn. New York: Doubleday, Anchor Books, 1962.

Baym, Nina. "Actually, I Felt Sorry for the Lion." In *New Critical Approaches to the Short Stories of Ernest Hemingway*, edited by Jackson J. Benson, 112–20. Durham, NC: Duke University Press, 1990.

Beck, Warren. "The Shorter Happy Life of Mrs. Macomber." *Modern Fiction* 1.4 (1955): 28–37.

Bloom, Harold. *The Anxiety of Influence: A Theory of Poetry*, 2nd edn. New York/Oxford: Oxford University Press, 1997.

Blume, Lesley M. M. *Everybody Behaves Badly: The True Story behind Hemingway's Masterpiece 'The Sun Also Rises'*. Boston, MA: Houghton Mifflin Harcourt, 2016.

Boulé, Jean-Pierre. *Sartre, Self-Formation and Masculinities*. New York/Oxford: Berghahn Books, 2005.

Brasch, James D., and Joseph Sigman. *Hemingway's Library: A Composite Record*. New York/London: Garland Publishing, Inc., 1981.

Bruccoli, Matthew J., and Judith Baughman, eds. *Hemingway and the Mechanism of Fame: Statements, Public Letters, Introductions, Forewords, Prefaces, Blurbs, Reviews, and Endorsements*. Columbia: University of South Carolina Press, 2006.

Burstow, Bonnie. "How Sexist Is Sartre?" *Philosophy and Literature* 16.1 (1992): 32–48.

Cadegan, Una M. *All Good Books Are Catholic Books: Print Culture, Censorship, and Modernity in Twentieth-Century America*. London: Cornell University Press, 2013.

—. "Hemingway's Dark Night: Catholic Influences and Intertextualities in the Work of Ernest Hemingway by Matthew Nickel." *American Catholic Studies* 125.4 (2014): 87–8.

—. "Modernisms Theological and Literary." *U.S. Catholic Historian* 20.3 (2002): 97–110.

Calabi, Silvio. "Ernest Hemingway on Safari: The Game and the Guns." In *Hemingway and Africa*, edited by Mandel Miriam B. Rochester, 85–121. New York: Boydell & Brewer, 2011.

Calarco, Matthew. *Zoographies: The Question of the Animal from Heidegger to Derrida*. New York: Columbia University Press, 2008.

Camus, Albert. *The Myth of Sisyphus and Other Essays*. Translated by Justin O'Brien. New York: Vintage Books, 1959.

—. *The Rebel: An Essay on Man in Revolt*. Translated by Anthony Bower. New York: Vintage International, 1991.

Catholic Church. "The Dignity of the Human Person." In the *Catechism of the Catholic Church*, 2nd edn. Vatican: Libreria Editrice Vaticana, 2012.

Collins, Margery L., and Christine Pierce. "Holes and Slime: Sexism in Sartre's Psychoanalysis." *Philosophic Forum* 5 (1973): 112–27.

Cotkin, George. *Existential America*. Baltimore, MD: Johns Hopkins University Press, 2003.

Daly, Mary. *Gyn/Ecology: The Metaethics of Radical Feminism*. Boston, MA: Beacon Press, 1978.

Dawkins, Richard. *The Blind Watchmaker: Why the Evidence of Evolution Reveals a Universe without Design*. New York/London: W. W. Norton & Company, 1986.

Dearborn, Mary V. *Ernest Hemingway: A Biography*. New York: Vintage Books, 2017.

De Beauvoir, Simone. *Adieux*. Translated by Patrick O'Brian. New York: Pantheon Books, 1984.

Donaldson, Scott. *By Force of Will: The Life and Art of Ernest Hemingway*. New York: Viking, 1977.

—. "Hemingway and Suicide." *The Sewanee Review* 103.2 (1995): 287–95.

Eagleton, Terry. *Culture and the Death of God*. New Haven, CT: Yale University Press, 2014.

Earle, David M. *All Man! Hemingway, 1950s Men's Magazines, and the Masculine Persona*. Kent, OH: Kent State University Press, 2009.

Eby, Carl P. *Hemingway's Fetishism: Psychoanalysis and the Mirror of Manhood*. Albany, NY: State University of New York Press, 1998.

Evans, Robert. "Hemingway and the Pale Cast of Thought." *American Literature* 38.2 (1966): 161–76.

Ferrando, Francesca. "Posthumanism, Transhumanism, Antihumanism, Metahumanism, and New Materialisms." *Existenz: An*

International Journal in Philosophy, Religion, Politics, and the Arts 8.2 (2013): 26–32.

Gellman, Jerome. "Jean-Paul Sartre: The Mystical Atheist." *European Journal for Philosophy of Religion* 2 (2009): 127–37.

Geroulanos, Stefanos. *An Atheism That Is Not Humanist Emerges in French Thought*. Stanford, CA: Stanford University Press, 2010.

Gillespie, John. "Sartre and the Death of God." *Sartre Studies International* 22.1 (2016): 41–57.

Gordon, Peter E. "The Place of the Sacred in the Absence of God: Charles Taylor's *A Secular Age*." *Journal of the History of Ideas* 69.4 (2008): 647–73.

Green, James L. "Symbolic Sentences in 'Big Two-Hearted River.'" *Modern Fiction Studies* 14.3 (1986): 307–12.

Grimes, Larry. "Hemingway's Religious Odyssey: The Oak Park Years." In *Ernest Hemingway: The Oak Park Legacy*, edited by James Nagel, 37–58. Tuscaloosa, AL: University of Alabama Press, 1996.

—. *The Religious Design of Hemingway's Early Fiction*. Ann Arbor, MI: UMI Research Press, 1985.

—. "Things They Carried: Nick, Hemingway, and Oak Park Connections to the Western Front." *Midwestern Miscellany* 47 (2019): 16–28.

Grudem, Wayne. *Systematic Theology: An Introduction to Biblical Doctrine*. Grand Rapids, MI: Zondervan, 2000.

Gurpegui, José Antonio. *Hemingway and Existentialism*. Valencia: Publicacions de la Universitat de València, 2013.

Guss, Nathan. "Danger and Literature: Michel Leiris and the Corrida." *MLN* 124.4 (2009): 951–69.

Halteman, Matthew C. "Ontotheology." *Routledge Encyclopedia of Philosophy*, edited by Edward Craig. https://www.rep.routledge.com/articles/thematic/ontotheology/v-1.

Hardt, Michael, and Antonio Negri. *Commonwealth*. Cambridge, MA: Harvard University Press, 2009.

Harris, Sam. *The Moral Landscape: How Science Can Determine Human Values*. New York: Free Press, 2010.

Harrison, Peter. "Science and Secularization." *Intellectual History Review* 27.1 (2017): 47–70.

Hart, William David. "Naturalizing Christian Ethics: A Critique of Charles Taylor's *A Secular Age*." *Journal of Religious Ethics* 40.1 (2012): 149–70.

Hediger, Ryan. "Becoming with Animals: Sympoiesis and the Ecology of Meaning in London and Hemingway." *Studies in American Naturalism* 11.1 (2016): 5–22.

—. "The Elephant in the Writing Room: Sympathy and Weakness in Hemingway's 'Masculine Text,' *The Garden of Eden*." *The Hemingway Review* 31.1 (2011): 79–95.

Hemingway, Ernest. *Death in the Afternoon*. London: Arrow Books, 2004.

—. *A Farewell to Arms*. New York: Charles Scribner's Sons, 1929.

—. *Fiesta: The Sun Also Rises*. London: Vintage Books, 2000.

—. *For Whom the Bell Tolls*. New York: Scribner, 1940.

—. *The Garden of Eden*. New York: Scribner Paperback Fiction, 1995.

—. *Green Hills of Africa*. New York: Charles Scribner's Sons, 1935.

—. *In Our Time*. New York: Scribner, 2003.

—. *Men Without Women*. New York: Scribner Paperback Fiction, 1997.

—. *A Moveable Feast*. New York: Charles Scribner's Sons, 1964.

—. *The Old Man and the Sea*. London: Vintage Books, 2000.

—. *Under Kilimanjaro*. Edited by Robert W. Lewis and Robert E. Fleming. Kent, OH: Kent State University Press, 2005.

—. *Winner Take Nothing*. London: Arrow Books, 1994.

Hemingway, Mary Welsh. *How It Was*. New York: Alfred A. Knopf, 1976.

Holman, C. Hugh. "Hemingway and Emerson: Notes on the Continuity of an Aesthetic Tradition." *Modern Fiction Studies* 1.3 (1955): 12–16.

Horan, Daniel P. "Deconstructing Anthropocentric Privilege: *Imago Dei* and Nonhuman Agency." *The Heythrop Journal* 60 (2019): 560–70.

—. "A Rahnerian Theological Response to Charles Taylor's *A Secular Age*." *New Blackfriars* 95.1055 (2014): 21–42.

Hotchner, A. E. *Papa Hemingway: A Memoir.* New York: Bantam Books, 1967.
Hunt, Lynn. *Inventing Human Rights: A History.* New York: W. W. Norton & Company, 2007.
Jay, Martin. "Faith-Based History." *History and Theory* 48.1 (2009): 76–84.
Journey, Anna. "Earn the Vomit: Employing the Grotesque in Contemporary Poetry." *The American Poetry Review* 43.5 (2014): 15–19.
Kennedy, J. Gerald. "Hemingway's Gender Trouble." *American Literature* 63.2 (1991): 187–207.
Kert, Bernice. *The Hemingway Women.* New York: W. W. Norton & Company, 1983.
Killinger, John. *Hemingway and the Dead Gods: A Study in Existentialism.* New York: Citadel Press, 1965.
Kirkpatrick, Kate. *Sartre and Theology.* New York/London: Bloomsbury T&T Clark, 2017.
—. *Sartre on Sin: Between Being and Nothingness.* Oxford: Oxford University Press, 2017.
Kokobobo, Ani. *Russian Grotesque Realism.* Columbus, OH: Ohio State University Press, 2018.
Kotsko, Adam. *Agamben's Philosophical Trajectory.* Edinburgh: Edinburgh University Press, 2020.
—. *Neoliberalism's Demons: On the Political Theology of Late Capital.* Stanford, CA: Stanford University Press, 2018.
—, and Carlo Salzani, eds. *Agamben's Philosophical Lineage.* Edinburgh: Edinburgh University Press, 2017.
Latham, Aaron. "A Farewell to Machismo." *New York Times*, October 16, 1977. https://www.nytimes.com/1977/10/16/archives/a-farewell-to-machismo-a-story-by-any-other-name-hemingway.html.
Linde, Mauricio D. Aguilera. "Hemingway and Gender: Biography Revisited." *Atlantis* 27.2 (2005): 15–26.
Linsenbard, Gail. "Sartre's Criticisms of Sartre's Moral Philosophy." *Sartre Studies International* 13.2 (2007): 65–86.
Love, Glen A. "Hemingway's Indian Virtues: An Ecological Reconsideration." *Western American Literature* 22.3 (1987): 201–13.

Lynn, Kenneth Shuyler. *Hemingway*. Cambridge, MA: Harvard University Press, 1987.
McGill, Christopher. "A Reading of Zoomorphism in 'The Short Happy Life of Francis Macomber.'" *The Explicator* 70.1 (2012): 57–60.
Maier, Kevin. "Hemingway's Hunting: An Ecological Reconsideration." *The Hemingway Review* 25.2 (2006): 119–22.
Mansfield, Harvey. "Manly Assertion." In *Hemingway on Politics and Rebellion*, edited by Lauretta Conklin Frederking, 91–103. New York: Routledge, 2010.
May, Charles E. "Introduction." In *The New Short Story Theories*, edited by Charles E. May, xv–xxvi. Athens, OH: Ohio University Press, 1994.
Menand, Louis. *The Free World: Art and Thought in the Cold War*. New York: Farrar, Straus and Giroux, 2021.
—. "Stand by Your Man: The Strange Liaison of Sartre and Beauvoir." *The New Yorker*, September 19, 2005.
Meyers, Jeffrey. *Hemingway: A Biography*. New York: Harper & Row, 1985.
—. "Hemingway's Primitivism and 'Indian Camp.'" *Twentieth-Century Literature* 34.2 (1988): 211–22.
—. "Hemingway's Second War: The Greco-Turkish Conflict, 1920–1922." *Modern Fiction Studies* 30.1 (1984): 24–36.
Nickel, Matthew. *Hemingway's Dark Night: Catholic Influences and Intertextualities in the Work of Ernest Hemingway*. Wickford, RI: New Street Communications, 2013.
Nietzsche, Friedrich. *The Gay Science*. Translated by Thomas Common. New York: Dover Publications, 2006.
—. "On Truth and Lying in a Non-Moral Sense." In *The Norton Anthology of Theory and Criticism*, edited by Vincent B. Leitch, 870–95. New York/London: W. W. Norton & Company, 2001.
O'Donnell, Angela Alaimo. "Death & Life in the Afternoon: A Meditation on Bullfighting." Americamagazine.org, October 2, 2017, 42. Available at https://www.academia.edu/34647926/Death_and_Life_in_the_Afternoon_A_Meditation_on_Bullfighting.
Perry, Michael J. "The Morality of Human Rights." *San Diego Law Review* 50.775 (2013): 793.

—. "The Morality of Human Rights: A Nonreligious Ground?" *Emory Law Journal* 54 (2005): 104–5.

Pienkos, Angela T. "Slaughterhouse: Chicago's Union Stockyard and the World It Made." *Polish American Studies* 74.1 (2017): 93–5.

Pollan, Michael. "An Animal's Place." In *The Norton Reader: An Anthology of Nonfiction*, 14th edn, edited by Melissa A. Goldthwaite et al., 681–96. New York/London: W. W. Norton & Company, 2017.

Prud'homme, Joseph. "Hemingway, Religion, and Masculine Virtue." In *Hemingway on Politics and Rebellion*, edited by Lauretta Conklin Frederking, 104–32. New York: Routledge, 2010.

Regan, Tom. "The Case for Animal Rights." In *The Norton Reader: An Anthology of Nonfiction*, 14th edn, edited by Melissa A. Goldthwaite et al., 670–80. New York/London: W. W. Norton & Company, 2017.

Reynolds, Michael. *Hemingway in the 1930s*. New York/London: W. W. Norton & Company, 1997.

—. *The Young Hemingway*. New York: Norton, 1986.

Sanderson, Rena, Sandra Spanier, and Robert W. Trogdon, eds. *The Letters of Ernest Hemingway Volume 3, 1926–1929*. Cambridge, UK: Cambridge University Press, 2018.

Sanderson, Richard K., and Rena Sanderson. "Suicide and Literary Biography: The Case of Hemingway." *Biography* 20.4 (1997): 405–36.

Sanford, Marcelline. *At the Hemingways, Centennial Edition*. Moscow, ID: University of Idaho Press, 1999.

Sartre, Jean-Paul. "American Novelists in French Eyes." Accessed August 26, 2019. docs.sartre.ch/American%20Novelists.pdf.

—. *Being and Nothingness*. Translated by Hazel E. Barnes. New York: Washington Square Press, 1953.

—. *Existentialism Is a Humanism*. Edited by John Kulka. Translated by Carol Macomber. New Haven, CT: Yale University Press, 2007.

—. *No Exit and Three Other Plays*. New York: Vintage International, 1989.

—. "Reply to Albert Camus." In *We Have Only This Life to Live: The Selected Essays of Jean-Paul Sartre 1939–1975*, edited by Ronald Aronson and Adrian Van Den Hoven, 210–35. New York: New York Review Books, 2013.

—. *The Wall and Other Stories*. Translated by Lloyd Alexander. New York: New Directions Publishing Corporation, 1948.

—. *War Diaries: Notebooks from a Phony War 1939–40*. Translated by Quintin Hoare. New York: Verso, 1984.

—. *The Words: The Autobiography of Jean-Paul Sartre*. Translated by Bernard Frechtman. New York: Vintage Books, 1964.

—. "The Wretched of the Earth." In *We Have Only This Life to Live: The Selected Essays of Jean-Paul Sartre 1939–1975*, edited by Ronald Aronson and Adrian Van Den Hoven, 384–402. New York: New York Review Books, 2013.

Saunders, Judith P. *American Classics: Evolutionary Perspectives*. Boston, MA: American Studies Press, 2018.

Schmitt, Carl. *Political Theology*. Translated by George Schwab. Chicago, IL: University of Chicago Press, 1985.

Schweiker, William, et al. "Grappling with Charles Taylor's *A Secular Age*." *The Journal of Religion* 90.3 (2010): 367–400.

Slaughter, Joseph. *Human Rights, Inc.: The World Novel, Narrative Form, and International Law*. New York: Fordham University Press, 2007.

Spanier, Sandra, and Miriam B. Mandel, eds. *The Letters of Ernest Hemingway Volume 4, 1929–1931*. Cambridge, UK: Cambridge University Press, 2018.

—, eds. *The Letters of Ernest Hemingway Volume 5, 1932–1934*. Cambridge, UK: Cambridge University Press, 2020.

Spanier, Sandra, and Robert W. Trogdon, eds. *The Letters of Ernest Hemingway Volume 1, 1907–1922*. Cambridge, UK: Cambridge University Press, 2011.

Stoltzfus, Ben. *Hemingway and French Writers*. Kent, OH: Kent State University Press, 2010.

—. "Sartre, *Nada*, and Hemingway's African Stories." *Comparative Literature Studies* 42.3 (2005): 205–28.

Stoneback, H. R. "For Whom the Flood Rolls: Ernest Hemingway and Robert Penn Warren—Connections and Echoes, Allusion,

and Intertextuality." *North Dakota Quarterly* 76.1/2 (2009): 7–21.
—. "In the Nominal Country of the Bogus: Hemingway's Catholicism and the Biographies." In *Hemingway: Essays of Reassessment*, edited by Frank Scafella, 105–40. New York: Oxford University Press, 1991.
—. "Pilgrimage Variations: Hemingway's Sacred Landscapes." *Religion and Literature* 35.2/3 (2003): 49–65.
—. *Reading Hemingway's 'The Sun Also Rises': Glossary and Commentary*. Kent, OH: Kent State University Press, 2007.
Sullivan, Marek. "Cartesian Secularity: 'Disengaged Reason,' the Passions, and the Public Sphere beyond Charles Taylor's *A Secular Age* (2007)." *Journal of the American Academy of Religion* 87.4 (2019): 1,050–84.
Taylor, Charles. *A Secular Age*. Cambridge, MA: Belknap Press of Harvard University Press, 2007.
Thomas, Dylan. "Do not go gentle into that good night." Poets.org, accessed May 28, 2021. https://poets.org/poem/do-not-go-gentle-good-night.
Tillich, Paul. "Relation of Metaphysics and Theology." *The Review of Metaphysics* 10.1 (1956): 57–63.
Warren, Robert Penn. "Hemingway." *The Kenyon Review* 9.1 (Winter 1947): 1–28.
—. "Hemingway's World." In *Readings on Ernest Hemingway*, edited by Katie De Koster, 34–8. San Diego, CA: Greenhaven Press, 1997.
Weeks, Jr., Lewis E. "Mark Twain and Hemingway: 'A Catastrophe' and 'A Natural History of the Dead.'" *Mark Twain Journal* 14.2 (1968): 15–17.
West, Jr., Ray B. "Ernest Hemingway: The Failure of Sensibility." *The Sewanee Review* 53.1 (1945): 120–35.
Winter, J. M., and D. M. Joslin, eds. *R. H. Tawney's Commonplace Book*. Cambridge, UK: Cambridge University Press, 1972.
Wolfe, Cary. "Fathers, Lovers, and Friend Killers: Rearticulating Gender and Race via Species in Hemingway." *boundary 2* 29.1 (2002): 223–57.
Young, Philip. *Ernest Hemingway*. New York: Rinehart, 1952.

INDEX

Titles of works are filed at, or cross-referenced from, authors' names. Fictional characters are indexed by surname. Notes are indicated by page numbers with the suffix 'n'.

Adams, Doctor (fictional character), 125–6, 127, 193–200
Adams, Nick (fictional character)
   "Big Two-Hearted River," 127, 183
   "Indian Camp," 193–5, 196–200
   "Now I Lay Me," 178–9, 180, 181–4, 185–8
   "Ten Indians," 125–6, 127
Africa, 123, 158, 239, 242
afterlife
   Hemingway's depictions of, 114, 169, 178, 182, 186, 198
   Sartre, 57, 173, 176
   secularization, 16
   war, impact on Hemingway's beliefs, 101, 104, 105
   see also human soul
Agamben, Giorgio
   "Beyond Human Rights," 160
   Homo Sacer: Sovereign Power and Bare Life, 160
   human identity, 67–84, 160, 212, 224, 247
   humanism, 21, 145, 160–1, 259n178
   The Open, 160, 247
   Profanations, 17–18
   Remnants of Auschwitz, 248
   The Sacrament of Language, 68, 82
   secularized theism, 60–1, 78–9, 83, 161, 224
   The Time That Remains, 247
   see also *bare life*
Althusser, Louis, 70
American Civil War, 88, 89, 126, 136, 206
American existentialism, 8, 13
animal cruelty, 132–3, 137–8, 155–6, 171, 187, 207–8; see also bullfighting; fishing; hunting
animal equality
   Death in the Afternoon, 154, 156, 167–8
   For Whom the Bell Tolls, 149–50, 154
   The Garden of Eden, 240
   "Now I Lay Me," 187
   positive and negative egalitarianism, 157–61
   "The Short Happy Life of Francis Macomber," 155–6, 218
animal rights, 148, 156–60, 187, 238, 242
animalization/dehumanization
   Agamben, 74, 78, 160, 248
   conclusions, 247–9
   Death in the Afternoon, 213
   A Farewell to Arms, 147
   The Garden of Eden, 241
   hunting, 158
   "A Natural History of the Dead," 138–9, 142, 144–5

"Now I Lay Me," 187–8
"On the Quai at Smyrna," 129–30, 133–5, 145
Sartre, 85–7, 227
Anselmo (fictional character), 148–52, 153
anthropocentrism
  A Farewell to Arms, 147, 171
  For Whom the Bell Tolls, 152, 154
  introduction to, 15, 16, 20, 26
  moral purpose of humans, 15, 77
  "A Natural History of the Dead," 140, 143
  "The Short Happy Life of Francis Macomber," 155–6, 219
  see also human exceptionalism; *imago Dei*
anthropogenesis, 73–6, 86, 160, 161
anti-humanism, 143, 246, 258n178
Aronson, Ronald, 85
assertive manliness, 39–40, 191–2, 218
Assman, Jan, 12, 30
atheism
  Death in the Afternoon, 107–9
  failed atheism, 59, 61–7, 81, 115–16, 247
  A Farewell to Arms, 169
  For Whom the Bell Tolls, 136, 153–4
  Hemingway, biographical study, 96, 98, 104, 105, 112, 113
  introduction to, 2–3, 11–12, 14, 16, 22, 32
  "A Natural History of the Dead," 145–6
  Nietzsche, 21
  "Now I Lay Me," 178, 180, 184, 186
  Sartre, 2, 11–12, 25, 26–31, 57–61
  The Sun Also Rises, 230
  Woolf, 8
  see also materialistic atheism
Atlantic Monthly, 4
Augustinian tradition, 28–9, 66
Austin, J. L., 68

autonomy see human autonomy; masculine autonomy
avant-garde modernists, 7–8, 9, 13, 14

Bache, William, 1
Baker, Carlos, 10, 23, 89, 100, 101–2, 104
baptism
  of Hemingway, 10, 89, 90, 100, 108
  Hemingway's depictions of, 169, 230, 231
  of Sartre, 62
bare life
  colonialism, 85
  definition, 76, 81, 248
  killing, 213
  sovereign leaders, 78, 83
Barkley, Catherine (fictional character), 169, 188
Barnes, Jake (fictional character)
  bullfights, attendance at, 214, 229, 235–6
  dephallused, 36, 124
  lost generation, 8
  Roman Catholicism, 24, 229–33, 235
Barton, Bruce, 90
Barton, Clara, 90
Barton, Reverend William E.
  baptisms, 89, 90
  beliefs, 33, 34, 37–8, 41, 90–2, 97
  letter to Hemingway, 104
  missed by Hemingway, 96
Baudrillard, Jean, 70
Baughman, Judith, 5
Baym, Nina, 156
bears, 149–50, 154, 158, 244
Beck, William, 215
Being and Nothingness (Sartre)
  atheism, 26, 66, 81
  Hemingway's link to, 6, 106
  in-itself, for-itself, for-others, 29, 31, 66, 81–2, 85, 87
being-for-itself, 27, 29, 76, 80–4, 212
being-for-others, 85, 221, 227–8

being-in-itself, 27, 28, 76, 82, 83, 212
being-in-itself-for-itself, 27, 31, 66, 82–4, 87, 212, 248–9
Bérulle, Pierre de, 28
birth *see* childbirth
birth control, 110–12
Bloom, Harold, 48n41
Blume, Lesley M. M., 186
Bourne, Catherine (fictional character), 238–9
Bourne, David (fictional character), 237–41
Brasch, James D., 4
The Brooklyn Daily Eagle, 110, 111
Bruccoli, Matthew, 5
Brumback, Ted, 101
buffaloes, 158, 216, 221, 222, 223, 243
bullfighting
   Death in the Afternoon, 107, 136–7, 168, 207, 208–13
   matadors, 173, 208–15, 237, 245
   The Sun Also Rises, 214, 229, 235–6
Butler, Judith, 37

Cadegan, Una M., 9, 24
Calarco, Matthew, 161
Camus, Albert, 4, 8, 86, 189, 190, 247
Captain Doctor (fictional character), 143–6, 246
Catechism of the Catholic Church, 67
Cesarean sections, 110–12, 193–4, 196, 197–8, 199
Chekhov, Anton, 195
Chicago, 88, 147
childbirth
   Hemingway's other depictions of, 135, 169, 200
   Hemingway's son, 110–12
   "Indian Camp," 193–4, 196, 197–8, 199
Christianity
   Donne, 135–6
   human soul, 51, 185, 201
   modernist rejection of, 10

Taylor, 16–17, 19–20
war, 105
see also Oak Park Congregationalism; Protestantism; Roman Catholicism
citizenship, 20, 78–9, 132, 160, 213
code heroes *see* existential heroes (code heroes)
colonialism, 85, 239
concentration camps, 86, 247, 248
Confucius, 234–5
Congregationalism, 23; *see also* Oak Park Congregationalism
Constantinople, 130
constitutional law, 78, 83, 84
correspondence theory of language, 68, 69, 70
Cotkin, George, 7–8
courage
   bullfighting, 211, 213
   hunting, 155, 215, 217
   in war, 102, 126, 144, 147
cowardice
   Hemingway's father, 93, 190, 191
   Hotchner, 38
   Jordan, Robert (fictional character), 202–4, 206
   Macomber, Francis (fictional character), 216–17, 221–2
   No Exit (Sartre), 227–8
   suicide, 190, 191, 200, 202–4, 206, 211
creation
   God as creator, 27, 50n52, 57–60, 63–4, 67, 71, 77, 79
   humans as creators, 3, 10, 30, 221, 224
   intelligent design, 58, 64, 141, 146, 218
culture, Eagleton's definition, 21

Daily Mail, 131
de Beauvoir, Simone
   Adieux (interviews with Sartre), 27, 30, 57–60, 65, 81, 87
   Hemingway, links to, 4, 5

Index

Dearborn, Mary, 88, 93
death *see* killing; mortality; suicide
Death in the Afternoon (Hemingway)
   animal equality, 154, 156, 167–8
   bullfighting, 107, 136–7, 168, 207, 208–13
   mortality, 107–8, 114, 167–8, 185, 207, 208–13
   "A Natural History of the Dead," 106, 136–46, 148, 241, 246
Decalogue, 78, 212
decisionism, definition, 75; *see also* sovereign decisionism
dehumanization *see* animalization/dehumanization
Derrida, Jacques, 37, 69
Dietrich, Marlene, 39
doctors, 110, 134, 175–7; *see also* Adams, Doctor (fictional character); Captain Doctor (fictional character)
Donaldson, Scott, 100, 188–9, 190
Donne, John, 135–6
Dostoevsky, Fyodor, 58, 80

Eagleton, Terry, 21
Earle, David M., 33–4
Eby, Carl P., 37
ecstasy, 176, 181, 209–10, 216, 229
egalitarianism, positive/negative definition, 157–61
Ejxenbaum, B. M., 195
Electra (mythical character), 224, 228
elephants, 237–44
Eliot, T. S., 8–9
emasculation, 93, 97, 124, 190–1, 218
Emerson, Ralph Waldo, 13–14
England, 107
equality *see* animal equality
Evans, Robert, 6
evolution, 73–6
executions, 172–5, 176, 189
existential heroes (code heroes)
   fishing, 236–7
   For Whom the Bell Tolls, 200, 203, 204
   The Hemingway hero, 106, 178, 186
   hunting, 155, 157, 215–18, 222–3
   "Indian Camp," 193, 196, 200
   matadors, 208–15
   Orestes (mythical character), 224–5
   suicide, 192
   war, 101–2, 104, 126–8, 147
existentialism
   nihilism as first stage of, 190, 210, 211, 219, 222, 229
   see also American existentialism; French existentialism; Sartre, Jean-Paul; secular existentialism

faena, 208–10, 214, 235–7
failed atheism, 59, 61–7, 81, 115–16, 247
A Farewell to Arms (Hemingway)
   animals, 146–7, 171
   Barkley, Catherine (fictional character), 169, 188
   human souls, 179, 180
   religious feeling, 169–70, 178, 186, 210
   Roman Catholicism, 22, 169–70
   romantic narrative, 168–9, 185
   war and loss of faith, 146–7, 151
fascism, 148, 150, 172, 176, 202, 245; *see also* Nazism
fatherhood
   Hemingway as father, 110–12, 185, 187
   Hemingway's depictions of, 125–7, 193–200, 203–6, 238–40
   Hemingway's father, 33–5, 88, 93, 94, 190–1, 193
femininity, 36, 37, 92, 125
feminist studies, 34–5, 37, 123
Ferrando, Francesca, 259n178
First Congregational Church of Oak Park, 11, 89, 90, 96, 104
First World War *see* World War I
fishing
   Hemingway's experience of, 33, 34, 93, 157, 158, 235
   "Now I Lay Me," 182, 183, 187

The Old Man and the Sea, 154, 234, 236–7
"The Short Happy Life of Francis Macomber," 216
The Sun Also Rises, 229, 233
Fitzgerald, F. Scott, 7, 35
Fleming, Robert E., 242–3
For Whom the Bell Tolls (Hemingway)
   imago Dei, 151–5, 202
   Jordan, Robert (fictional character), 135–6, 148–52, 154, 191, 200–6
   Prud'homme's reading, 52n57
   romantic monogamy, 185
   suicide, 191, 193, 202–4
Fornaci, Italy, 10, 100, 108
France, 76–7; *see also* Paris
Franco, Francisco, 172
Frederking, Lauretta Conklin, 52n57
free will
   Hemingway, 26, 33, 90, 92, 98, 237
   Sartre, 20, 26, 50n49, 227
freedom
   Agamben, 83, 224
   Hemingway's depictions of, 221–2, 234
   radical freedom, 3, 7, 8, 28, 202
   Sartre, 2–3, 28–30, 80–2, 84–6, 224, 225–7
French existentialism, 2–9, 11–14; *see also* Sartre, Jean-Paul

Gellhorn, Martha, 190
Gellman, Jerome, 26–8
gender, 33–40, 92–3, 125, 238–9; *see also* masculinity
Geroulanos, Stefanos, 246
Gillespie, John, 29–31, 78
God
   and human moral purpose, 10, 15, 58, 64, 77
   modernist rejection of, 2–3, 7–8, 10–11
   word of, 70–2
   see also atheism; creation; secularization
God-function/God-surrogates
   definition, 12, 14–15
   Eagleton, 21
   Hemingway, 13, 245
   Sartre, 12, 30, 72, 88
Gorton, Bill (fictional character), 229–30, 232
Greco-Turkish War, 128, 130–1
Greek refugees, 130–5, 145, 208
Greffi, Count (fictional character), 169–70
Grimes, Larry, 22–3, 89–92, 94, 98
Gris, Ramon (fictional character), 172, 173
grotesquerie, 134, 139, 141–6
guns
   hunting, 187, 220
   suicide, 190, 203, 204
   war, 98, 139, 144, 204–5
Gurpegui, José Antonio, 2, 3
Guss, Nathan, 255n95

Haeckel, Ernst, 73
Hail Mary prayer, 1, 183, 234
Hall, Ernest, 88, 94
Hall, Grace, 35, 89, 93–4, 95–6, 97, 190
Halteman, Matthew C., 56n102
Harris, Sam, 48n42
Harrison, Peter, 16
Haskell, Henry J., 94–5
Hediger, Ryan, 155, 239–42
Heidegger, Martin, 45n7, 56n102
Hemingway, Clarence, 33–5, 88, 93, 94, 190–1, 193
Hemingway, Ernest
   "Big Two-Hearted River," 127, 183
   "A Clean, Well-Lighted Place," 1, 146, 194, 234
   death by suicide, 24, 189, 192–3
   "The Doctor and the Doctor's Wife," 127
   "The End of Something," 127
   "Fifty Grand," 4
   The Garden of Eden, 35–6, 237–42
   Green Hills of Africa, 48n41, 123–5, 243

Index

"In Another Country," 175–8, 184–5, 250n14
In Our Time, 126–8, 137, 174–5, 195, 200, 253n65
"Indian Camp," 127, 193–200
introduction to, 1–11, 13–14
journalism, 5, 11, 94–5
"The Killers," 1, 250n14
letters, 95–7, 102–3, 105, 108–13, 180
Men Without Women, 175, 178, 186
A Moveable Feast, 4, 35, 208
"A Natural History of the Dead," 106, 136–46, 148, 241, 246
"Now I Lay Me," 178–9, 180, 181–4, 185–8
The Old Man and the Sea, 23, 52n57, 154, 233–4, 235, 236–7
"On the Quai at Smyrna," 127–8, 128–36, 137–8, 145, 200
Papa myth (Hemingway myth), 22, 33, 34–5, 36, 123, 124, 125
"The Short Happy Life of Francis Macomber," 1, 106, 155–6, 215–18, 219–23
"The Snows of Kilimanjaro," 1, 106, 218
"Soldier's Home," 175–6
"Ten Indians," 125–6, 127
"Three-Day Blow," 127
True at First Light, 23
Under Kilimanjaro, 180–1, 237, 242–5
Winner Takes Nothing, 136, 215
World War I, 24, 98–106, 146–7, 180
see also *Death in the Afternoon* (Hemingway); *A Farewell to Arms* (Hemingway); *For Whom the Bell Tolls* (Hemingway); *The Sun Also Rises* (Hemingway)
Hemingway, Gregory, 110
Hemingway, Marcelline, 89, 94
Hemingway, Margaux, 190
Hemingway, Tyler, 94–5
Hemingway, Ursula, 192

Henry, Frederic (fictional character)
animal cruelty, 171
human souls, 179, 180
religious feeling, 169–70, 178, 186, 210
war and loss of faith, 146–7, 151
heroism see existential heroes (code heroes)
history, modernist rejection of, 8, 9, 10
Holy Ghost, 66–7, 150
homosexuality, 35, 36, 37, 159
Horan, Daniel P., 51n52
Hotchner, A. E., 38–9
human autonomy, 30, 81
human exceptionalism
Agamben, 161, 224
conclusions, 218–19, 224, 245, 249
definition, 41, 61, 79
Hemingway's depictions of, 171, 188, 235, 240
see also anthropocentrism; *imago Dei*
human identity
Agamben, 67–84, 160, 212, 224, 247
Barton's liberal theology, 91
as creators, 3, 10, 30, 221, 224
Death in the Afternoon, 212
A Farewell to Arms, 147, 171
For Whom the Bell Tolls, 136, 149–52
Hemingway, biographical study, 92–3, 97–8, 102, 104, 113–15
language, 68, 73–5, 76, 77
moral purpose of humans, 10, 15, 58, 64, 77
"A Natural History of the Dead," 143–6
"On the Quai at Smyrna," 129, 132, 133
Sartre, 27, 60, 64–5, 78–88, 212, 213, 246
"The Short Happy Life of Francis Macomber," 215, 221–3
sovereign decisionism, 33, 34, 75–6, 78–88, 213, 224
see also *imago Dei*

human rights
  Agamben, 160–1, 248
  A Farewell to Arms, 147
  For Whom the Bell Tolls, 148, 152, 173
  human vs. non-human/animal, 76–7, 136, 156–7
  imago Dei, 21, 79–81, 83, 88, 147
  "A Natural History of the Dead," 144–5, 246
  "On the Quai at Smyrna," 132
  secularization, 15
  self-evident, 76–7, 81, 245
human soul
  Hemingway, 108, 171, 178–82, 185
  positive egalitarianism, counter-argument, 159
  Roman Catholicism/Christianity, 51, 185, 201
  Sartre, 57, 64
humanism
  Agamben, 21, 145, 160–1, 259n178
  anti-humanism, 143, 246, 258n178
  Hemingway, 140–1, 143–6, 237, 239
  posthumanism, 158–61, 258n178
Hunt, Lynn, 76–7
hunting
  For Whom the Bell Tolls, 148–9
  The Garden of Eden, 238–40
  Green Hills of Africa, 123–5
  Hemingway's experience of, 33, 34, 93, 157–8
  "Now I Lay Me," 187
  "The Short Happy Life of Francis Macomber," 155–6, 215–18, 220–3
  Under Kilimanjaro, 242–5
hypermasculinity, 33–6

Ibbieta, Pablo (fictional character), 172–4, 176, 201
idealist atheism, 58, 65
imago Dei
  Agamben, 161, 213, 224, 248
  definition, 26, 50n52, 60, 67
  A Farewell to Arms, 147, 170–1
  For Whom the Bell Tolls, 151–5, 202
  Hemingway's suicide, 192
  human rights, 21, 79–81, 83, 88, 147
  vs. humanity's animal nature, 208
  "A Natural History of the Dead," 140, 142
  "Now I Lay Me," 188
  positive egalitarianism, 159
  Roman Catholicism/Christianity, 41, 51n52, 64, 67, 202
  Sartre, 60, 66, 79–81, 83, 85–8, 171, 213, 224
  secularization, 19, 21
  "The Short Happy Life of Francis Macomber," 218–19
  The Sun Also Rises, 235
immanence, 15, 16–17, 18, 19–20, 161
immortality
  Death in the Afternoon, 208–10, 212
  "The Short Happy Life of Francis Macomber," 215, 218, 219, 223
  Sartre, 65
  The Sun Also Rises, 235–6
  Under Kilimanjaro, 245
  war, impact on Hemingway's beliefs, 101, 103–4, 105
  see also afterlife; human soul
intelligent design, 58, 64, 141, 146, 218
Italy, 10, 100, 101, 108, 175, 179, 186

The Jazz Journal, 94
Jordan, Robert (fictional character), 135–6, 148–52, 154, 191, 200–6
Journey, Anna, 134
Joyce, James, 8
Juma (fictional character), 240–2

Kansas City, 11, 95
The Kansas City Star, 94–5, 101

Index

Kennedy, J. Gerald, 35, 93
Kert, Bernice, 35
Key West, 110
Kierkegaard, Søren, 2
killing
   For Whom the Bell Tolls, 148–52, 205–6
   The Garden of Eden, 238–42
   Hemingway, other mentions, 44, 211–12, 224, 247, 249
   Sartre, 59, 65, 87, 227–9
   "The Short Happy Life of Francis Macomber," 216–18, 220–3
   Under Kilimanjaro, 242–5
   see also bullfighting; fishing; hunting; war
Killinger, John, 2–4, 6–7, 105–6, 108, 213
Kirkpatrick, Kate, 28, 227
Kokobobo, Ani, 134
Kotsko, Adam, 12, 161
Krebs, Harold (fictional character), 175–6
Krutch, Joseph, 8

language
   correspondence theory of, 68, 69, 70
   human identity, 68, 73–5, 76, 77
   oaths, 68, 69, 70–2, 82
   poststructuralism, 68–70, 72
Latham, Aaron, 35
law
   Agamben, 71, 73, 78, 83, 160, 161
   constitutional law, 78, 83, 84
   legal authority, 20, 225, 245
   Sartre, 20, 60, 78, 82–3, 224, 225, 229
   Schmitt, 18, 20, 84
Lewis, Robert W., 242–3
liberal theology, 23, 91, 98
Linde, Mauricio D. Aguilera, 36
linguistics, 68, 69, 73; *see also* language
lions, 155–6, 216, 217, 219–21, 242–3, 244

literary modernism, 7–10, 11, 13–14, 113
Locke, John, 16
Lord's Prayer, 1, 184, 234
lost generation, 7–8, 9, 195
Love, Glen, 158
Lynn, Kenneth, 23, 35

McGill, Christopher, 155
MacLeish, Ada, 10–11
Macomber, Francis (fictional character), 155, 215–18, 219–23
Macomber, Margot (fictional character), 155, 215–16, 217, 218, 221–3
Maier, Kevin, 157
Mansfield, Harvey, 39–40, 191–2
marriage motif, 176–7, 183, 184–6
masculine autonomy
   American existentialism, 13
   "Indian Camp," 195
   and religion, 33–4, 39, 40, 95, 97, 146
   suicide, 192
"Masculine Christianity," 90, 92
masculinity, 33–41
   assertive manliness, 39–40, 191–2, 218
   competence/mastery, 193–4, 205, 209–11, 244
   Hemingway myth, 123, 124, 125
   hypermasculinity, 33–6
   Oak Park Congregationalism, 33, 34, 37–8, 39, 41
   Papa myth (Hemingway myth), 22, 33, 34–5, 36, 123, 124, 125
   self-mastery, 90, 92–4, 96–7, 98, 196
   toxic masculinity, 37, 52n57, 124
   see also courage; cowardice; existential heroes (code heroes); fatherhood; killing
matadors, 173, 208–15, 237, 245
materialistic atheism
   Hemingway, 237
   Sartre, 28, 50n49, 58–9, 79, 82–4, 87

May, Charles, E., 195
meaninglessness
   of life/human insignificance, 171, 189–90, 202
   meaning created from, 210, 213, 215
   modernism, 8, 10
   and mortality/immortality, 103–4, 105, 107
   see also nothingness/nada
Melville, Herman, Moby Dick, 136
Menand, Louis, 4
metaphysical authority
   Agamben, 18–20, 72, 84
   For Whom the Bell Tolls, 151–2
   introduction to, 10, 12, 32, 39
   sovereign decisionism, 18–20, 82–3, 84, 87
Meyers, Jeffrey, 23, 100, 130, 138
Milan, 101, 175, 179, 186
Miller, Reverend William Edward, 94
Mirbal, Juan (fictional character), 172, 174–5
Mitchell, Prudence (fictional character), 125, 126
modernism, 2–3, 7–11, 13–14, 113
moment of truth, 213, 214, 218, 223, 229, 235–7
monogamy, 168, 185–6
moral absolutes
   Agamben, 78
   conclusions, 247
   The Garden of Eden, 240, 241
   Sartre, 20, 30–1, 57–9, 65, 81, 84–5, 87, 229, 246–7
   Schmitt, 20, 78–9, 84
   and secularization, 14–15, 20–1
   Under Kilimanjaro, 244–5
moral authoritarianism, 247, 249
moral authority
   Agamben, 78, 83, 248
   The Garden of Eden, 242
   Sartre, 30, 60, 62, 63, 84, 87, 225–9
moral codes
   Oak Park Congregationalism, 33, 34, 37, 39, 92–4, 97
   Roman Catholicism, 9, 32, 110–13
   see also animal rights; human rights; secular morality; Victorian morality
moral law
   For Whom the Bell Tolls, 151–2
   Roman Catholicism, 9
   Sartre, 78–81, 84–5, 224–5, 228
moral purpose, of humans, 10, 15, 58, 64, 77
mortality
   Death in the Afternoon, 107–8, 114, 167–8, 185, 207, 208–13
   A Farewell to Arms, 147, 169–71, 180, 185, 186, 188
   "The Flies" (Sartre), 229
   "In Another Country," 175–8, 184–5
   introduction to, 1–3, 6, 10–11, 32
   "A Natural History of the Dead," 138–46
   "Now I Lay Me," 178–9, 180, 181–4, 186, 188
   "On the Quai at Smyrna," 128, 133–5
   "The Short Happy Life of Francis Macomber," 215–18, 222–3
   The Sun Also Rises, 235–6
   "The Wall" (Sartre), 172–5, 176, 201
   war, impact on Hemingway's beliefs, 100–6, 180
   see also afterlife; human soul; immortality; killing; suicide
mules, 132–3, 137–8, 155–6, 207–8
murder
   Hemingway, 131, 144, 206, 212, 217, 240
   Sartre, 65, 86–7, 224, 228
muscular theology, 33, 37, 92
mysticism
   Hemingway, 25–6, 32–3, 181, 234–5
   Sartre, 27–9

nada see nothingness/nada
natural theology, 137, 139–42, 145, 218

Nazism, 17, 78
negative egalitarianism, definition, 157–61
Nickel, Matthew, 22, 24–5, 32, 98–9, 105, 108, 181–2
Nietzsche, Friedrich, 15, 21, 29–30, 78, 84, 119n86
nihilism
  existentialism's first stage, 190, 210, 211, 219, 222, 229
  Hemingway, 1, 3, 11, 114
  literary modernism, 10
Norton, William J., 89
nothingness/*nada*
  Hemingway's depictions of, 1, 2, 32, 106, 146, 234
  Roman Catholicism, 25, 115, 234–5, 237
  Sartre, 9, 28–9, 81, 246, 247–8
Nouvelle Revue Française, 4

Oak Leaves, 90
Oak Park Congregationalism
  and Hemingway's later views, 114, 115, 237
  Hemingway's youth, 89–98, 99, 104, 180
  masculinity, 33, 34, 37–8, 39, 41
  self-determination, 33, 34, 37, 40, 94
  suicide, 190
Oak Park, Illinois, 11, 33, 91
oaths, 68, 69, 70–2, 82
O'Donnell, Angela Alaimo, 210, 214
Old lady (fictional character), 136, 137–8, 142, 167–8
Orestes (mythical character), 224–5, 228–9
original sin, 67, 90, 92, 98

Paley, William, 137
Pamplona, 214, 229
Papa myth (Hemingway myth), 22, 33, 34–5, 36, 123, 124, 125
papal authority, 110–11, 112
Paris, 4, 5, 6–7, 13, 98–9, 108–10
Park, Mungo, 139–42, 145

paternoster, 1, 184, 234
Percival, Philip, 157–8, 243–5
perspective, literary
  "Indian Camp," 195, 199
  "A Natural History of the Dead," 143, 145, 148
  No Exit (Sartre), 227–8
  "The Short Happy Life of Francis Macomber," 155–6, 219–21
Pfeiffer, Pauline, Hemingway's marriage to
  Roman Catholic influence, 10–11, 99, 108–12, 113
  works during, 24, 106, 108, 123, 186, 215
phallic symbolism, 36, 124, 205
phallogocentrism, 37
Pienkos, Angela, 147
Piggott, Arkansas, 110
pilgrimage, 23–4, 214–15, 235–6
Poe, Edgar Allan, 195
Pollan, Michael, 159, 168
positive egalitarianism, definition, 157–61
posthumanism, 158–61, 258n178
poststructuralism, 68–70, 72
Pound, Ezra, 7, 13
prayers
  Hemingway's depictions of, 1, 178, 183–4, 186, 232–4
  Hemingway's Roman Catholicism, 98
  Oak Park Congregationalism, 88–9, 95–6
profanation, 17–18, 61, 160–1
Protestantism
  differences with Roman Catholicism, 232
  Hemingway, 11, 22–3, 26, 33, 88, 90–1, 108
  Sartre, 62
Prud'homme, Joseph, 1, 52n57

queer studies, 34–5, 37, 123

racism, 125, 159, 239
radical freedom, 3, 7, 8, 28, 202

Ray B. West, Jr., 136
Red Cross, 90, 98, 101
refugees, 130–5, 145, 208
Regan, Tom, 158–60
relativism, 58, 65, 79, 84–6, 212, 229
religious feeling
   Death in the Afternoon, 209–10
   A Farewell to Arms, 169–70, 178, 186, 210
   The Old Man and the Sea, 233, 237
   ritual practice, 186, 230, 233, 235
   The Sun Also Rises, 230, 233
Reynolds, Michael, 90, 101
rights, 86; see also animal rights; human rights
ritual practice
   bullfighting, 207, 213, 214–15, 235–7
   fishing, 234–5, 237
   hunting, 187, 218, 235, 243–4
   "Now I Lay Me," 178, 182–4, 186, 187
   pilgrimage, 23–4, 214–15, 235–6
   Roman Catholicism, 230–4
   see also prayers
River Forest High School, 94
Roman Catholicism
   A Farewell to Arms, 22, 169–70
   Hemingway's contested conversion, 10, 13, 22–6, 98–100, 108–15, 181, 235
   Hemingway's marriage to Pauline, 10–11, 99, 108–12, 113
   imago Dei, 41, 51n52, 64, 67
   Mass, 98, 109, 214, 230, 231, 256n101
   modernist rejection of, 8, 9–10
   mysticism, 25–6, 28, 32–3, 181, 234–5
   "Now I Lay Me," 178, 181, 182, 183–4, 186
   The Old Man and the Sea, 233–4
   Sartre, 62, 66–7
   suicide, 203
   The Sun Also Rises, 22, 24, 229–33, 235

romantic attachments, 125–6, 127, 168–70, 185–6
Roosevelt, President Theodore, 157–8

safaris, 123, 157–8, 215–17, 242–5
salvation, 90, 171, 199, 214, 228–9, 232
Sanderson, Richard and Rena, 192
Santiago (fictional character), 154, 233, 236–7
Sartre, Jean-Paul
   Adieux (de Beauvoir's interviews), 27, 30, 57–60, 65, 81, 87
   "American Novelists in French Eyes," 4
   Existentialism Is a Humanism, 20, 79, 81, 82
   failed atheism, 59, 61–7, 81, 247
   "The Flies," 224–9
   human identity, 27, 60, 64–5, 78–88, 212, 213, 246
   introduction to, 2–7, 11–13
   moral absolutes, 20, 30–1, 57–9, 65, 81, 84–5, 87, 229, 246–7
   Nausea (*La nausée*), 5, 6
   No Exit, 227–8
   preface to *The Wretched of the Earth* by Frantz Fanon, 85
   as religious believer, 26–32, 57, 62–3, 66–7
   secularized theism, 28–30, 59–60, 61, 65–7, 78–9, 88, 171, 229
   "The Wall" (*Le mur*), 5, 172–5, 176, 200, 201
   War Diaries, 60, 62–3
   The Words, 27, 61–2, 63, 65
   see also *Being and Nothingness* (Sartre)
Saunders, Judith P., 1
Saussure, Ferdinand de, 68
Schmitt, Carl, 17, 18–19, 20, 78–9, 84
science, 15–17, 137, 145
screaming, 128–33, 144, 145, 193, 196, 200
searchlights, 128–9, 131–2, 133

Index

Second World War, 5
secular existentialism, 1, 13, 22, 25–6, 32–3, 114
secular morality, 64, 81
secularization
  Agamben, 17–20
  conclusions, 245–6, 249
  definition, 14–15
  overview, 12–13, 14–21, 29–31
  and transcendence, 13, 14–21, 34
secularized theism
  Agamben, 60–1, 78–9, 83, 161, 224
  Death in the Afternoon, 209
  A Farewell to Arms, 151, 170
  The Garden of Eden, 238, 242
  killing, 224, 229, 235, 237, 249
  Oak Park Congregationalism, 33, 34, 39
  overview, 13–14, 19, 20, 25–6, 171
  Sartre, 28–30, 59–60, 61, 65–7, 78–9, 88, 171, 229
  "The Short Happy Life of Francis Macomber," 216
  The Sun Also Rises, 230, 232
self-assertion *see* assertive manliness
self-determination
  "The Flies" (Sartre), 228
  Hemingway's later views, 97, 128, 192, 229, 234
  Oak Park Congregationalism, 33, 34, 37, 40, 94
self-mastery, 90, 92–4, 96–7, 98, 196
Shakespeare, William, 100
short story form, 195–6, 199
Sigman, Joseph, 4
sin
  Augustinian tradition, 28–9
  killing, 151
  original sin, 67, 90, 92, 98
  pride, 212
  suicide, 203
Sinclair, Upton, 147
Singer, Peter, 159
Slaughter, Joseph, 76

sleep, 129–30, 179, 181–3, 185–6, 188, 233
Smith, Adam, 16
Smyrna, 130, 145, 207–8
sovereign decisionism
  Agamben, 19, 73, 75–6, 78, 80, 82–4, 212, 218–19, 247–8
  conclusions, 247–9
  human identity, 33, 34, 75–6, 78–88, 213, 224
  metaphysical authority, 18–20, 82–3, 84, 87
  Oak Park Congregationalism, 33, 34, 37, 39, 92–3
  Sartre, 20, 31, 66, 81, 82–3, 85, 212–13
  Schmitt, 17, 18–19, 20, 78–9, 84
  suicide, 190–2, 202
  see also existential heroes (code heroes); killing
sovereign subject, 20, 72–3, 82–4, 87–8, 212–13, 239
Soviet Union, 86, 247
Spain, 107, 136, 207, 211, 213, 214, 229
Spanish-American War, 157
Spanish Civil War, 148, 172–3
state governance, 17–20, 78, 83
Stein, Gertrude, 7, 35, 48n41, 136, 137, 207
Steinthal, Heymann, 73
Stoltzfus, Ben, 2–3, 6, 106–7, 108, 215, 222
Stoneback, H. R., 22–4, 25, 98–9, 108, 231–2, 234–5
suicide
  "A Clean, Well-Lighted Place," 1
  cowardice, 190, 191, 200, 202–4, 206, 211
  Death in the Afternoon, 185
  For Whom the Bell Tolls, 191, 193, 202–4
  Hemingway's death, 24, 189, 192–3
  Hemingway's family members, 190–1
  "Indian Camp," 193–4, 196–200

The Sun Also Rises (Hemingway)
   bullfighting, 214, 229, 235–6
   dephallused males, 36, 124
   lost generation, 7–8
   Roman Catholicism, 22, 24, 229–33, 235
   swords, 204–5, 213

Taylor, Charles, 16–17, 18, 19–20
Ten Commandments *see* Decalogue
theism, 12, 13, 16, 25–6, 66, 104
theology, 12, 14, 16, 28; *see also* liberal theology; muscular theology; natural theology
Third Congregational Church of Oak Park, 89
Thomas, Dylan, 191
Tillich, Paul, 12
The Times, 131, 133
Toklas, Alice, 35, 207
Toronto Star, 130
toxic masculinity, 37, 52n57, 124
transcendence
   Agamben, 17–20, 160–1
   conclusions, 245, 249
   introduction, 3, 8, 10, 26, 31–2
   and secularization, 13, 14–21, 34
trauma, psychological, 104, 127, 185, 195, 198, 238, 249
Turkey *see* Constantinople; Greco-Turkish War
Tyler, Anson, 88

United States of America (USA), 8, 13, 33–4, 37, 76–7, 107, 158; *see also* American Civil War; Oak Park, Illinois

Victorian morality, 91, 94, 97, 98

war
   animal cruelty, 132–3, 137–8, 207–8
   existential heroes (code heroes), 101–2, 104, 126–8, 147
   grotesque deaths, 134, 139, 141–6
   loss of faith, 100–1, 105, 146–7, 151, 184, 186
   postwar trauma, 104, 127, 185, 195
   see also American Civil War; Greco-Turkish War; Spanish-American War; Spanish Civil War; World War I; World War II
Warren, Robert Penn, 1, 2
weapons
   searchlights used as, 132
   see also guns; swords
Weeks, Lewis E., Jr., 136
Welsh, Mary, 5–6, 242–3, 244–5
Wilson, President Woodrow, 90
Wilson, Robert (fictional character), 155, 215–18, 219, 220–3
Wolfe, Cary, 36, 87, 238–9, 242
Woolf, Virginia, 8
World War I
   Hemingway as ambulance driver, 98, 101, 146–7
   Hemingway's injury, 24, 98, 99, 100, 101–5, 180
   "In Another Country," 175–8
   modernism, 7, 9
   searchlights, 132
World War II, 5

Young, Philip, 6

Zeus (mythical character), 224–7, 228–9

EU representative:
Easy Access System Europe
Mustamäe tee 50, 10621 Tallinn, Estonia
Gpsr.requests@easproject.com

www.ingramcontent.com/pod-product-compliance
Lightning Source LLC
Chambersburg PA
CBHW050210240426
43671CB00013B/2281